COAL BLACK HEART

By the Same Author

Citizens Irving: K. C. Irving and His Legacy
The Last Best Place: Lost in the Heart of Nova Scotia

JOHN DeMONT

COAL BLACK HEART

The Story of Coal and the Lives it Ruled

Doubleday Canada

Doubleday Canada and colophon are trademarks

LIBRARY AND ARCHIVES CANADA CATALOGUING IN PUBLICATION

DeMont, John, 1956-
    Coal black heart : the story of coal and the lives it ruled / John DeMont.

ISBN: 978–0–385–66504–9

    1. Coal trade--Nova Scotia--History. 2. Coal miners--Nova Scotia--History. 3. Coal mines and mining--Nova Scotia--History. 4. Nova Scotia--History. I. Title.

TN806.C22N6 2009   338.2'72409716   C2008-906888-2

Printed and bound in the United States of America

Published in Canada by Doubleday Canada,
a division of Random House of Canada Limited

Visit Random House of Canada Limited's website: www.randomhouse.ca

10 9 8 7 6 5 4 3 2 1

To the coal miners and the DeMonts (and Demonts),
MacKeigans, Brierses and Browns,
wherever they might be.

"I guess your people have been on the coal over there
   for a long time?" asks the voice beside me.
"Yes," I say, "since 1873."
"Son of a bitch," he says after a pause, "it seems to
   bust your balls and it's bound to break your heart."

The Vastness of the Dark, Alistair MacLeod

Contents

PROLOGUE

A Colony of Miners

I was living in Halifax—a married father of one looking through French windows into a curtain of drizzle—when an editor from Toronto called early one Saturday morning in 1992. Only something momentous made *Maclean's* magazine, where I worked, start ripping up pages at a time when the latest issue should have been heading for the printers. Saddle up, he said, because a fireball had shot up a coal-mine shaft in a place called Plymouth, trapping twenty-six men underground. Reporters know that bad things happen in this world. The shock to my system was nonetheless extreme. It hurt to imagine the agony of those men and their families. Yet to this day I remember, more than anything, my disbelief that men were still risking subterranean death thousands of yards from blue skies so that our lights would go on. At that instant, my universe perceptibly tilted. I felt both stupid and craven. And an obsession was born.

This kind of disconnect from the comforts of everyday life isn't unusual in our time and place. We rarely gaze around the kitchen and reflect that the paper we're reading, the coffee we sip and the chair on which we're parked have all come from far away, and by virtue of someone else's labour. I, of all people, should have known better. To my knowledge I had never laid eyes on a single miner who worked the Pictou County coal seams. Yet at that moment I realized that these were my people as surely as if we owned the same surname, gait, and DNA. Somehow, in the headlong rush of life, I'd managed to forget that generations of my ancestors had taken the long ride underground to hack out the black stone that has transformed societies and launched empires. And that even the non-miners who shared my genes lived in coal's grimy shadow.

This wasn't just some dusty historical connection, either. An hour later, as I headed north from Halifax in my Toyota, one of my cousins could have been working a shift in one of the last operating collieries on Cape Breton. I, however, was a city boy brought up with the expectation that I would pursue some occupation that kept my face clean and the family's narrative line moving upward. Everything I knew about coal came from the old stories that had hung in the air while I was growing up: the back-breaking, dangerous work; the pitiful wages; the years of indentured servitude to companies that not only controlled where the miners and their families worked, and when and for how much, but also owned their homes, even the stores where they bought their food and clothes.

Lord, it sounded cruel, this world of damp and dust and lethal cave-ins that began with something as simple as a whiff of gas, a few unstable rocks, a spark from two pieces of machinery brushing together. This world where children like my grandfather—who went into the mines at age eleven—spent their days working in pitch-black tunnels. A world where a good year meant new shoes for the kids and a bad one a casket in the parlour and a roomful of mourners in the dining room. I devoured those stories of shining heroes with inconceivable names like Tugger Head, Noodle Neck, Jimmy Oh-My-Back and Shiver the Pit, who could put in a day in the colliery, wash off the coal dust, then guzzle hooch and dance the night away to Scottish fiddle tunes that hadn't changed since the days of Bonnie Prince Charlie; of base villains like Roy "the Wolf," who starved women and children for an extra penny of profit, and the company goons who shot good miners dead in the street.

Then somehow, over time, I put some of the old stories aside. I now knew that energy meant oil derricks and guys in stetsons, not the sooty black stuff that used to get shovelled into Grammy's cast-iron stove. I always loved the reflected glory of having a coal miner for a cousin; it sounded tough and exotic, like being born in Tuktoyaktuk. But it never really dawned on me, as I fired up my laptop for a day of serious typing, that my younger cousin, Kenneth, was donning his helmet and going underground to do a job that didn't offer much in the way of a career arc, or a cushy retirement around the pool in Sarasota.

I knew the facts to be these: at 5:20 that morning—May 9, 1992—an explosion had erupted in the Westray coal mine in the village of Plymouth, Nova Scotia. The blast had been so strong that it had blown the top off the mine entrance and shattered steel roof supports throughout the mine. Twenty-six men were trapped in the mile-long shaft. Draegermen—coal miners specially trained in rescue techniques—were on the way from Cape Breton and elsewhere. The mine company operatives and the politicians who had paved the way for the Westray mine's existence were already ducking for cover.

Which is why I was taking the turnoff on the Trans-Canada and driving east down Foord Street, named after the coal seam that had settled the town. Past the blocky little semi-detached homes—built a century earlier by the coal company—that had been shaken by the explosion early that morning. I drove beyond the war memorials and the monument to the men who had died in Pictou County coal mines. Past half-empty store windows, a derelict movie theatre, the old-timers in their windbreakers and tractor dealership ball caps killing time in front of the government buildings.

The town's main drag was mostly empty, adding to the funereal air. So I just kept driving, not noticing the signs marking where a village ended and the open country began. Across a narrow river and beyond stands of second-growth forest, a collection of silos appeared. I headed straight for them until a Mountie waved me up a road. I parked on the shoulder behind the radio and television vans, and walked up the hill to the building where the reporters had been corralled.

I aimed some borrowed binoculars at the fire hall and watched family members and their supporters—clerics, social workers, counsellors, I imagined—arrive at the community centre. They came in ones and twos, walking stiffly and slowly as if to avoid what waited inside, or in small knots, clutching each other for support. Watching these people, stripped of any pretense about fairness in life, seared my eyes but I couldn't look away.

Everything is surely connected. I believe that statement as fully as any Buddhist or conspiracy theorist. It's now generally accepted by scientists that the world is 4.5 billion years old. Within that context, 300 million years ago, when the first vegetation covered what would become Nova Scotia's Pictou County, was just yesterday. Those plants died, began to decay, were covered in layers of dirt, sand, silt and mud, and were eventually flooded by overflowing rivers and seas. When the cycle had occurred enough times, coal—made from plants that last saw sunlight 100 million years before dinosaurs trod the earth—was formed. It's the connective tissue of time. Because of coal—ancient fossils, really—lives have been altered; families changed; the entire world reconfigured. Or to put it another way: a piece of vegetation blooms, and 300 million years later twenty-six men are trapped underground, and the pall of tragedy hangs over a hollowed-out place at the eastern edge of North America.

As the draegermen searched for life underground, I had to bone up quickly on coal mining in Nova Scotia. I read. I walked around. I talked to ex-miners like James Linthorne, a fifteen-year mining veteran whose father was the last man to die in a Pictou County coal mine before the Westray tragedy. I visited people like James Cameron, a wonderful Pictou County historian who wrote the best book ever penned about coal mining in this province. Often I just drove around. I wasn't quite sure where to go, because I barely recognized the world any more.

The lights, I finally understood, don't just automatically turn on. In provinces like Alberta, Saskatchewan and Nova Scotia, in countries like the United States, China and Germany, electricity usually means coal, a mineral that emerges from the earth pretty much ready for use. Coal, along with oil and natural gas, the other immensely concentrated fossil fuels, run most modern economies and power virtually every action of modern life.

Energy used to depend upon growing crops for humans and animals to eat and wood, brush and other vegetable matter to burn. Fossil energy, as environmental writer Bill McKibben explains, "depended on how much plant matter had grown eons before." It was all there, waiting to be discovered and to be unleashed. And that unleashing required real men doing hellishly dangerous jobs that would leave the rest of us soft-handed paper-pushers and keyboard jockeys—us dislocated souls stunned by the news that a young calf has to die because we simply must have osso bucco—curled up in the corner bawling for Mama.

This, in a small way, I now knew. I also understood that coal had once been king in this province. That under the ground I now trod had once thrived amazing subterranean worlds straight out of Jules Verne. And that at some earlier time one hell of an interesting story took place in coal towns like this throughout Nova Scotia. I tried to imagine what the tangle of thick forest running down to the Pictou County rivers and seashore must have looked like to the English Protestants arriving from Philadelphia, to the Highland Scots lured by free passage, a farm lot and a year's provisions, and the soldiers who fought for the Loyalist side in the American Revolution. One of their group, a local surveyor, is given credit, in some circles, for discovering the first coal outcrop in the area. But members of the Mi'kmaq First Nation, who told of lighting fires igniting outcrops of black rock, knew about it long before the whites arrived.

Coal lifted Pictou County—and most of the rest of this province—out of its pioneer existence. In time the true extent of the Pictou coalfield was sketched out: 165 square kilometres within which lay twenty-five seams of bituminous coal, one atop the other, separated by rock strata and faults. Some of those seams—notably the Foord—were as thick as any in the world. "The most striking features of the coal seams and enclosing strata," an early mining expert wrote about the Stellarton seams, "are the irregular folds and numerous faults in different directions which together with the rapid variation in thickness makes the most difficult mining conditions your investigator has observed in any of the coalfields of North America or in Europe." Translation: the whole structure was shot through with thick clouds of explosive gas and, therefore, prone to spontaneous combustion.

Chances are that John McKay, "son of the Squire, usually known as Collier," had no inkling of this when he dug the first coal mine in Pictou County in 1807. I had to assume that the Englishmen who followed twenty years later were better informed. I read about how an outfit called the General Mining Association (GMA) built the first steam engine in the province, which was used to pump water out of the mine and hoist coal to the surface. How they imported skilled British help to operate their mines. And how, in 1839, the company opened the Albion Mines–Abercrombie Railway—its English-made locomotives the first to run on iron rails in Canada— to carry coal to the piers.

I can't be sure after all this time, but I think my heart started to thump as I discovered this stuff. As the new mines opened—the Acadian, the Cage, Thom and Stellar pits, the Drummond pit— emigrants came from the British Isles, Europe, Newfoundland or elsewhere in the Maritimes. Coal industry service companies flocked to Albion Mines and throughout Pictou County. Eventually, the coalfields brought the Industrial Revolution—in the form of iron-works, steel mills and other heavy industry—to the backwoods of Nova Scotia. With time, brand new settlements emerged: Westville, the site of a major coal discovery in 1866 and within a few decades one of the fastest-growing towns in the country; Trenton, which came into being two decades later, after some blacksmiths founded an ironworks to make anchors and iron fittings for sailing ships; Thorburn, where a mine opened in 1872. It was enough to make one writer observe, twenty years after the GMA's arrival, that it had founded "a colony of miners."

One morning four days after the Westray explosion, I drove through Stellarton, past what's left of Mount Rundell—the mansion where the mine manager and his chatelaine once entertained British tycoons, Canadian prime ministers and visiting royalty. Past the long-closed mine entrances and what remained of the coal company shacks. With time, the inexorable forces of "progress" and global economics had intervened in Pictou County and the other coalfields of Nova Scotia. Capital fled elsewhere. Oil began to replace coal as the choice to power the world's electrical grid. By then, many of Pictou County's coalfields were simply exhausted: the collieries too old, deep and expensive to operate; the coal deposit more heavily mined than any comparably sized area anywhere on the continent. A few mines managed to live a hand-to-mouth existence. Eventually, the last miners punched out there too. People drifted away. Businesses closed. As the rest of the world hurtled toward the new millennium, anyone could tell that the towns of Pictou County were redolent of the past, not the future. Even if stories of great drama and heartbreak lingered just below the dust.

It's an unseasonably warm spring day, as if the land barely remembers what happened just days ago. By the time I arrive, mourners have already filled the white clapboard United Church in the settlement of Eureka, at the forks of the East River. So I stand outside amidst the bulky men with the ill-fitting suits, the women in their Sunday dresses, the haunted-eyed seniors and confused kids. "Amazing Grace" sounds through two loudspeakers mounted outside the church. Birds chirp in the nearby trees. Heads bowed, we listen to the voice of the Reverend Marion Patterson eulogizing Lawrence Bell, twenty-five, whose body was one of the first to be pulled from the Westray mine. Patterson speaks of Bell's love of hockey and the guitar, his zest for life. "Let us not say goodbye to Larry," she concludes, "just good night." Then the five hundred or so mourners walk to their cars and begin snaking their way to the cemetery.

Throughout the day, in the churches and graveyards of Pictou County, the heartbreaking scene will be repeated. By then the bodies of fifteen men have been recovered. For a couple of days the families of the remaining trapped miners will cling to the slim hope that the rescue crews working night and day in the pitch-black, rubble-strewn shaft will find more alive. Six days after the explosion, Curragh Resources, the owner, will call off the search, leaving the last eleven bodies underground.

Best estimates are that 500 million tons of coal have been harvested in the history of Nova Scotia. About 2,500 men—more than the province lost in the Great War—have died in the process. That works out to about five lives lost per million tons of coal—about triple the death rate in modern-day China, where the number of coal-mining deaths is viewed as a global scandal. The Nova Scotia total doesn't even include the victims of silicosis, emphysema and a host of cancers and heart ailments related to a lifetime in the pit.

The Pictou collieries have claimed their share of the dead. The weird faulting and dramatic variations in seam thickness have caused frequent roof collapses and made the timber, coal and rock roar down with a terrible sound. There are other ways to die, too. In 1866 someone named McCarney perished because he "fell 15 ft. and struck a timber." Four years later the paradoxically named John Luckman was "crushed by cage." In 1873 Malcolm McIsaac died by virtue of being "crushed by back balance." A year later W.C. Jackson and John Potts both died due to "rope breaking in shaft." Four years after that, Francis Colin was "run over by a pit tub," while in 1883 D. Baillie was "killed by run away rake." Men went to meet their maker because of "suffocation," because of being "crushed by machinery," being "run over by train of hoppers," due to a "premature explosion of shot from use of iron tamping bars," being "caught by box on balance while putting his clothes on for home" or after being "whirled around a shaft."

Official numbers are sketchy, but best estimates are that since 1827, some six hundred men have died in the Pictou mines. The "damps"—the term English miners used to collectively refer to all foul, noxious, poisonous gases found in collieries—have taken many away. By itself, methane, found in huge quantities throughout the field, is merely flammable; when mixed in the right concentrations with oxygen—9.5 percent methane being the mixture's most volatile point—the gas becomes explosive. A spark is all it takes: a pick hitting a piece of scrap iron, a shovel striking coal contaminated with pyrites. Historian James Cameron figures that the Pictou field has suffered forty-eight major fires over the years. At one time or another, virtually every mine in the Stellarton area has been shut down because of fire or explosion.

Sometimes it's impossible to know precisely what happened; other times the stories read with grim clarity. On May 13, 1873, a miner named Robert McLeod set a routine gunpowder charge in the uppermost coal face of the Drummond Colliery, in Westville, a few kilometres from Plymouth. According to accounts, an unusual amount of gas was ignited, filling the mine with smoke. Making matters worse, the ventilation system stopped working. The manager ordered an evacuation. As the miners were leaving and a squad of firefighters were entering the mine, an explosion ripped through the tunnels. Miners from nearby collieries arrived and tried to rescue the trapped men and boys, whose moans echoed upward through the airshaft. A second explosion hit, killing one of the rescuers. In desperation, the mine was sealed to starve the fire of oxygen. On the surface, "men and women wander about in groups," the newspapers reported in the days following the catastrophe, "their saddened countenances betokening the great grief that has fallen upon them."

Five years later, an explosion occurred in the Foord Pit in nearby Albion Mines, killing Jason Nering, James Mitchell, Lewis Thomas and Edward Savage. The rolls of the dead included Donald McKinnon, Charles Boram, the MacDonald boys— Alexander, Angus, Murdoch and Ronald—Angus McGilvary and Hugh McElvie. Also no more were Laughlin Morrison, Thomas Sullivan, Dan Cummings, Merles Benoit, Rory McKinnon (father and son) and twenty-three others.

On January 18, 1918, the Allan Shaft—the most dangerous in a risky lot of seams—exploded. This time the Pictou County church bells rang out for Thomas Adderly Jr. and Clement Barcey, for Robert Winton and Peter Zomoskie, for Isaac Luther and Victor Humblet. Some families suffered more than most: the Bartholomews (Louis and Joseph), the Hanuses (Alfred and Cammile), the Kayenses (Felican and Joseph). Joseph and John McAulay were also among the dead, alongside William and John McLellan, Floriand, Louis and August Vaast, and Desire and Sylvia Laderie. All told, eighty-eight men died that day. Most every family felt the pain—including the Johnsons, who lost a clan member named James.

I noticed, examining the rolls of the dead, that another Johnson, Peter, was a solo fatality during an accident in the McBean Mine in 1957. I have no idea if he and James were related. But I'm still willing to bet that there was some sort of connection between the two of them and Eugene Johnson, who was laid to rest in a lovely treed cemetery in a nearby hamlet on the same day that I attended Lawrence Bell's funeral.

Illumination does not come often to someone like me. But somehow and somewhere in those grim days after the disaster I had a vision of the black residue that coal has left everywhere in this province. Without coal, whole sections of Nova Scotia might not have been settled at all, or at least might have been settled more slowly. Without coal, Nova Scotia might still be just a collection of scattered farms and fishing villages. Without coal, the province's people would lack their edge and urgency—their spirit forged by a flame that comes from betting everything, year after year, on the vagaries of a single commodity.

But the trade-offs! Jesus, the trade-offs. All those names on the miners' monuments in Westville, New Waterford, and Springhill. All those old men coughing their lungs out at Cape Breton Regional Hospital. All those shattered communities, devastated wives and fatherless children. All those economies locked in the last century even as the new one begins. Coal has a lot to answer for in Nova Scotia: whenever one of us grouses about our province's fractious politics, we're on some level talking about coal. Anyone who laments the state of our hard-luck economy is really complaining about coal's legacy. Why are the rural towns and villages emptying out? What's responsible for the pockets of abject poverty dotting the countryside? Where do our appallingly bad health statistics come from? The deeper I dug through my job as a reporter, the more likely I was to find that coal was the answer.

The Westray disaster, as much as any single event, showed how coal, politics and have-not economics intersect in Nova Scotia. It was hard, for example, to sit in a Toronto high-rise office with Clifford Frame, as I did a year after the Westray tragedy, and not feel the crushing injustice of life. The Curragh Resources Inc. CEO—all Foghorn Leghorn elegance in his dark suit, green tie, handkerchief and cufflinks—seemed precisely the kind of guy who would be hailed as a saviour by the Nova Scotia government when he arrived in the 1980s, offering to create jobs in a place that sorely needed them. "They wanted somebody they thought they could work with and not be pushed around by," Frame said. "The province and the feds gave me the encouragement. If I didn't have that encouragement, I wanted nothing to do with that project."

Encouragement, in this case, meant a total of $12 million in federal and provincial funding, loan guarantees and interest rate subsidies for Curragh. There were lots of people who told the governments not to do it. But the coal industry has always been adept at backing just the right legislators and politicians to make its sooty dreams reality. And there's always the jobs card. The money was well spent as far as the politicians were concerned. The province's Conservative government had been rocked by a wave of mishaps and tawdry scandals. Its popularity was plummeting. Even Donald Cameron, the party's Pictou County strongman, was in the midst of a close battle for his seat. What a stroke of unimaginable luck, then, that five days before election day a Curragh subsidiary announced it was creating three hundred jobs by developing a $127-million mine in the midst of Cameron's riding. When the polls closed, Cameron had held onto his seat by a few hundred votes and the Tory government—will miracles never cease—had been returned to power with a slim four-seat majority.

Eugene Johnson, I later discovered, had voted Tory. When I went to see his widow on the one-year anniversary of the disaster, she told me that he had been happy to finally follow his forebears underground. By the time the mine officially opened on September 11, 1991, Eugene's excitement was fading. He told his wife, Donna, about the sections of roof collapsing. He was sparing her the worst: the endless list of flouted safety violations, the sub-par ventilation, the dangerously high levels of methane gas and coal dust. The managers who intimidated the crew, and even tampered with safety equipment, in an effort to pull more coal out of the seam, to keep the revenue coming for a parent company that badly needed cash flow.

On the night of May 8, Eugene said goodbye to his wife and hugged his two sons, both under ten. Once the twelve-hour shift ended, Eugene, who played the guitar and even wrote some poetry, was due for four days off. The Commission of Inquiry's report into the explosion—*The Westray Story: A Predictable Path to Disaster*—picks up the story from here. The spark was probably caused when the continuous miner—an electrical machine that literally carves the coal from the working face of the mine—struck either pyrites or sandstone in the coal wall. The tiny flame should have faded harmlessly. Instead, it ignited a cloud of methane gas that had been allowed to accumulate in the shaft due to improper ventilation. Some of the miners may have had a ten-second head start. It's hard to think of them racing down the shaft as the rolling flame—which consumed all the oxygen in the roadways and left poisonous carbon monoxide in its wake—licked above their heads. Breathing in the carbon monoxide, they would have fallen on the spot. When the fireball hit a thick layer of coal dust—another contravention of provincial mining regulations—it triggered a massive explosion that burst through the entire mine, devastating everything in its path.

I've thought a lot about coal since Westray. And that has led to a revelation. It took time to merge together our extended storyline. But noodle around a little—with the help of the Internet, the archives and some energetic distant relatives—and a pattern becomes clear. My family's tale is no different from that of millions of other Canadians: centuries of struggle in the underclass of the old country, a decision to take a flyer on a new life in a new world, then a long slog making some other guy rich, until we finally abandon the muck, woods and subterranean depths for the expanding middle class. In between, the usual mix of heartbreak, triumph and tedium. There is, as far as I can discern, only one constant thread running through our collective yarn. Coal.

Coal brought my people here from the farmlands of Scotland and England's industrial heartland, and drew us inexorably to Cape Breton. Coal mining brought our disparate tribes together and then, for better or worse, gave our lives an organizing principle. Without coal, no me; at least, not someone with the same genetic topography, the same inherited molecules, predilections and phobias. It made us all who we are. When coal mining disappeared we scattered to the winds; a century after the Brierses, DeMonts, McKeigans and Browns arrived, they're mostly gone again, to Halifax, the outskirts of Chicago, Toronto and Montreal. As I write these words, I have precisely one uncle, an aunt and two first cousins—including the only remaining member of my people who has worked a coal seam—still living in Cape Breton.

So the story of coal is my story too, which means that the best way to understand my family's storyline is to understand the history of that soft, sooty black mineral in this province. There was a sense of urgency; time was wasting. The links between family members had invariably started to fray. The elders with any direct connection to coal were dwindling. My father had Alzheimer's; the last of my uncles still living in Cape Breton underwent bypass surgery; during the writing of this book their other brother went to bed one night and did not wake up, and the final Cape Breton uncle on my mother's side also died. I wanted to make sense of their stories while they still echoed in the air.

So much about the story of coal mesmerized me. I'm far from the first writer with a thing about the subterranean life, those unimaginable passageways and cities where thousands of men led parallel lives inside the earth. I also got hooked on the story because it seems to encapsulate everything about Nova Scotia: its geology, settlement and economic development, along with its social history, place in the world and aspirations for the future. It's a story that's connected to the great events of the world, but at the same time remains an extraordinarily human journey. The chronicle of coal in Nova Scotia is the story of how a simple black rock irrevocably changed a society and its people. It's a narrative of outrage, but also a drama filled with heroism, loss, the cruel but hypnotic spectacle of time and the inexorable force of economic progress. As much as anything, it's a story that ends with a question: what happened to these people after their land was eviscerated and emptied out?

Not everyone sees them the way I do. "Grim" is a word often used to describe coal miners and coal-mining towns, particularly in the thirty years since the industry began its inevitable decline in these parts. It's not a word they necessarily use to describe themselves—even if few of them would wish a job in the pits on their sons. Weirdly, at least in the view of the rest of the world, they talk mostly in positive terms: of the camaraderie of soldiers, professional athletes and other men who have shared intense, dangerous work; of the professionalism that comes from doing a difficult job well. There is a swell of pride evident even in the voices of broken old men when they say, "I am a Cape Breton miner," a "Springhill miner" or a "Pictou County collier."

People in Calgary or Toronto or even, to a lesser degree, Halifax, seem to think of coal miners as quaint, kinda sad relics of our industrial past—their stories relegated to the songs of Rita MacNeil and the occasional earnest CBC drama. Or as brutish throwbacks out of D.H. Lawrence, who do what they do for a living because they're too backwards or set in their ways to have another choice.

The other popular refrain about Nova Scotia coal miners nowadays is that they were lazy parasites. They were forever on strike. They wasted "our" money in an industry that had no good economic reason to exist. Just writing those words makes my bowels churn. I fully understand that, in this day and age, people who can't justify their paycheques in economic terms have no real excuse for living. I'm also willing to accept that going into the pits at the start of the twenty-first century—even if you're desperate for a decent paycheque in a place where a 20 percent unemployment rate is the norm—demonstrates a certain lack of originality.

Yet what about perseverance? What about duty? What about valour? Because that more than anything was what kept me coming back to the miners. When I spoke earlier of being utterly stunned upon learning that men were still coal mining in Nova Scotia, I forgot to mention my next thought: wonderment that someone actually had the courage for such a thing. I've kept coming back to their stories because I admire the miners and their families for the most childish reason possible: because they strike me as heroic.

It's hard to imagine a more savage and inhuman industrial environment in which to make a living. Their fate was never their own to control. Someone else—adventurers in London, profiteers in Boston, corporate villains in Montreal—always signed their paycheques, owned the food they ate and the shacks in which they lived. Yet rather than fleeing it, or surrendering to it, they transcended "the deeps" with their humanity, their collective strength—their courage, which lingers long after the last whistle on the last shift has sounded. Not showy reality TV–style courage. A quieter, workmanlike heroism, which doubtless appeals to me in this deep, visceral way because I've never done anything remotely brave myself.

Unlike the bulky guys who were huddled around the flaming, hollowed-out oil drums one January day eight years after the

Westray disaster, blockading the Lingan power generating station just outside of Sydney to protest the closure of one of Cape Breton's two remaining coal mines. A few of the workingmen's hands lacked thumbs and index fingers. Even the non-smokers among them hacked and coughed, their lungs flayed by decades of inhaling coal dust. Most of them were in their forties. But all coal miners look older than they are. "Ancient ahead of our time," one of them said. "Our bodies ruined by the mines just like our fathers' and grandfathers' before us."

Fighting to be heard above gale-force winds, I yelled a question about the treatment they were getting from the federal government, which was closing down their mine, and the importance of telling readers their side of the story. Somebody laughed mirthlessly. One miner couldn't meet my eyes, as if embarrassed to be in the presence of someone making a living in such an unmanly way. The flames made their faces look timeless, tribal, somewhat dangerous. "For what it's worth," I finally said, "I've got a cousin in the mines: Kenneth Demont."

A pause.

"Well, Kenny Demont's cousin," a voice from the dark said, "you know much about coal mining?"

"Not as much as I should."

Rugged Angus Davidson, forty-one years old, the third generation of his family to work the coal face, stepped into the light where I could see him. "Maybe it's about time you learned," he said.

I couldn't have agreed more. Even if it meant connecting that moment with another, hundreds of millions of years before humans climbed out of the trees. It happened in a place called Pangaea. Which, I guess, is where we will start.

CHAPTER ONE

No Vestige of a Beginning

John Calder—who has a doctorate of geology in his pocket and a tiny silver hoop in his left ear—sees things way differently than you or I. Let me illustrate. Late morning on a mild fall day; the year is 2007, which means the airwaves bulge with hos and booty, George Bush and Paris Hilton, get-rich-quick and hours-long erections. The icecaps are melting. Governments everywhere seem mean and dim. Yet there stands Calder—greying hipster hair, blue mackinaw, green army pants, distressed hiking shoes—on a beach that is canted on an angle of a couple of degrees into the waters of Chignecto Bay, putting everything in its proper perspective.

When Calder looks at a section of cliff, he doesn't just see rocks. He considers the looping bands of land—the messy stuff that looks to an untutored eye like a dragon's spine, interspersed with feature-less layers that even I recognize as sandstone—and sees entire continents shifting, grinding together and colliding. He glimpses chains of mountains erupting skyward and then covering unimaginable chunks of the earth. He sees the world pulling apart and superoceans rushing in. When Calder looks at a rock on the beach with a couple of squiggles on it—or at least that's how it looks to me—it triggers in his temporal lobe images of plants shaped like feather dusters stretching high into the prehistoric sky. Or it bombards his brain with visions of six-foot-long insects, mandibles snapping like nunchuks, struggling through the primordial muck. When he walks over coal, I imagine, his liver starts to quiver.

I'm here because I want him to teleport me back, oh let's see, about 300 million years. Because only by understanding what happened then on this piece of geography can I grasp everything that followed. The best place to see the epochal story of how coal came to be formed in Nova Scotia is at the cliffs of Joggins, a next-to-nothing of a place that stares across Chignecto Bay at southern New Brunswick. Luckily I've got the perfect guide. Calder, a respected geologist with Nova Scotia's department of natural resources, understands the science. He also has what geologists call "the picture": the ability, as John McPhee, the writer, explains, to take lingering remains, connect them with dotted lines and then fill in the gaps to "infer why, how and when a structure came to be." Calder possesses yet another gift: an unwavering eye for the narrative line. He can see the big story along with the big picture. "We're walking in the footsteps of giants here," he says, starting down the beach toward the Joggins cliffs. Miraculously, I actually know what he means.

The Joggins cliffs failed to transport me the first time I saw them—on a high school field trip. So today I'm trying to make up for that youthful myopia, that failure of imagination. I'm not the first person to search for enlightenment here. In 1842, by design and coincidence, the pioneering thinkers on the emerging scientific field of geology descended on Joggins, the place Calder likes to call the "coal-age Galapagos." Picture two mutton-chopped men picking their way over the rocks. Abraham Gesner, the one with the broad shoulders, dark hair and piercing eyes, came from German stock via the Netherlands and New York's Hudson Valley. He was a restless sort who had bigger ambitions than a farming life in Nova Scotia's luminous Annapolis Valley. Just out of his teens he had tried shipping horses from Nova Scotia to the West Indies, but had been twice shipwrecked. Chastened, he had returned to his father's farm and, in 1824, married the daughter of a local doctor. Legend has it that the only way the father would consent to the union was if Gesner accepted his financial help and enrolled in a London medical school. Eventually, he returned to Nova Scotia with a medical diploma—and also an abiding interest in geology, probably due to exposure to some of the powerful lecturers in the new science in the United Kingdom.

So it was entirely logical that Gesner picked a seaport called Parrsboro, on the Minas Basin, as the place to start a medical practice. He visited his patients by horse or on foot, travelling along a section of coastline where, twice a day, 100 billion tons of seawater—more than the combined flow of all the freshwater rivers in the world—pours in and out of a 200-million-year-old rift valley cradled between Nova Scotia and New Brunswick. The Mi'kmaqs, Nova Scotia's first people, felt the Bay of Fundy a holy place. Gesner also discovered something transcendent in the way the surging water had stripped away millions of years of land, until the cliffs and shore shimmered with layers of geological time.

While visiting patients, Gesner made notes and gathered specimens. Before long, he was finding reason to edge along the Minas Basin all the way up Chignecto Bay to Joggins, to peruse the area's mineral wealth. He read whatever geological books he could get his hands on, learning enough to publish his first work, *Remarks on the Geology and Mineralogy of Nova Scotia*, in 1836. "Let the great extent of the Coal fields of Nova Scotia," he wrote in his over-heated, biblical prose, "the beds of Iron Ore, Sandstone, Gypsum, Limestone; with every kind of material proper for building both the massive cathedral and the humble cottage, be considered."

The book made enough of a splash that a year later Gesner was hired by the New Brunswick government to conduct a geological survey of its province. By then he was in his early forties. Yet he spent much of the next five years alone, except for his native guides, pushing his way up turbulent streams and over rugged mountains that had seldom been seen by white men. By the standards of the day his geological work was decent enough. The man just had no head for business. ("With no experience in practical mining, he was not able to make a realistic appraisal of the economic potential of the mineral occurrences he discovered," geologist Loris Russell wrote in his entry about Gesner in the *Dictionary of Canadian Biography*. "Thus his enthusiasm saw in every galena vein or coal seam a lead mine or a coal field.") By 1842 the man who would later usher in the modern petroleum industry was just about broke. In desperation, he opened a museum that included his vast collection of minerals, fossils and wildlife specimens. It failed. Gesner's creditors took over his fabled collection, in lieu of payment.

All of which is to say that Gesner may have been overjoyed at the distraction of playing tour guide for an illustrious guest anxious to see the fossil cliffs of Joggins. Sir Charles Lyell—bony of visage and possessing the visionary's thousand-mile stare—was on a side trip during his first visit to the United States and the British province of Canada. At almost forty-five, the most famous scientist in the English-speaking world was near the pinnacle of his career. Nine years earlier he had published the first edition of his seminal book,

Principles of Geology: being an inquiry how far the former changes of the earth's surface are referable to causes now in operation—which, more than any other work, had defined geology as a science.

By 1842, Lyell was smack dab in the middle of one of the great scientific/religious debates of the millennium: how old is the earth? Before the nineteenth century there was still relative unanimity in the Eastern, Christian world that God had created the world in six days. Then heretical new theories began to appear: that the earth was the result of a collision between a comet and the sun, or had condensed over eons from a cooling gas cloud. By the time Lyell arrived in Nova Scotia, the debate within the scientific community had hardened into two distinct camps. On one side were the "catastrophists," who believed that earthquakes, volcanic eruptions, floods or other calamities were responsible for the formation of the world's surface. On the other side stood the "uniformitarians," of whose cause Lyell was the world's leading proponent.

Lyell's view can be boiled down to his famous dictum "The present is the key to the past." Or, to put it another way, the earth's crust changes now for the same reasons and at the same rate as it always has. And geological changes are the steady accumulation of minute changes over enormously long spans of time—not the result of some calamity sent by a righteous God. By 1842 this wasn't the prevailing scientific view—far from it—so Lyell was forever searching for proof. Which brought him to Nova Scotia.

Lyell had another equally weighty question on his mind when he arrived in nearby Parrsboro to meet Gesner: what exactly was coal? Strange to think that on something so fundamental—the nature of the mineral fuelling the Industrial Revolution that was then transforming the world—there was no consensus. Many, including a young naturalist named Charles Darwin, thought the shiny black rock that extended for miles and miles must have formed in the only suitably vast location on the planet: under the sea. Two years earlier a Canadian geologist named William Logan had presented a paper that had knocked the scientific world for a loop; coal beds he had examined in South Wales were persistently underlaid with a layer of clay containing numerous fossil tree roots. In 1841 Logan had travelled to Pennsylvania and Joggins and found the same plant roots that were present in Wales. In his view, those were the roots of landlocked plant matter that was the source of the coal beds.

Lyell came to Joggins to see for himself. "I was particularly desirous, before I left England of examining the numerous fossil trees alluded to by Dr. Gesner as imbedded in an upright posture at many levels in the cliffs of the South Joggins," he wrote in *Travels in North America,* his book about the journey.

> I felt convinced that, if I could verify the account of which I had read, of the superposition of so many different tiers of trees, each representing forests which grew in succession on the same area, one above the other; and if I could prove at the same time their connection with seams of coal, it would go further than any facts yet recorded to confirm the theory that coal in general is derived from vegetables produced on the spots where the carbonaceous matter is now stored up in the earth.

Calder, who knows Joggins like a grizzled beat cop, understands precisely where to go: past the reddish-grey sandstone and the silt-stone and shale smoothed by the winds and waters of the Bay of Fundy. Beneath the cliffs with their thick depths of clay, interspersed with boulders left during the retreat of the last ice sheet, thirteen thousand years ago. At one point, at least in theory, those layers of geological strata exposed in the cliffs were orderly and horizontal;

older strata underneath, each newer layer being laid atop the older ones. Then something happened that knocked the world askew and folded the leading ends of the strata into the earth. When I turn to look at the cliffs, I see layers slanting downwards—at times almost on a 90-degree angle—from left to right. Which means that we're now travelling through geological time as we move from west to east. "About a million years," says Calder, agile as a mountain goat on the rocky surface. "Which, of course, is nothing in the overall scheme of things."

Geological thinking has made quantum leaps since the era of Lyell and Gessner. For a layman like me the important thing is that Calder tells me I'm not hallucinating when I stare at a map of the world: Africa's west coast does look like it could snuggle up against South America's east. Slide everything together and you'd expect to hear a click as the continents lock near-perfectly into place. Geologists used to believe in continental drift, that the earth's continents were slowly drifting across the surface of the globe. With time, that premise was supplanted by a new world view that goes by the snappy sounding title of "plate tectonics." The continents—along with the ocean basins—are part of the earth's crust, which is divided into some twenty segments called plates, which have nothing to do with continents. The African plate, for example, covers all of Africa, but most of its 62 million square kilometres are sea floor beneath the North and South Atlantic and Indian oceans. The North American plate—Nova Scotia's home—is 76 million square kilometres running from the mid-Atlantic right to the west coast.

Wherever they lie, these plates are rock-solid, up to 150 kilometres thick under the continents while just 8 kilometres deep beneath the oceans. Beneath them is a softer, hotter layer of solid rock that, because of its red-hot temperatures, can bend slowly like a bar of Turkish Delight. The plates of the earth's crust float on this layer. It's enough to give a fellow vertigo, the way these plates are forever changing positions and moving. No one's absolutely sure why, but over the malleable layer the plates grow, shrink, combine and disappear, their number changing through time.

This means that, considered through the widest possible lens— eons rather than years, centuries or millennia—the earth isn't some hunk of unchanging rock. Everything, even at this very moment, is moving and in flux. At a rate of just a few centimetres a year, mind you. Still, in a time frame where a million years is like nothing, big things happen: the earth's crust migrates, oceans open and close, continents collide; land buckles, skids into the planet's molten core and shoots miles into the skies forming mountains.

Some 275 million years ago, before dinosaurs or mammals roamed the land, an ocean of unimaginable size closed and the earth's latest and greatest merger took place. Geologists christened the end result "Pangaea," meaning "all earth" in Greek. In the middle of the new supercontinent, cheek by jowl with what would become North Africa and the Cornwall coast of England, lay Nova Scotia.

It's a staggering notion: when Pangaea formed, Nova Scotia was on or near the equator, and continued to inch its way northward as the supercontinent slowly broke apart and the continents continued to assemble. In time, as the continents collided, mountain belts formed—and, eventually, small deep basins between them. This mosaic of interconnected mountains and basins extended from central Nova Scotia northward across the Gulf of St. Lawrence to the present-day shore of the Gaspé Peninsula, east to Newfoundland. The region, by then completely emerged from the sea, was crossed by northeasterly flowing rivers. The rivers carried gravel, sand and mud from the adjacent primordial mountains down into the luxuriant rainforest swamps and bogs flourishing across the tropical lowlands. As the climate warmed, vegetation formed, not just in present-day Nova Scotia but elsewhere in Pangaea's spreading land mass. And ever so slowly, in the river valleys and freshwater lakes between the remains of those mountain ranges in what would become England and Wales, Pennsylvania, Virginia and Nova Scotia, coal formed.

What Calder seeks are the remnants of the vegetation that grew on the flood plains. The tectonic plates continued to grind, collide, recede and collapse, the continents to assemble. Rock bent into folds, or split, causing great slices of plate to rise and fall relative to each other. The Cumberland Basin, where Joggins lies, was one of the low-lying areas that settled between the faults. The exposed sediments we're looking at are the 300-million-year-old wash from the rivers in the uplifted highlands to the west and south.

It doesn't take Calder long to find what he's after: a brownish column, maybe a yard around, suspended perpendicularly within the cliff face. All these hundreds of millions of years later, it's still possible to make out elongated, diamond-shaped scars that span the trunk. Today, the tree's only living relative is common club moss, which grows just a few centimetres high. In its heyday, that Lepidodendron, one of the most common types of lycopod, stretched thirty metres into the steamy prehistoric sky. Calder's on a bit of a roll now, pointing out thin stems that indicate a once-thick undergrowth of calamites, ancient horsetails; running a finger along the remains of a cordaite, which had roots like today's mangrove and metre-long leaves that resembled the amaryllis. Each remnant tells a similar story of the ancient crust of the earth sinking and sediment quickly—by geological standards—accumulating overtop.

Lyell and I have something in common. What he saw in 1842—Lepidodendrons suspended as if in aspic, lycopods haphazardly dotting the sedimentary rocks, calamites peeking out at weird angles—astounded him. "Just returned from an expedition of 3 days to the strait which divides Nova Scotia from New Brunswick," he wrote to his sister after a Joggins visit similar to my own, "whither I went to see a forest of fossil coal—trees—the most wonderful phenomenon perhaps that I have seen, so upright do the trees stand, or so perpendicular to the strata, in the ever-wasting cliffs, every year a new crop being brought into view, as the violent tides of the Bay of Fundy, and the intense frost of the winters here, combine to destroy, undermine, and sweep away the old one—trees twenty-five feet high and some have been seen of forty feet, piercing the beds of sandstone and terminating downwards in the same beds, usually coal."

I have to tell you: it's a humbling thing to look at the remains of a 300-million-year-old plant. The intricate, perfect design, for starters. Then there's the notion I first encountered in Barbara Freese's book *Coal: A Human History,* that when you look at an ancient fern you're indirectly gazing upon prehistoric sunlight. All those ancient trees, ferns and mosses were sophisticated machines that captured solar energy, and converted it into chemical energy and carbon that stayed stored within their cells until they decayed, burned or got eaten. Usually, when plant material dies, it decomposes more rapidly than it accumulates. Peat, the precursor to coal, forms when the reverse is true—when the wetland has a waterlogged surface with little access to oxygen, and this protects the plant matter from bacteria, fungi and other organisms that cause decomposition.

Whether or not peat will form depends mostly on climate and geology. Precipitation has to exceed evaporation. The buildup of plant matter has to keep pace with the subsidence of the earth's surface, so sedimentary deposits or rising water levels don't overwhelm the peat. Let's assume optimum conditions. Beneath the ever-deepening layers of sand, silt and mud, most of the peat moisture is squeezed out. More heat and pressure furthers the transformation, first into lignite, a soft, brownish-black coal with a low carbon content, then black or bituminous coal, the type found in Nova Scotia and in most of the coal-bearing areas on the planet. A mineral that fuels economies, launches kingdoms and revolutionizes worlds.

Coal wasn't the only rock formed in the Carboniferous—the name given by scientists to the period running from 360 million to 280 million years ago—world. Basins were subsiding, infiltrated by upland streams that deposited their coarse sand and gravel loads, covered by rising seas that eventually retreated, leaving coastal plains that were again colonized by peat-forming vegetation. The pattern—coal seams, flood-plain mudstones, lake or marine limestones and riverbed sandstones—is visible in outcrops around the world, and is thought to be linked to the rising and falling sea level as the ice caps of the South Pole melted and grew when the climate shifted. Nowhere, though, can match Joggins as a time-lapsed snapshot taken as the world's great coalfields were being formed.

No wonder Joggins was so deeply embedded in Lyell's thinking from that moment on. In 1852 he returned with another illustrious Nova Scotian scientist in tow. They had met a decade earlier, when Lyell made a brief stop before his trip to Joggins. In New Glasgow he dined at Mount Rundell, met the local mucky-mucks and paid a visit to a young man with a good fossil collection. "He looked over my specimens with appreciation," John William Dawson wrote in his memoirs, "and listened with interest to what I could tell him of the geology of the beds in which they occurred." Dawson, twenty-two, devoutly Christian, fluent in Latin and Greek and with a working knowledge of Hebrew, was freshly back from Edinburgh, Scotland, after his university studies had been interrupted by a family financial setback. At that point his startlingly varied career—geologist, paleontologist, author, publisher, politician, educational visionary, university president—was just beginning. His life-altering epiphany, on the other hand, had already occurred. "It happened, when I was a mere schoolboy," Dawson wrote, "that an excavation in a bank not far from the schoolhouse exposed a bed of fine clay-shale which some of the boys discovered to be available for the manufacture of home-made slate pencils."

Dawson and his classmates used to amuse themselves by digging out flakes of the stone and cutting them into pencils with their pocket knives. One day Dawson was surprised to discover that one of the flakes "had on it what seemed to be a delicate tracing in black, of a leaf like that of a fern." The riddle—real leaves or not, and if real, how did they come to be in the stone?—preoccupied his mind. Eventually his father sent him to the principal of a local grammar school, the astute Scotsman Thomas McCulloch. He "received me kindly, and assured me that the impressions were real leaves imbedded in the stone when it was being formed." And Dawson's life, quite simply, was never the same again.

He read everything he could get his hands on about geology and natural history. He began collecting the minerals, shells and fossils that he found in the Pictou County countryside and as far away as the petrified forest of Joggins. He expanded his collection by exchanging specimens with Gesner and other Nova Scotia geologists. At the University of Edinburgh he took courses in geology, taxidermy and the preparation of thin sections of fossil animals and plants for the microscope. Meeting Lyell was another turning point;

a friendship blossomed. Afterwards, Dawson went back to university and became British North America's first trained geologist.

That made him perfect company when Lyell returned to Joggins. There, within the sediment-filled trunks of three ancient trees, they discovered what turned out to be the remains of one of the world's earliest known reptiles—and the first evidence that land animals had lived during the coal age. Dawson named the discovery *Hylonomus lyelli*, after his mentor. The finding gave Lyell new ammunition against the catastrophists, and solidified his thinking that the planet's rock layers served as an archive of earth's evolution. What Lyell saw and concluded in Nova Scotia also had important implications in the greatest question of the day: evolution or creation?

Lyell's geological theories were already a primary influence on the thinking of Charles Darwin, who had been presented with a copy of the first volume of his *Principles of Geology* before departing on the *Beagle* in 1831. Darwin would lean heavily upon the lessons from Joggins in making the case for evolution in *The Origin of Species*:

> In other cases we have the plainest evidence in great fossilized trees, still standing upright as they grew, of many long intervals of time and changes of level during the process of deposition, which would not have been suspected, had not the trees been preserved: thus Sir C. Lyell and Dr. Dawson found carboniferous beds 1,400 feet thick in Nova Scotia, with ancient root-bearing strata, one above the other, at no less than sixty-eight different levels. Hence, when the same species occurs at the bottom, middle and top of a formation, the probability is that it has not lived on the same spot during the whole period of deposition, but has disappeared and reappeared, perhaps many times, during the same geological period.

Lyell, in fact, changed Darwin's whole world view. As he was quoted as saying, "The greatest merit of the Principles was that it altered the whole tone of one's mind, and therefore that, when seeing a thing never seen by Lyell, one yet saw it through his eyes."

Since the tide is in, we don't see any stumps when we walk past the spot where Lyell and Dawson made their world-altering discovery. Otherwise, the scene is pretty much the same as it was 155 years ago. It gives me a familiar buzz. Like most people, I've often felt that I was born in the wrong time and place. There was my Alexandre Dumas phase, when I felt I should have had buckler and sword on my hip, a great cape trailing behind me, as I strutted through the rain-slicked streets of Paris. There was a period when I felt terribly cheated because I hadn't been at Minton's in New York in the 1940s, to hear Charlie Parker shoot bolts of lightning from his alto sax in situ rather than on vinyl. Nowadays I am more inclined to want to be one of those Victorian amateur scientists, those self-educated, restlessly inquisitive polymaths tromping around in their tweeds, with butterfly nets and microscopes, waiting for the flashes of insight that seem responsible for most of the scientific advances of the age.

Calder, an accomplished documentary photographer, seems to fit easily into the mould of the universal man. So did Lyell, a lawyer by profession but dedicating himself to the great questions of existence, and Gesner—notwithstanding the flawed personality that destined him to die broke and broken—with his eternal curiosity. Most of all I wanted to be like Dawson, but not when he was changing the world with Lyell. I preferred to imagine him, sketchbook in hand, prospector's hammer in a bag slung over his shoulder, making his way from one end of Nova Scotia to the other, whether working as a geologist or as the province's first superintendent of education, which involved meticulously visiting every school in every district.

Dawson was mad for rocks; he couldn't help himself, even though it nearly killed him. A trip he made one April, while trying to get to the root of the province's educational woes, was perhaps illustrative: travelling over the North Mountain in the Annapolis Valley in a light snowstorm, addressing an educational meeting in "that somewhat isolated locality," then convincing local fishermen to take him at daybreak through heavy seas to see a large fall from a cliff a few miles down the coast. Amidst the debris he found "an amazing quantity of fine zeolites with which we loaded the boat and returned to Black Rock in time to pack the specimens before breakfast." Then he left for Aylesford, twenty-five miles away, before continuing west to picturesque Digby Neck. He took the ferry to Long Island, "on which no conveyance was to be had." There he walked the island's entire ten-mile length, examining rocks as he went.

Dawson travelled mostly by horse, whether riding or via stagecoach, sometimes by boat or on foot, and, as he put it, "my educational and geological journeys were therefore not only attended with much labour, but occasionally with some risk." If you want to understand the extent of Nova Scotia's coalfields, it's instructive to see things through his eyes. To consider, for a moment, the awe he may have felt traversing the land near Sydney, on Cape Breton Island, where he was transfixed by fossilized rain marks—"the finest example yet known"—and by shales he declared "also much more rich than those at the Joggins in the leaves and other more delicate parts of plants."

Then there was the sheer immensity of the Sydney coalfield, within which thirty-four coal seams had by then been identified. At that point Dawson wouldn't have precisely understood how slowly the transformation of ancient wetlands into energy source occurred. Peat, we now know, accumulates gradually, growing only four millimetres a year in the modern tropics. A coal seam one metre thick was originally five to ten metres of peat, and took perhaps 2,500 years to accumulate; each of the coal beds of Joggins represents about 1,000 years of peat accumulation. By comparison, the coal seams of the Sydney coalfield, 4.3 metres at their thickest, were the product of roughly 10,000 years of natural history. Neither Dawson nor his guide, Richard Brown, the manager of the Sydney Mines, would have realized one key point about the formation. It would take deeper coal mines in the area, and the boreholes of offshore drill ships, to show that the coal-bearing rocks extend nearly to the south coast of Newfoundland. Fully 98 percent of the Sydney field is underwater.

At some point Dawson made his way to the island's southwest coast, where the coal seams spectacularly outcrop in the coastal cliffs. Near the Gaelic settlement of Mabou, the exposures rivalled the Joggins shore and the near-vertical position of the faults underscored the geological upheavals that had occurred there. Dawson explored the nearby Inverness field, where coal-bearing rocks occupy a land area of about nine square miles, along with the Mabou field, with its eight coal seams, just twenty-five kilometres away. In the seams near Port Hood he found sigillaria stumps that were almost as good as the ones found at Joggins.

In fits and starts he made his way through the coalfields of the mainland, to Joggins, where the seams rarely exceeded a metre in thickness and the coal itself contained troublesome amounts of sulphur and ash. Then to "a place called Springhill," where the coal is "of good quality" but the field's great distance from water meant it would be "waiting for their full development till railways extend across the country, or til domestic manufacturers demand supplies of mineral within the province." Back to Pictou County, near his boyhood home, he encountered a relatively small field—Albion Mines—boasting seams of unimaginable diameter.

For years he kept at it, fitting the mapping and surveying in between his important day jobs. Nights he hauled himself back to wherever he was staying and made notes in his elegant hand, sketching whole sections of rock, cliff and terrain with draftsmanship as precise as the drawings of a Renaissance understudy. He approached the job with the eye of a scientist but a poet's romantic heart. "Acadia ... signifies primarily a place or region," he wrote in his monumental 1855 opus *Acadian Geology,* which stood for more than a century as the best survey of the geology of Nova Scotia, New Brunswick and Prince Edward Island, "and, in combination with other words, a place of plenty or abundance."

Dawson was blunt about what he saw: "the Great Britain of Eastern America," an area with abundant resources that "must necessarily render them more wealthy and populous than any area of the same extent on the Atlantic coast, from the Bay of Fundy to the Gulf of Mexico, or in the St. Lawrence valley, from the sea to the head of the great lakes." I imagine him writing those words: the optimism, the excitement, the leap of faith and imagination. I am standing on a beach where the bones of the earth show through, a long time later. It's crazy, I know, but his words thrill me even now.

CHAPTER TWO

Beneath the Golden Salmon

I recollect seeing coal before I knew what it was: thick ebony chunks of rock near the cellar chute in my grandparents' backyard on York Street, in Glace Bay. I went digging there one day with a child's undeniable purpose; someone had told me that when they were kids my father and his brothers used to sometimes bury swordfish bills in the backyard. They would wait long enough for them to be picked clean by insects, dig them up, then brandish the skeletal remains like rapiers as they ran down the block past the miners' homes, playing at Zorro. Mabel and Clarie Demont's yard, I seem to recall, was lousy with the rock, making it hard slogging for a little kid with a plastic shovel. I imagine that, being a lazy boy at heart, I must have taken an immediate dislike to it—until, I guess, somebody around there set me straight.

I didn't know then that coal was a miracle for those who knew how to use it. That scholars think the first indisputable use of coal was for cremation in Bronze Age South Wales, or that, from the remains of Roman coal-fuelled fires along Hadrian's Wall, we understand that coal has been used in Europe on a small scale for thousands of years. European coal use seems to have disappeared for hundreds of years after the fall of the Roman Empire, until somehow, as the Middle Ages approached, it was rediscovered; the Venetian traveller Marco Polo marvelled at "stones that burn like logs" when he visited the court of the great Kublai Khan in the thirteenth century. Around then—after hundreds of years of being harvested from the surface by peasants looking to heat their hovels—coal began to be used commercially in Europe, to fuel blacksmith forges and for other metalworking. Liège in Belgium and Newcastle in England became some of the first coal centres. Because of its bulk and the high costs of transportation, coal was first only used in the area around where it was mined. But by the mid-1200s, it was being transported via sea the three hundred miles from Newcastle—home to England's most important seams—to London.

Coal was in such demand because other fuels were running out. As England's advancing population colonized and cultivated vast tracts of the country, the forests, marshes and moors disappeared at a startling rate. As wood became scarcer, demand for coal increased. So did supply, once Henry VIII decided, in 1527, to end his marriage to Catherine of Aragon because she couldn't provide him with a male heir. When Pope Clement VII refused to grant him an annulment, Henry broke with Rome. According to Barbara Freese, that "led to one of the greatest property shifts in English history." Many of the richest coal mines in England suddenly became the property of the Crown. It auctioned off the land. The mines ended up in the hands of profit-driven merchants and gentry.

By then, the downside of coal was already becoming evident in cities like London, which lay enshrouded in a cloud of choking black smoke and fumes. By the start of the fourteenth century men were refusing to work at night because of pollution from the coal fires, and a royal proclamation forbade the use of coal in lime kilns in parts of South London. The proclamation was such an abject failure that instructions were given to punish offenders with fines for a first offence and to demolish their furnaces for a second. Yet, as we will repeatedly see, economics almost always trumped all other concerns when it came to coal. As the British Empire gathered momentum, more and more landowners were cutting down woodlands to make room for sheep. By the sixteenth century the iron industry was consuming vast amounts of charcoal, using up even more of the English forests. As the century closed, England had only one option if it hoped to conserve its remaining forests. The coal age, officially, had dawned.

Which makes me wonder: how did they miss it? How did the coal plainly visible in Cape Breton's cliffs, bays and headlands manage. to escape the notice of the first Europeans who plied its waters? No mention from Giovanni Caboto (John Cabot), the Italian-born navigator who may have visited Cape Breton in 1497, claiming the land for England; not a peep, apparently, from the Breton fishermen who began arriving at the start of the sixteenth century; nary a word from João Alvares Fagundes, the Portuguese explorer who established a fishing colony with about two hundred settlers on the island's northwestern peninsula around 1520. Captain Strong of the *Marigold*, who visited Cape Breton in 1593, went into excruciating detail about the island, including the various kinds of trees and even the small shrubs found there; except not a word about coal. Captain Leigh of the *Hopewell*, who arrived in 1597 and landed, "as he tells us, at five different places all in the middle of the Sydney Coal-field," is equally silent on the subject. The famed explorer, navigator and geographer Samuel de Champlain circumnavigated the island in 1607; according to Richard Brown, he failed to "make the slightest allusion to the coal seams, although he notices such small matters as the abundance of oysters."

Sixty-five years later someone finally opened his eyes. Nicolas Denys, a restless merchant from Tours, France, who had been appointed governor of all of the eastern part of Acadia, received a concession from Louis XIV for the mineral rights of Cape Breton Island. "There are mines of coal through the whole extent of my concession, near the sea coast, of a quantity equal to the Scotch," he wrote in the preface to *Description géographique et historique des Costs de L'Amérique Septentrionale,* published in Paris in 1672. Denys added, "At Baie Des Espagnols (Sydney) there is a mountain of very good coal, four leagues up the river" and "another near the little entrance of the Bras d'Or Lakes," and also wrote that "at LeChadye on the north-west coast there is a small river suitable for chaloups, where there is a plentiful salmon fishery and a coal mine."

Denys, though, had one focus: establishing a thriving fur trade. During his long residence in Cape Breton he did nothing to exploit the coal seams. Neither did Jean Talon, the Intendant of New France, even after discovering good-quality coal in Cape Breton in 1670 and dispatching a functionary to inspect the seams. Yet coal's value simply couldn't be denied. Soon the French were using coal from Sydney Harbour to refine sugar in the West Indies and, perhaps as some sort of novelty, to fire the royal forges in France. By the early 1700s, both the French and their British rivals—mainly New England colonists who fished along the coast of Cape Breton in the summer—regularly stopped in Sydney. There they took loose coal from the base of the cliffs, or by cutting into the land with crowbars and shovels and loading the mineral directly onto their boats. In 1711 Rear Admiral Sir Hovenden Walker, commander of a British naval squadron, took refuge there after losing several ships and nearly a thousand men in a disastrous attempt to take Quebec. The coal reserves, he gushed, were "extraordinarily good here and taken out of the cliff with iron crow bars only, and no other labour."

Two years later Britain and France signed the Treaty of Utrecht, ending hostilities in Europe and America. Under the pact, France handed almost all of Acadia, the present-day Maritimes, over to England. It held onto only tiny Île Saint-Jean, later to become Prince Edward Island, and Île Royale—eventually known as Cape Breton—which suddenly became the key to French power in North America. The island had long been an integral part of a French cod fishery that stretched from the western shore of Newfoundland, around the Gulf of St. Lawrence and along the Atlantic coast of Nova Scotia. In Cape Breton, fishing crews from France and the Basque region arrived every spring and built temporary bases for the summer cod industry. A sheltered, ice-free harbour on Île Royale's south coast was the natural epicentre of France's Grand Banks fishery. The Treaty of Utrecht gave the harbour even more strategic import; the French needed a North Atlantic trade hub linking France, North America and the West Indies, and a sentinel to guard the entrance to the Gulf of St. Lawrence and Quebec. They renamed the harbour Louisbourg, after the Sun King, made it the administrative headquarters for Île Royale and stationed soldiers there.

In 1713, 150 French settlers arrived in Cape Breton from Placentia, Newfoundland, after Britain surrendered the south coast of that island to the English. Two years later Cape Breton's civilian population had swollen to 700, and energetic entrepreneurs were setting up shops and trading with visiting ships. To survive, though, Louisbourg needed something else: walls to keep the marauding English out; big guns to train on attacking navies. "If France were to lose this island," Louisbourg's Governor Pontchartrain wrote in a letter to Versailles, "it would be irreparable; and as a result, it would be necessary to abandon the rest of North America."

Louis XIV took his point. The end result was the great fortress of Louisbourg, with its mortared walls surrounded by moats, its mammoth bastions laid out in a star shape to protect against land assault, its batteries to repulse warships attacking from the harbour side. To protect this precious little town, France erected the largest, most sophisticated fortifications North America had yet seen. Back in the 1960s, partly to create jobs for displaced Cape Breton coal miners, the Canadian government decided to rebuild one-fourth of the stone-walled town. Walking down those reconstructed streets past musket-carrying "French" lookouts with BAs in folklore demanding that visitors "*Arrête,*" you get a sense of what the town must have been like: the trading houses and wharves bustling with commerce generated by one of North America's busiest seaports; the streets filled with soldiers and priests, merchants and tradesmen, privileged colony administrators and poor labourers indentured to service in the colony. A bustling, wide-open place full of drunken, brawling mercenaries, illicit traders willing to move anything that might turn a profit, and enough high-level corruption that, according to author Lesley Choyce, the fort's finances were irreparably weakened by all the money skimmed off in various ways by local officials.

No wonder construction work on the fortress cost thirty million French livres, and led Louis XV to wonder aloud whether he would one day see Louisbourg rising over the western horizon from his palace at Versailles. In spite of enduring everything from smallpox epidemic to famine, Louisbourg was a construction boom town as much as a commercial hub. Wood was needed for buildings and to fire ovens; stone for soldiers' barracks, the governor's apartment and the bakery and chapel. Wood and stone were easy to find. The coal to run the artillery forge to make ironwork for the cannon carriages proved a bit more difficult. The only known source was an outcrop at Cow Bay, a place that first appears on a 1580 map of the area, under the name Baie de Mordienne.

Port Morien, as it's been rechristened, is now a pretty little fishing village a few kilometres from modern-day Sydney. On a 2007 visit I drove around for a bit with a retired RCMP officer who was busy trying to stop a plan to strip mine what's left of the area's coal seams. After a while he pulled his van off to the side of the road and walked over to a cairn bearing a modest plaque noting that TWO THOUSAND FEET SOUTH EASTERLY FROM THIS PLACE ARE THE REMAINS OF THE FIRST REGULAR COAL MINING OPERATIONS IN AMERICA, ESTABLISHED BY THE FRENCH IN 1720.

Otherwise not a single hint, to my eyes, that for decades soldiers dug into the exposed seams and moved the coal twenty kilometres south to where workmen were fortifying Louisbourg. Somewhere around here were the remnants of the first blockhouse, built by the French in 1725 to protect their valuable coal reserves. The French-English rivalry, after all, extended to the coal seams. Twenty years later the English began building their own blockhouse to protect the seams they were working at Burnt Head, farther up the coastline. That didn't stop a raiding party of French soldiers and native warriors from seizing nine vessels and capturing nine British soldiers. The English forged on anyway, finishing the fortification and installing 148 officers and men to protect their vessels carrying coal between there and Louisbourg, which had been in English hands since 1745. In 1748 the fortress reverted to French control under the Treaty of Aix-la-Chapelle. A decade later, Wolfe seized Louisbourg again for the English.

In 1784 Cape Breton—expected to be the destination of a massive influx of Loyalists following the American Revolution—became a separate colony and received imperial sanction to use the island's coal to raise revenue. The colony's first Lieutenant-Governor, J.F.W. DesBarres, opened a mine at the Sydney Main or Harbour seam. It was hardly an auspicious beginning; DesBarres's selling price of eleven shillings and sixpence per ton meant he struggled to break even. His successors had an odd recipe for developing the coalfield: short-term leases in return for excessive royalties. In the decades to come, the leases changed hands at a wearisome pace: from Messrs Tremaine and Stout to William Campbell, the attorney general, John C. Ritchie, the superintendent of shipping, back to Campbell, then to two other fellows named Tremaine of Halifax who pulled out altogether after deciding the cost of extracting the coal was prohibitively high, back to Ritchie and someone named Timothy Leaver, before being assigned to G.W. Brown and J. Leaver until the lease expired in 1820. At that point the lease was taken up by two other Browns (T.S. and W.R.) They too didn't make a cent.

This wasn't the case in the coalfields of England, where something truly transformative was taking place. The country's coal operators faced a perplexing problem: demand for English coal was growing at breakneck speed. The trouble was that the bigger the industry grew, the deeper the operators had to dig in search of larger coal seams. And the farther each shaft punched into the ground, the more each mine filled with water. Enter a blacksmith from Dartmouth named Thomas Newcomen, who came up with a way to use the forces of nature to solve the drainage problem. By burning coal, Newcomen used steam pressure built up in a boiler to power a piston. The piston, in turn, drove a pump that drained water from coal mines, allowing them to operate far more cheaply and efficiently. Author Bill McKibben estimates that Newcomen's engine replaced the equivalent of a team of five hundred horses walking in a circle. The steam engine changed the whole energy equation forever; humans were freed from depending upon their puny muscles or the brawn of horses, oxen and other animals. Now they could use the pent-up energy buried underground to do the work for them.

In 1763 a Scotsman named James Watt went one step further, adding a separate cooling chamber to the machine. His innovation reduced the loss of heat and improved efficiency to the point where his steam engine could be applied to all kinds of industries. An old agrarian world based on manual labour and life on the farm was being replaced by one dominated by industry, machines and life in cities. Coal—which replaced the limited power of human and animal sweat and muscle with the unrelenting potency of soulless machinery—was the raw material that fired the transformation. Coal-fired boilers fired the factories and mills that turned out finished products, and ran the locomotives and steamships that widened the market for those manufactured goods. Coal, it was discovered, also had other uses. For centuries, the British had converted their iron ores to pig iron and steel by heating the raw material with charcoal, made from trees. By the mid-eighteenth century, the nation's timber supply was failing. Coke, formed by baking coal until the impurities burned off, turned out to be a better, cheaper fuel for iron-ore smelting anyway.

Without coal, in other words, no clouds of smoke forever billowing from the ironworks and smelters of the Western Midlands—the Black Country. No Lancashire and Yorkshire terrifyingly transformed into the world's greatest textile centres. No canals, roads and rail lines hacked out of the terrain.

All of which made coal-mining's lack of progress in Cape Breton even more puzzling. The steady procession of names on the leases continued. In 1820, the year that the British Colonial Office reannexed Cape Breton to Nova Scotia, the leaseholders of the day managed to sell less than ten thousand tons of coal, marginally more than their predecessors had sold twenty years earlier. For an island within striking distance of the fast-expanding cities of the eastern United States, that was a startlingly meagre amount. Some of the reasons were obvious. Bootleg coal stolen with picks and shovels from Cape Breton's uninhabited coastal cliffs ate into commercial production. According to historians of the day, the Nova Scotian product was sent to market in such poor condition that it couldn't compete against English coal. Economics also conspired against the leaseholders: wages, which accounted for 80 percent of costs, were thought to be breathtakingly high. The shortage of return freight ratcheted up the price of shipping. That left the Cape Breton mine owners relying on local demand in Halifax, which consumed about three-quarters of output, and St. John's, which took the rest. Even then the high price of Cape Breton coal made it barely competitive against British coal shipped to North America as ballast.

As the new century dawned, the administration's approach— short-term leases coupled with exorbitant royalties—was as myopic as ever. "It could not be expected," Richard Brown wrote half a century later, "that men of capital would employ their money in an undertaking of magnitude under a lease of five or seven years; and it is equally certain that, without capital, the mines could not be worked for profit." The one way the authorities acted decisively— ensuring that the market for domestic coal remained a captive one— did no one any good. Landowners who discovered coal on their acreage found it was the property of the Crown. If they "forgot" this, soldiers who were empowered to prevent the mining and smuggling of illegal coal arrived to remind them. "The action of the authorities," geologist Francis W. Gray wrote in 1917, "must have seemed cruelly foolish and inexplicable to those colonists who, every spring, saw the coal that the winter's frosts had loosened drop into the sea with the first thaws of spring, to be washed completely away by the first storm."

On the mainland, the nineteenth century opened with little obvious promise. The Cumberland County mines in Joggins and Springhill ran into the same problems. The Scots who had settled in Pictou County, where coal had been discovered in the early 1790s, stubbornly tried to seize their underground wealth; the result, though, was little different. The story of John MacKay, who dug possibly the first coal mine in Pictou County in 1807, is perhaps emblematic. Like the other early operators, he lacked the money and technical skills to turn the first pits into much. During the Napoleonic Wars, things were good for anyone who found a way to provision the garrison in Halifax. In the last year of the War of 1812, Nova Scotia's lieutenant governor ordered MacKay to ship coal to Halifax. Expecting such orders—and wartime profits—to continue, MacKay invested heavily in roads, bridges, wagons and lighters to move the coal. But peacetime brought a collapse in prices. In 1817 MacKay was forced into bankruptcy and thrown into debtor's prisoner for a year, leaving his wife and children in "greatest distress." While in jail, MacKay petitioned the government in Halifax for help. Instead, while MacKay was in the brig, a local Pictou merchant and MLA named John Mortimer was handed the right to mine coal in Pictou County. Political patronage—another practice long associated with the province's coal industry—had its start.

The postscript was no cheerier: MacKay died without making a cent off the coal. The next few years, as new mines were tentatively opened and leases moved back and forth between owners, brought little improvement. A succession of local worthies took a shot at turning the leases into something. By 1820 total production was 7,762 tonnes. Five years later, production had dropped to a point where the leaseholder of the moment said his overall profit amounted to a grand total of £200.

One summer day I went looking, in the town of Stellarton, for an explanation of what happened next: how, within a few decades, coal mining in Nova Scotia went from nothing to an industry capable of bringing the Industrial Revolution to Canada. I wanted to start with a forgotten symbol: Mount Rundell, the twenty-room brick-and-wood official residence that the local manager of the General Mining Association had erected on a seventy-five-acre estate in the centre of the Pictou coalfield. Back in England it would have been a comfortable gentry house. "In the wilderness that Nova Scotia then was, in 1827," James Cameron wrote, "it was a mansion." The property included orchards, hothouses, a large park, a pigeon coop, stables, a porter's house and a coach house. Some of the acreage had been cleared and planted with ornamental trees, shrubs and flowers. A cricket crease stood in one corner of the property; another corner, with a dance platform, chairs and tables, was lent to churches and charities for fundraisers and picnics. Large visitors' houses marked the north and south ends of the property. Staff—some of them former slaves who had escaped from the United States—lived in small cottages elsewhere on the estate.

As much as anything, what intrigued me was the way Richard Smith and his wife, Elizabeth, the daughter of an important coal and iron master from England's Midlands—had entertained like old-country royalty. At its peak, Mount Rundell rivalled the provincial legislature as the most historic and important building in the province. At one point Lord Stanley visited, as did the Earl of Musgrave; and Sir William Fenwick Williams, a hero of the Crimean War. Prime Minister Charles Tupper eventually put in an appearance. So did Joseph Howe, the reformer and newspaper publisher. Fittingly, the great men of the burgeoning field of earth science—Dawson and Lyell—also appeared, drawn by the area's fabulous coal seams.

To my mind you couldn't beat the symbolism: this estate with its sweep of green lawn and long, curved carriage drive, completely surrounded by a hawthorn hedge, standing atop a hill on the edge of a scruffy little colliery town.

Two hundred years later, the grand buildings had been ripped down, and the grounds subdivided. It was near-impossible to find a hint of the mansion's existence.

"Mount what?" a local old-timer said, when I asked about the house.

When I mentioned the General Mining Association, that rang a bell, but he was sketchy on the details. So I went home and tried to piece together the story of the GMA and coal-mining in Nova Scotia. That quest led me to London somewhere around the middle of the eighteenth century, when a man named Hart dealt in toys and fishing tackle in St. Paul's Churchyard, "at the sign of the golden salmon." "Business prospering, he moved to no. 32 Ludgate Hill, where he added the sale of cheap, light jewelry and box and other combs" to his line of merchandise. A man named Theed took over from Hart, took in a partner named Pickett and introduced "the sale of plate." Somebody invited Philip Rundell, the youngest of sixteen, who had served his apprenticeship with a Bath jeweller, to work in their silversmith's shop. Pickett, it developed, had political ambitions—serving as a London alderman in 1782, sheriff in 1784 and lord mayor in 1790—and increasingly left the business to Rundell, who wasn't devoid of ambition himself. One day, finding Theed in a "dissatisfied humour," he persuaded him to sell out. "And thus," wrote George Fox, the author of what may well be one of the earliest corporate histories in English, "he [Rundell] placed himself at the head of the House which afterwards was to become the object of envy to all the Trade and the wonder almost of the World."

In time Rundell was joined by John Bridge, who had served his apprenticeship with the same Bath jeweller. Rundell, who Fox wrote "was naturally of a violent disposition, very sly, and cunning and suspicious," minded the shop; charming, urbane Bridge was the outside "contact" man, a "complete courtier," well fitted for "beating the bush to drive the game to Ludgate Hill." In Georgian England a little charm could get a person a long way; in 1797 Rundell and Bridge were appointed one of the royal goldsmiths, and seven years later they received the royal warrant to supply the Crown with plate, jewels, medals, insignia and even works in ormolu and bronze.

By the 1820s—thanks to Bridge's charm, Rundell's ruthlessness and the sheer beauty of their product—the pair headed a vast enterprise with agencies in Paris, Vienna, St. Petersburg, Baghdad, Constantinople, Bombay, Calcutta, and various cities in South America. The British royal family—particularly George III, who used to shower jewels on his mistresses and members of his inner circle and was as mad for silver-gilt and gilt bronze as his rival Napoleon—adored their plate and jewels. With time, according to antiques scholar Christopher Hartop, it got so that "the affable Bridge would leave Ludgate Hill every morning with his trademark blue bag to show the king a selection of the firm's latest creations."

Why am I telling you all this? Because George's son Prince Frederick, the Duke of York and Albany, also had a thing for baubles. When he saw his brother, George IV, dressed for the coronation in 1821, he admired the profusion of jewellery (not all real) and exclaimed, "By God I'll have everything the same at mine." His biographer called Frederick the king's favourite son, "inattentive to his pecuniary affairs, in consequence of which he fell into many difficulties, and in some instances his name stood on tradesmen's books." The death of George III in 1820 meant that the prince was without the £10,000 a year he had received for looking after his father. When he died in 1827, he left such staggering debts that the Duchess of York approached Christie's to sell his extensive silver collection to cover them. By 1825 Messrs Rundell and Bridge of Ludgate Hill were holding a big slice of the £250,000 in debts which the Duke could barely cover.

The jewellers had another problem: what to do with the money that filled their coffers at a time when the world seemed decidedly short on sound investment opportunities. A year earlier, Rundell and Bridge had been persuaded to form a company with the intriguing title of Colombian Pearl Fishery Association. They raised £120,000 on the stock market, then sent two ships to Latin America in search of lucrative pearl beds. Their ships didn't find anything that would yield the kind of return the London jewellers needed on their investment. They went back to the drawing board, rounded up some more London investors and formed the General South American Mining Association. The company moved quickly, sewing up mineral rights in Brazil and Colombia. A year later—with Latin American mining companies failing everywhere—the GSAMA abandoned its adventure. Which is precisely where the Duke of York and his marker with Rundell, Bridge and Rundell (Philip's nephew, Edmond, had joined them in 1803) came in.

In 1788—even though his mental illness had yet to explode into full-blown mania—George III had drafted a lease to all the mineral rights in Nova Scotia that he fully intended to give to the Duke of York. The documents, for one reason or another, were never completed and the lease seemed to have slipped the duke's mind—until Parliament and his moneylenders at some point started looking askance at his dissipated ways. By then the paperwork had been mislaid, the king was too far gone to recall the past, and all the officials from 1788 were dead or gone. No one put any stock in the duke's claim. So you can imagine the bafflement when the document was found in the Crown's patent office. And in 1826 the Duke immediately turned around and sublet the mining leases to the London jewellers. Then he no doubt issued a royal "whew." Everyone was happy. He had reduced his debts and acquired a 25 percent cut in the anticipated profits from a new foreign venture. Rundell, Bridge and Rundell, who had shortened the name of their offshore company to the General Mining Association, must have been relieved not to have to write off the royal debt. When the deal was examined from one angle the people of Nova Scotia had lost out: their minerals, and the riches that went with them, had been cavalierly handed away to old-country landlords in an act of outrageous royal whimsy. On the other hand, the pragmatists in Nova Scotia understood that suddenly there was capital and mining expertise—in short, an industry—where before there had been none.

There was no denying that the arrangement started poorly. The GMA had been misinformed; they expected to find veins of copper, since Nova Scotia's soil was supposed to teem with it. In 1825 they sent out a Cornish mining engineer named Blackwell to tally up the vast colonial riches. He spent a summer considering every known copper deposit in the province. According to Brown, he found small pieces in the igneous trap rocks in the Bay of Fundy and some "trifling deposits" in the harder sand stones on the shores of the Northumberland Strait—never enough, though, to be worth the expense and bother of extraction. His message for the bosses back in London was clear: forget about copper. Focus on coal. Coal, by God, that was the future.

CHAPTER THREE

A Ponderous Pyramid of Ruins

L oaded to the gunwales with mining machinery, supplies and equipment, the brig *Margaret Pilkington* entered Pictou Harbour on June 4, 1822. Her deck was a sea of dark wool greatcoats and pale whiskered faces. Among the hundred colliers and their family members arriving from the north of England one man, by dress and demeanour, would have stood out from the others. A painting presumably done during Richard Smith's thirteen-year tenure as "general mine superintendent for Messrs. Rundell, Bridge, and Rundell of Ludgate Hill, in the City of London" shows a balding man with a fringe of white hair fashioned into a whirling comb-over. Thin lips, an elegantly formed nose festooned with a spiderweb of broken blood vessels, an old man's sunken cheeks even though he was at most in his early fifties. The eyes get you: slightly bored, condescending maybe—as if it's all beneath him—which seems about right for the scion of a prominent Staffordshire coal-steel family with something still to prove. Smith, who could trace his ancestry to a courtier in William of Normandy's entourage, said he knew about coal "from my youth upwards." That didn't stop him from going broke when the coal and iron boom collapsed at the end of the Napoleonic Wars. Smith rebuilt his reputation by managing mines in Wales and Portugal. At forty-four, he still had enough fire in his belly to accept when the GMA asked him to help establish their coal-mining operations in Nova Scotia.

There, he supervised the assembly of Nova Scotia's first steam engine—with pump, hoisting drum and chain and a boiler—at John MacKay's blacksmith shop in Pictou. Once complete, it was thrown into the harbour, where, to the astonishment of all, it floated rather than sank. From there it was towed seven miles up the East River, an apparition on the black waters, until it reached the spot where the GMA would create the colony of Albion Mines—named, Cameron writes, after the ancient name for Great Britain, Allbyn.

Smith had hardly arrived before petitioning Lieutenant Governor James Kempt for the eviction of settlers who lived on land atop or adjacent to the outcrop of coal. Within days of the *Margaret Pilkington*'s arrival his men were sinking a new pit, the Storr, into the Foord seam; three months later the GMA had its first shipment of coal. Smith described the gas he discovered in the seams as "abundant, almost beyond precedent" and the water as "exceedingly troublesome." With his employers' blessing, he forged ahead anyway, using the steam engine instead of the usual horses to pump water out of the mine and to hoist coal to the surface. Under Smith's direction the men built the first steamship in Nova Scotia, using an engine built in the GMA's own foundry. They built coke ovens, brickworks, mills, carpenter's shops and a foundry, run by imported British foundry men. They made wharves, railways and roads. They erected houses for the workingmen, barns and stables for the horses.

Smith was bringing the same forces that were transforming England to the backwaters of Nova Scotia. In that way, the coming of the GMA was rather like the arrival of the banana company in Macondo, the jungle town in Gabriel García Márquez's *One Hundred Years of Solitude:* "Endowed with means that had been preserved for Divine Providence in former times they [the company] changed the pattern of the rains, accelerated the cycle of harvests and moved the river from where it had always been." In time, coal provided cargo for the wooden ships built in Pictou County. The ensuing decades brought heavy industries—machine shops, bridge and structural steelworks, factories that manufactured mining machinery, heavy wagons and trucks, marine and stationary motors, glass products, marble and granite. For a time, as the twentieth century dawned, Pictou County was one of the steelmaking capitals of Canada.

The natives—like newspaperman Joseph Howe, who visited the Albion Mines in 1830—were left gape-mouthed by what they beheld: the store "in which is kept a more various and extensive stock of goods than is to be found in any mercantile Establishment in the country;" the foundry, which resembled a "Vulcan's workshop" in which "the swarthy artisans are busied adding link to link, and fashioning, by the cunning of their hands and the sweat of their brows those mighty chains to which the ship of some 'great admiral' may be indebted for her safety." Most of all, by the pits themselves, which, once entered, make a visitor feel like "Captain Symmes traveling through the opening at the Poles." Inside, a visitor would encounter "a lot of Beings, looking more like Demons than men" the lamps on their cap making them appear "like the Cyclops, who has but one glaring eye in his forehead." From head to toe, he went on to write, "these people are covered with coal dust, which mixing with the perspiration drawn out by their hard toils, gives their features a singular and rather melodramatic expression."

Howe's stomach fluttered during the descent into the pit. "Are we blown to a thousand atoms?" he wrote. "Are we suffocated by sulphur and fire damp? Are we not lying, like an Egyptian Mummy, beneath a ponderous pyramid of ruins?"

Smith watched the early days of this metamorphosis unfold from the comfort of Mount Rundell. The man who would become his chief lieutenant in Cape Breton, on the other hand, began his tour of duty in an old framed house—"perfectly innocent of paint"— built over some mine workings that had settled and thrown the floor so far out of whack that one side of the sitting room was two feet below the other. His name was Richard Brown. When he arrived at the Sydney Mines in 1826, the conditions must have seemed squalid to someone with a grammar school education who had grown up on a viscount's estate. The four hundred acres of land belonging to the mines had fallen into neglect. The roads were "scarcely passable," he later wrote; before 1830 the only means of transportation was by foot on paths through the woods. There wasn't a single school. The only place of worship: a small Roman Catholic chapel where the priest from Sydney officiated "once, or perhaps twice, in the course of a year."

Brown was there to work, not to seek redemption. I've been able to find only a single drawing of "Lt.-Col. Richard Brown, 'F.G.S., F.R.G.S.'" In it he wears a dark coat, patterned bow tie and white, stiff, high-collared shirt. He is seated, looking off to his right, holding some sort of document in his left hand, his right hanging nonchalantly off the back of his chair. There's a touch of Captain Ahab to that hooked nose, lank swept-back hair, thin lips and haunted stare. He had a hunger that even developing and running the most productive coalfields in the British colonies couldn't fill.

In his spare time he scoured the island's cliffs and outcroppings and wrote the definitive book on Cape Breton's coalfields—along with an authoritative history of the island, which he illustrated with hand-drawn pencil sketches that historians and geologists were still marvelling over a century later. He was a self-taught paleobotanist—someone who uses fossilized plant remains to reconstruct bygone environments—before anyone had coined a word for the specialty. He was visionary enough, as the *Canadian Mining Journal* put it, to be the first person to "see and appreciate the value of the Island's under sea [sic] coal measures," which account for about 98 percent of Cape Breton's coal seams.

Back in 1826, though, he was just a green kid from Westmoreland, in the Lake District of England. His father was a bailiff to a viscount who owned, among other things, coal mines. There, Brown trained as a mining engineer. It was under the nobleman's aegis that he left for Canada, at the age of twenty-one, to "survey and report upon the coal fields of Nova Scotia and Cape Breton." Landing in Nova Scotia, he discovered something alarming: the best seams in the Pictou and Sydney coalfields—in other words, the best seams in the whole empire—were already under charter to others, and therefore exempt from the Duke of York's lease.

He needn't have worried. George Smith and William Liddell, the owners of the other Pictou County leases said their small mines were no match for the "superior skills and capital of his royal highness' sub-lessees." Then there were the favourable terms the GMA squeezed out of the colonial government. Comparisons are hard, because a single standardized unit of coal measure was not yet the norm in the early nineteenth century. But economic historian Marilyn Gerriets found a way to consider how the GMA deal stacked up against a five-year lease three men named Bowen struck in 1822 to develop the Sydney coal mines. The royalty they paid—seven shillings sixpence per Winchester chaldron (thirty-six bushels)—was more than seven times the royalty paid by the GMA, which by 1828 controlled most of the coalfields in Nova Scotia.

It's easy to look at things two centuries later and say the government gave way too much and got too little in return. Consider, though, the backdrop. At the start of the nineteenth century, Cape Breton was thinly settled—with an estimated 2,500 inhabitants—extensively forested and economically underdeveloped. Most of the non-indigenous people—Acadians, United Empire Loyalists, Newfoundland Irish and some Gaelic-speaking Scots—lived along the coast and worked in the cod fishery. The arable land in the interior remained pristine, almost untouched. Then, in 1802, the first shipload of ragged settlers from the Western Highlands and islands of Scotland made land. At that point the infamous Highland clearances—in which tens of thousands of men, women and children were evicted from their homes to make room for large-scale sheep farming—were over. The peripheries of Scotland, where most people now lived as subsistence farmers on the estates of a few clan chieftains, were still undergoing wrenching change. Many tenant farmers emigrated, hoping to recreate overseas something of the life that was dying in Scotland. Some of them were so destitute that their Scottish landlords cancelled their rents and debts and even paid their way, just to free up the land.

The exodus from the outer islands was almost biblical in scope. Historian Stephen Hornsby has written that at the peak of the migration, during the late 1820s and early 1830s, more Highland Scots were moving to Cape Breton than anywhere else in North America. By his estimation, some 20,000 Highlanders, many of them speaking exclusively Gaelic, moved there before the influx petered out in the 1840s. By the time Brown arrived, Scots were in the majority. Half a century later, nearly two-thirds of Cape Breton's 75,000 people were of Scottish origin. "In large part," Hornsby writes, "Cape Breton had become a Scottish island."

Let us for a moment imagine one of them, Alexander Beaton—originally from the Isle of Skye—standing on deck in his sackcloth and baggy trousers with his wife, Mary, and his five children (Anne, Ket, Donald, Isobel and John) as their ship approaches the Cape Breton coastline in 1830. From there they can see the slate-grey sky, the rocky headlands, the impenetrable forest. The ship will have been overcrowded, underprovisioned and unsanitary, with small-pox and "ship fever," or typhus, taking their toll.

The passengers had no choice; no longer needed back in Scotland, they are among the first of Great Britain's rural poor to be "shovelled out" to the new world, in the memorable phrase of one writer at the time. Most of them arrived destitute, with barely the clothes on their backs. Some of them were supported by friends and relatives, others by government relief. The government was spending so much on immigrant aid that in 1832 it instituted a head tax, to get some of its money back and slow the flow of newcomers to Nova Scotia. That just made the poverty worse. Arguing for the repeal of the tax, one Cape Breton member of the provincial House of Assembly declared that he had seen "the bedding sold from under a poor woman, to raise the money to pay back [to] the shipmaster the amount of that tax—and he has seen poor children begging through the streets of Sydney for the means of paying that exaction to which they become liable, by venturing from one part of the Empire to another."

It would be nice to say that all the hardship was worth it. Cape Breton in 1827 was a wild, foreboding, yet heart-stoppingly beautiful place: rough, glaciated uplands from the old Appalachian mountain range, gently rolling lowlands covered with thick layers of boulder clay and pockmarked by glaciated lakes, everything else blanketed by a sea of coniferous and deciduous forest. The first settlers got the few good patches of farmland. Later arrivals were forced onto the uplands, where they struggled to cobble together a bare existence as best they could, working part-time as wage labour on someone else's farm or crewing on a cod schooner. Abraham Gesner estimated that most of the 1,500 people who arrived in Cape Breton in 1842 ended up as squatters on private property and, when they were kicked out, simply wandered elsewhere.

Sometimes they even took work in the Cape Breton mines. Not that there was a lot of that in 1827. The earliest mines in the area—the French at Port Morien, the English at Burnt Head, the mine at Sydney Mines opened by Governor DesBarres in 1784—consisted of adits, levels driven horizontally into the coal seams. The operators of Sydney Mines couldn't afford a steam engine to drain the mine. Rather than dig deeper, they moved westward, sinking shallow shafts every two hundred metres or so for ventilation and to haul up the coal. When Brown arrived there were six to ten of those shafts, the deepest about thirty metres.

The miners hacked the coal out of the seam with picks and wedges. Then it was dumped into two-bushel tubs and hauled over a narrow log roadway "by strong-active young men" who were paid by the tub. At the bottom of the shaft the coal was emptied into a larger tub, which was hauled the ninety feet to the surface. There it was emptied into a hopper and discharged into twelve-bushel carts. If a ship happened to be at the local wharf, the carts were driven along a narrow road to dockside for loading. If no vessel was around—or during the long winter months—the coal was simply dumped at the wharf in a big heap.

By then, eighty to ninety men worked the Sydney Mines. Most were young and Irish—many of them veterans of the Newfoundland cod fisheries. To a man they were footloose, itinerant and, to Brown's eye, frighteningly unskilled. "All that had been done was worse than useless as the property, instead of being improved, was seriously damaged," Brown wrote, perhaps self-servingly, years later, about the scene when he arrived. "About seventy-five acres of the main seam had been worked out, leaving the pillars behind, which, owing to the settling of the roof could not be recovered. To show the wasteful, reckless way in which the works had been conducted, it need only be stated that from seventy-five acres of a six-foot-seam, which ought at least to have yielded 500,000, only 275,000 tons had been raised since the mine was commenced in 1785."

Brown held the miners in low esteem. Their unwillingness to properly differentiate between big and small coal, he said, was responsible for Cape Breton coal's inability to make any headway in the United States market. As for the compensation arrangement, well, come on: "All the workmen of the establishment, consisting of overmen, mechanics, colliers, haulers and labourers, in addition to their wages, whether by the day or by contract, were allowed rations of beef, pork, bread and molasses, which were given out weekly. If a man was absent from his work, of course he had to pay for his rations; but whether a man worked faithfully or not he received the same allowances, thus placing the industrious and skilful men on the same level as the idle and ignorant."

Such, then, was the cushy life of Cape Breton coal miners in the early nineteenth century: the soot and damp, the back-breaking toil in pitch-black tunnels amidst rats and rockfalls. The workdays that began, whether on the surface or in the pit, at five a.m. and ran through to seven p.m., broken up by short breaks for breakfast and dinner, each meal punctuated by a glass of raw rum belted back before they picked up tools again. (For good measure, they received another dollop of spirits at quitting time.) Wages were doled out at two paydays per year: one for "four months' men" on May 1, the other for "twelve months' men" on December 31. There was no exchange of cash in Nova Scotia's pioneer economy. Instead, anyone working in the mining industry, fisheries or shipbuilding depended upon merchant credit—an arrangement known as the truck system. But normally, there wasn't much left after the men had settled up for their clothing, stores and rum.

A lucky few lived in nearby cottages with their wives and kids or, if they were overmen or mechanics, in a log or sod hut. The rest of the men bunked down in one of the barracks or "cook-rooms" where they ate their meals, and slept in berths along the sides of the room. "It may easily be imagined what sort of a place the cook-room was, where forty men ate, slept and washed—when they did wash which was only once a week—in a single apartment," wrote Brown.

In winter it is true they had abundant means of making it warm enough, which is about all that can be said in its favour; in summer it became so very "lively" that most of the men preferred sleeping during the fine weather under the spruce trees in the vicinity. It could hardly be expected that either harmony or good order prevailed in two rooms occupied by eighty or ninety men under such conditions, where all were upon equal terms and free from restraint. Brawling and fighting seemed to be the order, or rather the disorder, of the day, from Monday until Saturday. Sunday being truly a day of rest, which, strange to say, was devoutly observed. The writer, who had the misfortune to occupy a house for more than twelve months about 100 yards from the cook-rooms, can testify that he rarely enjoyed an undisturbed night's rest during the whole of that period.

I can see him lying in his bed at night, thin mouth crinkling in disgust at the smells and sounds emanating from the bunkhouse next door, head spinning with what he'd accomplished that day—and everything that lay ahead. Brown had a 30-horsepower engine built to raise the coal to the surface, and another 20-horsepower model to pump water from the shaft. He erected new workshops, warehouses and barracks. Worried that an accident to the steam engines would shut down the whole operation, he had an iron foundry, with fitting shops, lathes and "everything necessary for repairing all kinds of mining machinery" built "as there was at that time no place, within a distance of 800 miles, where such repairs could be efficiently made." Shiploads of skilled workmen and colliers arrived from England. A light temporary railroad materialized, from the pit to the old wharf. Small vessels continued to load at the old wharf; the larger ones were loaded by schooner lighters carrying some sixty tonnes of coal, each "at a secure place of shipment some distance from the harbour." On nights when sleep wouldn't come he could stare out at the GMA ships, winking in the dark, before they weighed anchor and glided east, bound for the United States market his GMA bosses coveted so.

CHAPTER FOUR

Who Could Live in Such a Hole?

My great-great-great-great-grandfather, James Briers, was born twice, as far as I'm concerned. The first time was sometime around 1767, depending upon which tombstone or church registry you consult. The second time was 240 or so years later, when I discovered that he had come into this world amidst the flat farmland, ancient hedges and stone walls that mark the land like inukshuks in the south corner of England's Lancashire County. How his people got there, I don't precisely know; according to the family genealogist, the first mention of the Briers name was in Dumfriesshire, Scotland, where they were some kind of border clan—a mixture of Gaels and Celts "whose original territories ranged from Lancashire in the south, Northward to the south bank of the Clyde river in Scotland." Not a lot is known about James Briers, either, other than that he was a coal miner and had a son named Peter who followed his father into the pit. Andrew Alston, my redoubtable third cousin and a whiz with a family tree, figures Peter and his wife Ann moved around a bit in the Lancashire area.

One thing's certain: in 1842 they had a son named John who was baptized at St. Mary's church in the town of St. Helens. And somewhere along the line John took up pick and shovel, and he too became a coal miner.

It makes perfect sense. In mid-sixteenth-century England the locals, unaware of the immense coal seams which ran beneath their feet, were still burning turf when they couldn't get timber to heat their homes. The move to coal, when it came, was rapid. By the early seventeenth century St. Helens coal was travelling by pack horse to fuel the salt factories in Cheshire and Liverpool. Within decades, as the country's transportation revolution bloomed, coal from there was travelling via road, canal and railroad to new markets and customers. St. Helens—which later used its coal to build a great glass-making empire—was one of the miracles of the Industrial Revolution. There were so many. England, with its capital, technological know-how and global empire that provided a built-in market for homegrown manufactured goods, had a huge lead on other countries as this massive cultural, economic and social shift occurred. An economy based on manual labour was being replaced by one built around machines and dominated by heavy industries: shipbuilding, coal-mining, steel production and textiles. In the process, England became the workshop for the world. And at the very centre of it—coughing and wheezing, clanking and hissing—was Lancashire, whose cotton mills emerged as one of the most telling symbols of epochal change.

Before the rise of the factory, Lancashire's towns already had a tradition of small textile workshops and cottages where hand-loom weavers made yarn into cloth. Then along came a couple of Lancashire men with big ideas—John Kay, who invented the flying shuttle, and James Hargreaves, the creator of the spinning jenny—who took the spinning industry out of the cottages and countryside and into the mills. Not everyone was overjoyed. Throughout the country, Luddites—followers of a mythical leader named Ned Ludd, who was rumoured to live in Sherwood Forest—ran amok, breaking into factories and smashing machines that threatened to take textile industry jobs. In 1813, fourteen of them were hanged. Others were jailed, fined or deported to Australia. Ultimately, of course, the power lay with the mill owners. "We may see in a single building a 100 horse power steam engine (which) has the strength of 880 men, set in motion 50,000 spindles," one mill owner observed in 1835. "The whole requires the service of but 750 workers. But these machines can produce as much yarn as formerly could have hardly been spun by 200,000 men."

Lancashire, damp enough to ensure the necessary moisture for raw cotton to be spun into yarns and made into clothes, became the centre of the world's cotton trade. Manchester became England's first industrial city. By 1830 it boasted 101 mills employing more than 28,000 people. Another 18,000 worked at Oldham's 89 mills, 13,000 toiled at Rochdale's 63 mills, and Ashton-under-Lyne's 35 factories had a workforce of 8,400. Twenty years later, almost all of the cottage cotton weavers in Lancashire were working in "manufactories," and there was undeniable truth when the county's cotton masters bragged that they satisfied the home market before breakfast, and catered to the rest of the world afterwards. A decade later, an incredible 446,000 people toiled in Lancashire's cotton mills, as country folk crowded into towns that had seldom known a second of prosperity. Peter Briers, with his son John, daughter-in-law Ellen and their five children (Ann, Elizabeth, Samuel, Ellen and John William), eventually moved north to one of them: Chorley, with its rolling roadways and grand old manor houses, at the foot of the haunting West Pennine Moors.

Life changed, the world changed. The new, citified existence was better in so many ways than their old lives. Yet my heart still sinks when I picture the country folk arriving that first day in sprawling, soulless Liverpool or Manchester. Imagine them walking through mouldering landscapes unbroken by plants or green space, everything overlaid by a layer of soot. See their defeated body language when they discover that home is now some dirt-floor cellar with no light or ventilation, or a single room in a townhouse deserted by well-off owners anxious to put some distance between themselves and the encroaching lower classes.

The squalor wasn't limited to the metropolises. In the smaller towns of Lancashire a similar picture emerged; one writer described the cellars in Bolton as "the fever nests of town," where people, donkeys and even pigs lived side-by-side. In Bury, a survey discovered sixty-three households where five members of the same family slept in one bed. In the Rossendale region, rows of back-to-back houses were built clinging to the steep valley sides, leaving them damp, dark and airless. In Bacup, tenants paid a shilling a week to rent small cheek-by-jowl dwellings with a view of a communal yard where mangy, diseased wildlife wandered. Historian Andrew Taylor writes that the single privy shared by several households was a 170-yard walk for some, and the nearest well a half-mile distant. Finding room in a lodging house left tenants in no better shape; investigators found one household where a whole family and their dogs shared one bed in a single room.

Disease, as you can imagine, ran rampant. Housing conditions were so unsanitary that during the early part of the Industrial Revolution, 50 percent of infants died before the age of two. Work, the whole point of being there, provided no comfort. Skilled artisans suddenly found themselves reduced to routine labourers as machines began to mass-produce the products that, until then, had always been made by hand. Working in a cottage surrounded by family gave way to labouring on the factory floor among strangers. There, life was governed by the constant pumping of the combustion engine, and the employees' need to produce as much as possible during their long working hours. To many, the transformation was something magical: the triumph of man over nature, city over country, middle-class capitalists over the landed class of nobility and gentry. Yet it's the ghastly images of Blake's "dark satanic mills," Zola's Germinal, Tocqueville's Manchester—which he described as a "new hades" with its "heaps of dung, rubble from buildings" and "vast structures" enshrouded in "black smoke" that "keep air and light out of the human habitations which they dominate,"—that linger. It's Dickens's Coketown from *Hard Times*—from which the following passage is taken—that has stayed with us through the years:

> It was a town of red brick, or of brick that would have been red if the smoke and ashes had allowed it; but, as matters stood, it was a town of unnatural red and black, like the painted face of a savage. It was a town of machinery and tall chimneys, out of which interminable serpents of smoke trailed themselves forever and ever, and never got uncoiled. It had a black canal in it, and a river that ran purple with ill-smelling dye, and vast piles of building full of windows where there was a rattling and a trembling all day long, and where the piston of the steam-engine worked monotonously up and down, like the head of an elephant in a state of melancholy madness. It contained several large streets all very like one another, and many small streets still more like one another, inhabited by people equally like one another, who all went in and out at the same hours, with the same sound upon the same pavements, to do the same

work, and to whom every day was the same as yesterday and tomorrow, and every year the counterpart of the last and the next.

Inside the factory, the crueller lessons of capitalism were instilled. Productivity trumped people in a time when owners, unfettered by government regulation, were free to pursue whatever path was the most profitable, without considering human safety or well-being. The spinners boiled, the weavers froze. Cotton dust clogged the air and the lungs. Constant noise frayed the nerves and battered the eardrums. Mill workers suffered from chest complaints, headaches and stomach ailments, according to a Manchester history. One day a nobleman visited Manchester and spent a day wandering around "this great nasty manufacturing town." "Who," he wondered, "could live in such a hole where the slave, working and drinking a short life out, is eternally reeling before you from fatigue or drunkenness."

He had to know the answer: people without a choice in the world. In 1841, 2,350 women—their families stretched by the higher cost of urban living—worked in the coal mines of the United Kingdom, one third of them in Lancashire. Often they toiled side-by-side with their own offspring. An 1833 survey considered nearly 8,000 workers in the Lancashire mills and discovered that one-third were under the age of sixteen and 400 less than eleven years old. Children, after all, were part of the workforce in the 19th century United Kingdom where, in most households, they followed their parents into their respective industries. It was 1870 before schooling was made compulsory, and the 20th century before the allowable age for leaving school was raised to fourteen.

Life was truly lamentable for the youngest workers. Since they had no rights to speak of, they got the most tedious, dangerous jobs: as piecers tying yarn strings together when they broke, or scavengers picking up ends of loose cotton from underneath the heavy, dangerous machinery. They worked from six a.m. to seven p.m. Monday to Saturday, with an hour for dinner for the princely sum of a few pence a week. According to a locally published history of Manchester's cotton industry, if children were late they were fined. If they made a mistake or fell asleep on the job they were beaten, especially in the early years of the industry when it was common practice for children to be contracted out by workhouses as "pauper apprentices," leaving them open to all kinds of abuse.

"Any man who has stood at twelve o'clock at the single narrow door-way, which serves as the place of exit for the hands employed in the great cotton-mills, must acknowledge, that an uglier set of men and women, of boys and girls, taking them in the mass, it would be impossible to congregate in a smaller compass," Peter Gaskell wrote in 1833, in *The Manufacturing Population of England:*

> Their complexion is sallow and pallid with a peculiar flatness of feature, caused by the want of a proper quantity of adipose substance to cushion out the cheeks. Their stature low—the average height of four hundred men, measured at different times, and different places, being five feet six inches. Their limbs slender, and splaying badly and ungracefully. A very general bowing of the legs. Great numbers of girls and women walking lamely or awkwardly, with raised chests and spinal flexures. Nearly all have flat feet, accompanied with a down-tread, differing very widely from the elasticity of action in the foot and ankle, attendant upon perfect formation. Hair thin and straight—many of the men having but little beard, and that in patches of a few hairs, much resembling its growth among the red men of America. A spiritless and dejected air, a sprawling and wide action of

the legs, and an appearance, taken as a whole, giving the world but "little assurance of a man," or if so, "most sadly cheated of his fair proportions . . ."

So weary and malnourished were the child workers that in 1836 the average twelve-year-old boy was four foot four. (As I write this, my twelve-year-old son—a kid of average height in his peer group— is over five foot two.) With time, an outcry against the exploitation arose. Just not loudly enough; many factory owners claimed that employing children was necessary for production to run smoothly and for their products to remain competitive. John Wesley, the founder of Methodism, urged child labour as a way to head off youthful idleness and vice.

The only consolation for the textile workers was that their dismal lives could have been worse. By the early nineteenth century, the demand for coal had shifted from heating hovels to fuelling industry. Everywhere, boilers drove steam engines that pumped water from mines, powered machinery in mills, and transported materials, finished goods and people around the country and across the oceans. England's coal industry grew ten-fold between 1750 and 1850 as the Industrial Revolution spread to Europe and the United States. The United Kingdom raced to open new coal mines to meet skyrocketing demand; in one fifteen-year period—1842 to 1856—the number of coal mines in Britain quadrupled.

Such a thing would have been unimaginable in the early days, when the only mines were built around outcrops of exposed coal that were harvested by hacking away with picks. Suddenly, in places throughout Lancashire and elsewhere, it made sense to dig deeper, where the thick seams were found. Human power was needed to wield all those picks and shovels. The labour force soared, climbing from around 40,000 in 1800 to 143,000 within forty years. Women worked in the collieries of Scotland, Cumbria, Northumberland, Shropshire, Yorkshire and Lancashire. In Scotland and Northumberland they often carried coal in baskets on their backs as they climbed stairs out of the mine. Elsewhere, they hauled wagons on all fours, by means of a chain around the waist, through low passages.

Children also toiled in the mines. At this point one-third of those working underground in England's coal mines were under the age of eighteen. The 1842 Children's Employment Commission (Mines) Report noted that four-year-olds toiled in British mines, where the average age was between thirteen and eighteen. Often, they worked at jobs that would have made grown men wilt ("at six years old and upwards, the hard work of pushing and dragging the carriages of coal from the workings to the main ways, or to the foot of the shaft, begins"), in solitude ("solitary confinement of the worst order") and blackness ("many of them never see the light of day for weeks together during the greater part of the winter season").

The mind reels at what they faced: the total lack of sanitation; the eating, drinking, urinating and defecating that all went on side by side; the rats scurrying everywhere in such profusion that they sounded "like a flock of sheep." The 1842 report went on to conclude that the younger children "are roughly used by their older companions." Reading a description of the initiation ceremony experienced by a young Yorkshire miner, I tend to agree; his trousers were pulled down to examine his "little sparrow." Size mattered. If a boy was well endowed, he was treated with respect. Alas, if the newcomer had "a poor, weedy little thing, they used to cover it with fat and make fun of us for days, or else they used to paint it and hang a bit of band on it and all sorts of things."

The miners, regardless of age and gender, worked in tunnels tall enough to take the coal tubs but not tall enough for a person to stand. Often they had to crawl to the cutting face and lie down to work; in Lancashire and other areas, they worked seams less than eighteen inches high. The deeper the coal mine, the hotter the rock. According to historian John Benson, many workers—including females—worked naked, which increased their risk of accident only marginally. (An extra layer of clothes, after all, won't protect you from a fall of half a ton of rock.) The pits swirled with so much dust that even in the early nineteenth century the roadways had to be soaked with water to keep the miners from suffocating. Some miners, like Edmund Stonelake from South Wales, never forgot "the foul atmosphere of a nineteenth century coal pit where one's lungs got clogged with dust, and nostrils constantly assailed with foul smells from sweating stinking horses, and perspiring men." The colliers of Lancashire, declared the 1842 report, were in a particularly pitiable state:

> The adults are thin and gaunt. One or two colliers, somewhat corpulent, were pointed out to me as remarkable for being so. They have a stooping shambling gait when walking, no doubt acquired from their occupations in the low galleries of the mines. Their complexion, when washed, is pallid, approaching to a dirty yellow. Some of the children are decently clothed, and, according to their own statements, always have sufficient food. On the other hand many are in rags and in a disgusting state of dirt, and without enough to eat. The usual food of drawers is stated to be "cheese and bread, or bread and butter, and sometimes raisin pasties; they take what they have to eat in their hands, and take a bite now and again; sometimes they carry it until it is as black as coal."

Most miners never made it to age fifty. In a world without electricity, flame was the only way to produce light. The safety lamp had been invented at the beginning of the nineteenth century, but miners were expected to buy their own, and the light they gave off was feeble. Naked flames were the norm, making explosions of the methane that naturally gathered in the mines common. After an explosion, the danger was from afterdamp, the suffocating combination of gases that remained.

Some miners died en masse in highly publicized accidents in the Lancashire fields: thirteen at the Ince Hall colliery (1851); thirty-six at the Cappull colliery (1852); fifty-eight at the Arley Pits in Wigan (1853); another eighty-nine at Ince Hall (1854); forty at Ashton-under-Lyne (1857); fifty-three in the same district a year later; another twenty-five in Tyldesley (1858). Yet, as Benson points out, "the vast majority of deaths were caused not by famous disasters, but by isolated, and therefore almost entirely unpublicized accidents." From 1850 through to the First World War, an average of over a thousand miners per year died in the mines. A disproportionate number died in Lancashire, due to the rapid expansion of the industry there and the gassy nature of many of the seams.

I have no idea what John Briers, my great-great-grandfather, had to endure in the Lancashire mines—whether he was maimed by air spontaneously combusting, whether he ever suffered from photophobia (dread of the light), or the strange and awful miner's nystagmus, the chief symptom of which is a rotary oscillation of the eyeballs, or any of the other ailments that sometimes afflicted colliers. I don't even know how old John Briers was when he ventured underground for the first time. I just know that his life progressed in the usual fashion for a working man in this time at this place. In 1865, at age twenty-three, he married Ellen Margaret Pollard at St. George's church in Wigan. Four years later, they were living in St. Helens.

By the time the 1881 census was taken they were a family of eight. The patriarch, at forty-one, was still listed as a collier. The second-eldest boy, John William, now ten, was identified as a "scholar," which implied that things were going well enough in the household that, for now, he didn't have to join the 30,000 children under the age of fifteen working in British mines. Number 50 Chorley Lane, where they lived, was a plain, terraced home with two gable walls, surrounded by a garden. Not that home ownership made a measurable difference in a family's quality of life in eighteenth-century Chorley; freehold miners' homes were probably just as damp, dank and filthy as the worst coal company shack. Polluted water supplies and barbaric waste disposal meant the rapid spread of digestive complaints like diarrhea, and more serious infectious diseases like typhoid, scarlet fever, measles and whooping cough. Infant mortality was heartbreakingly high.

The cramped, crowded nature of virtually every miner's home— by the mid-nineteenth century five people was the norm in a house with only a couple of rooms—made day-to-day life maddeningly difficult. Beds were often located in the living room. Privacy was impossible: siblings slept in the same bed; the father and any sons and male tenants who worked in the pit bathed in a tin basin in the living room. Isolation in the case of illness was out of the question. In 1898, Benson recounts, a doctor called on a mining family in Derbyshire, in the middle of England. He found that the mother, "in a pathetic attempt to prevent the spread of infection in her overcrowded home," had placed three children with scarlet fever in one end of a bed and three more with typhoid in the other.

Considering the conditions at home, maybe they welcomed rising at 2:45 a.m. to leave the house by 3:15, then walking for half an hour to be at the pit by quarter to four. Long gone were the old bell pits—little more than deep wells opened to provide access to the coal, in which women and children humped the coal up ladders to the surface. Drift mines, driven into the side of a hill, allowed the miners to follow the seams farther underground. When deeper mines were needed to provide coal to fuel the factories that were changing the world, the room-and-pillar system—a network of work spaces carved into the seam with columns of left-over coal supporting the mine roof—held sway.

John William Briers's career, like his father's, probably followed the normal arc: starting out as a trapper boy, opening and closing the ventilation doors to allow men and coal to pass without disturbing the airflow through the workings; moving up the food chain a bit to perhaps becoming a "putter," pulling huge tubs that could contain a quarter of a ton of coal out to the main roadway. Around eighteen or nineteen he would have joined the ranks of hewers—those who actually dug coal with picks and shovels, the most aristocratic of colliery occupations. At this point his future would have been preordained: the next thirty years as a pick-and-shovel man; then, if he was still able, finishing out his days above the surface, among the women and children, doing less physically demanding work.

Above ground, despite the stereotype of the day, not every miner hustled to the pub once the end-of-shift whistle blew to swill down grog until he saw double. Not everyone left his wages in the back alley on the way home, betting on everything from cards and marbles to games of pitch-and-toss. There were other diversions, particularly after Parliament passed legislation in 1847 limiting the workday to ten hours. Suddenly the sporting life—whether bare-knuckle boxing, bull-baiting and cockfighting, or more civilized pastimes like football, rugby and cricket—became more popular. Some went to church—mainly the Church of England, although by the mid-1800s virtually every mining community had its own Catholic chapel. Others raised animals, gardened, even competed in regular flower shows.

It wasn't a particularly learned society. Estimates are that by the early 1800s only 48 percent of men and 17 percent of women could sign their names to the marriage register. Nonetheless, some miners formed theatrical troupes and criss-crossed the coalfields. The most serious among them took to reading rooms and libraries and attended evening lectures at the miners' institutes that began to spring up. Music—in the form of brass bands that materialized wherever factories were opened and pits sunk—was particularly popular. The instruments were simple to master and relatively cheap to buy. In many places the employers sponsored their workmen. As early as 1827, every large colliery in Northumberland and Durham was said to have its own band. Some of them could even carry a tune. In 1869 a group of workers from the St. Hilda Colliery, located in South Shields, an industrial town on the northeast coast, got it in their heads to form a brass band even though not one of them played an instrument. With the help of professional trainers they won England's national brass band championship in 1912, 1920, 1921, 1924 and 1926.

So miners and their families weren't—as the educated classes seemed to feel at the time—just knuckle-draggers and subhumans. The colliery folk of Lancashire and Lanarkshire, of Durham and Derbyshire, of Northumberland and Yorkshire, had the usual hopes, dreams and ambitions. In their cold, brutish world they found warmth by banding together in friendly societies that insured them against accidents. Somehow, they managed to start co-operatives to fight the monopoly of the coal company's "truck" system. In virtually every coalfield in the land, they made their first steps toward forming unions to offset the immense power of the colliery owners.

Moving onward, however haltingly, was the defining theology in this age of aspiration and progress. My people were no different. One day in 1891, twenty-year-old John William Briers stood inside St. George's church—"majestic in its capacious design and originally built to seat 2,200 worshippers," according to the history section of the church's website—at the top of St. George's Street in Chorley. A.G. Leigh was likely seated at the organ that day; J. Alfred Pattinson—vicar from 1890 to 1903—may have been officiating. For it was an auspicious occasion: the day John William Briers married the woman who would become my great-grandmother, Margaret Rigby, a nineteen-year-old Chorley calico weaver whose family, like every Lancashire clan, had deep ties to coal mining.

Their courtship ritual likely followed a predictable path. After cleaning up after work—in a tin bath in front of the kitchen fire—John William would have joined the other lads and lasses strolling up and down Market Street, near the centre of town, eyeing the talent. In Chorley this was known as the monkey walk. And it was a necessity in a place where it was frowned upon for unmarried people to visit any of the local pubs: the Colliers' Arms, built in the late Victorian period; the Black Horse, built in 1820, named after the pit ponies that hauled the coal; the Blackamoor, almost certainly named as a pun on the black-faced miners who frequented it. Money for drink was scarce. John William would have handed his wages over to his mother, who, being a grocer's daughter, would have handed back a small allowance. Somehow, though, romance blossomed.

Number 20 Gillibrand Walks, where the couple set up house

after their wedding, was a brick row house with a bay window and front garden—both considered posh in the day. It was a short walk to the Rigby grocery store in the central part of town. The couple was surrounded by Rigbys—Margaret's sister May Ann lived next door at number 18, Barbara at number 8, brother John at number 17 and Aunt Elizabeth at number 5.

Chances are that my great-grandfather worked at the nearby Birkacre colliery, opened to supply the local textile works. But that's only speculation; the huge number of collieries meant that labour was truly mobile in those days. Miners thought nothing of trekking a few miles to another colliery if it paid a couple of pence extra per ton. Heady ideas were in the air in England: for the first time ever, a working-class lad like John William might raise himself up with his own spirit, ambition, energy and good fortune.

I imagine him going to sober talks on serious subjects at the miners' lecture halls. He may have read Kipling, with his sentimental yarns about the inherent greatness of the Empire. He may have been a member of the Miners' Federation of Great Britain, just two years old in 1891 but already boasting over 250,000 members willing to fight and even die for their principles. Or, perhaps it was Margaret, a descendant of a long-established Chorley family, who dreamed of greater things. One fact is undeniable: at some point, for some unknowable reason, in the first years of the twentieth century they had a chat.

The news in the *Chorley Guardian* on May 10, 1902, must have been discouraging. "Some fourteen or fifteen collieries were stopped on Wednesday in South Lancashire owing to scarcity of orders, and 10,000 colliers are idle. . . . The Lancashire coal trade is now entering upon a spell of severe depression." A story less than six weeks later brought news that an arbitrator with the august name of Lord James of Hereford had ruled in favour of the mine owners on some wage question. "Accordingly, there will be a reduction of 10 per cent in the miners' wages from the first making up day in July."

Maybe it was that story that led Margaret and John William— beaten down by their Lancashire lives, or bursting with excitement about the future—to talk about the rumour that there was a need for colliery men in Nova Scotia.

Nova Scotia?

Nova Scotia—over there in Canada.

John probably knew someone who had joined the flood of Englishmen heading "across the pond" to work in the booming Nova Scotia mines and steel plants. Maybe he had read advertise-ments in the *Chorley Guardian* or *Wigan Observer,* placed by "appointed agents," encouraging immigration to Canada. Chances are that he had even heard about some of the disasters over there, which rivalled British tragedies for sheer carnage: the 73 who had died in the Drummond Colliery in a place called Westville in 1873, the 50 who had died at the explosion at the Foord Pit, in the same general area, seven years later. He would have certainly known about the explosion that had ripped through the Springhill Mine in northern Nova Scotia the same year he and Margaret were wed. On that February day, 125 died—the most in Canadian history to that point. Contributions to the Miners' Relief Fund had come from across Canada and the British Empire, including from Queen Victoria.

What ensued once the subject was opened I can only imagine: land is more than the ground we live on. Their people could trace centuries of history on that soil: here, some ancient member of the clan was claimed by the plague. There, a Rigby was once pilloried and pelted with rotting fruit for stealing rabbits from a nobleman's estate. Over behind that building, a Briers with milky skin had to step lively to avoid Jacobite pikemen passing through on the way back to Scotland. For them, every sad, gorgeous inch of geography was replete with meaning and shot through with memories so deep-rooted as to seem almost genetic.

They must have talked about the decision for days, even weeks. He was thirty, she twenty-nine—and the mines made people old before their time. They had to look toward the future, not the past. They had three children to consider: Amy, a one-year-old; the boys, Harold, now eight, and John, six. Did they dream of escape, of wide-open spaces and clean air where their children could grow up straight and strong and scrub the grime of generations from their faces? At a certain point, did they see life in this new land all spread out before them radiant with hope?

This, for certain, is all we know: at some point, a ship came.

CHAPTER FIVE

Greed and the Gilded Age

K now this about Henry Melville Whitney: he was stout, slouchy and partly deaf. An underachiever about whom, at thirty-three, it was written that his means "don't amount to much" and his first public utterances were characterized by "the Whitney reticence with short, vague and imprecise responses." Yet who possessed that most American gift of reinventing himself: three years later he was an "honourable, capable businessman" worth an estimated $500,000. A spellbinding orator. A man who, according to a contemporary, ran a business organization so adept at controlling the Massachusetts state legislature that by comparison "an average Tammany Gang," a "Chicago Combine" or a "St. Louis Syndicate" would look like a "hay-covered snowplough in August." Who, though his business endeavours usually carried the whiff of scandal, still managed to cultivate an image of public benevolence.

Maybe there's no direction other than forward when your brother is made undersecretary of the U.S. Navy and your family tree—yeah, *those* Boston Whitneys—is veined with the guy who came up with both the cotton gin and the general principle for the assembly line, and the owners of horses that have won every major thoroughbred race in the United States. What brought Whitney down in the end seems to have been the same fatal flaw as got his father, a merchant and manufacturer known as the General. Both had energy and vision, could start new things, but had trouble staying focused, hanging in for the long run. With time the son's early successes started to fade, his financial losses to accumulate. Whitney, who in his latter years, looked like a cross between Emperor Hirohito and Teddy Roosevelt, twice mounted unsuccessful runs for the Massachusetts State House. When Whitney died from pneumonia in 1925, the *New York Times* declared "that no American ever did more for Canada." When Whitney's estate was probated, it was discovered that he was almost a pauper.

Is a mental image starting to form? One of those freewheeling, Gatsbyesque characters of the Gilded Age? I forgot to mention one thing: Whitney brought my people here. Not directly, mind you. I'm not even sure if any member of my family ever actually eyeballed him. Yet had Whitney never strode the earth, John William Briers might never have ended up in Cape Breton. Ned Demont, whom you will soon meet, would have stayed in Windsor, Nova Scotia. And I'd be spinning a different yarn right now, instead of asking you to cast your mind back to where the Nova Scotia thread of the story left off—to the General Mining Association and its monopoly over coal-mining in the province.

The year 1837 is a good place to start. The GMA had been busy in the past decade. As historian Daniel Samson has written, its £200,000 investment represented an astounding sum for any British colonial mining operation, and would stand as the greatest investment in the history of Nova Scotia until Confederation in 1867. By 1833 some nine hundred men worked at its foundries and mines, a staggering workforce in a province where, as Samson put it, "a new grist mill was worthy of note." By then the GMA had doubled the province's coal production to 50,000 tonnes; by 1858 it would approach 300,000. For those smitten by the transformations then occurring in Great Britain and the northeastern United States in the mid-nineteenth century, it must have seemed like divine intervention that this miracle of progress had arrived in a place that seemed so mired in the eighteenth century.

Alas, there was another body of opinion about the GMA. I'm not talking of mild dislike. This was loathing—made all the more startling by the delight with which the company's arrival was greeted, still vividly evident in two-hundred-year-old newspapers. Can you really blame people? The arbitrary manner in which the Crown had handed over the mines to far-off developers smacked of the divine right of kings. The sweetheart nature of the GMA's deal—for most of the lease period it paid a magisterial £1 a year, plus a penny on each ton of coal—left people apoplectic.

The imperious way the Englishmen wielded their power rankled too. Technically, the duke's grant allowed mines to open under certain circumstances; if the GMA knew about a coal deposit and didn't, within a twelve-month period, open a mine at the site, the government was empowered to lease the deposit to a rival. In reality, as economist Marilyn Gerriets has pointed out, not one competing lease was ever granted. The GMA earned more enemies by wiping out the time-honoured common-law practice of treating coal and mineral deposits as public resources. Going after old Angus for hacking off a few bucketfuls of coal from an outcropping on his own land to heat his hovel was out of the question. But the GMA prosecuted with immense zeal anything that vaguely resembled a commercial mine. John Archibald, writing from Salmon River, Colchester County, in 1845, summed up the situation:

For a number of years I had good reason to believe that there
was a good coal field on my property, but I never did anything
towards opening the mine till the winter of 1843. . . . I then
sunk a shaft about 30 feet deep, which pierced a seam of coal
2 ½ feet thick, 30 feet from the surface. . . . At the time I sunk
this shaft I thought the Mines contained within this land had
not been reserved by the Crown at the time of granting the
land, but in the Spring of 1843 the Hon. S. Cunard in passing
left word at my house for me to take no further steps or he
would prosecute me for so doing.

Cunard, by the way, was the same Halifax-born Samuel Cunard
who went on to establish the world's first and greatest steamship
line. Before the GMA took over, he had made his own proposal to
lease and develop the Cape Breton coalfield. We know how that
turned out. Cunard, though, wasn't one to let an opportunity pass by.
While busy making money in the timber and tea trades and invest-
ing in everything from banking and iron to steamships, he became
a GMA director. His unprecedented access to Nova Scotia's business
and political elites made him the GMA's chief fixer in the province.

The Englishmen, you see, were relentless. They hired ships to
chase down vessels carrying coal from "smuggling mines." In retal-
iation, at one point, someone set fire to the GMA's Albion Mines.
So the province passed laws making it a felony to set fire to a coal
mine or to place "obstacles" across railroads. In 1845, in direct
response to the complaints of the GMA, the province brought in
new anti-smuggling laws. So browbeaten was the colonial government around then that it appointed four GMA agents as customs
agents for Sydney and Pictou. In 1849 the GMA paid a spy named
Matthew Roach to come up with a list of people illegally digging

coal in Cape Breton. His report advised the GMA that these people were "in poor circumstances, and that they are unable to pay even a moderate penalty, and would be ruined by the infliction of a fine of £20," and that they "use no caution to prevent his witnessing their operations, because the persuasion is universal among them that the taking away of coal is not illegal."

Slowly, almost undetectably, resentment grew. How could it not? One day, these Englishmen show up and inform the locals that they now own one of the few valuable resources in the colony. Oh, by the way—since you don't know what the hell you're doing, we'll operate the mines. We'll bring in people from the old country—England, Wales, Scotland—to run things properly. Everybody seemed overjoyed when the GMA—which was injecting £66,000 per annum into the Nova Scotia economy by the late 1830s—was spending. Once the association tried to actually take some profits from the mines . . . well, you can imagine.

The clamour of complaints against the royal monopoly grew louder as more and more potential operators applied to open up coal deposits only to have their requests repeatedly come back stamped "denied." The immense wealth some expected to accompany the GMA's arrival simply failed to materialize. Maybe it wasn't possible when an investor had to build everything from scratch in a place with no manufacturing facilities or skilled workforce. Whatever the reason, up until the 1860s, most of the GMA's manufacturing equipment—along with its men—came from England.

Mount Rundell, as much as any one thing, symbolized the GMA's public relations problem. The high-ceilinged Georgian building with its acres of groomed land loomed large over an eighteenth-century boondocks settlement. James Cameron wrote that the balls, dinners and parties there "did not go unnoticed in Halifax where Lieutenant Governors were expected to keep up a socially stylish front on a stipend never generous, and by repute, considerably less" than Mount Rundell's budget. In truth, the acrimony stemmed more from the power emanating from the place than from the grand grounds and expensive fixtures. Meanwhile, Mount Rundell's lord, the overbearing, pompous Richard Smith, seemed to rub everyone the wrong way. Joseph Howe's newspaper, *The Novascotian*, said that Smith left behind "some enemies as well as some friends" when he finally retired to England. Years later, his memory still evoked such vitriol that one of his successors quietly removed Smith's name from a GMA steamship and rechristened it *Albion*.

Smith's sole foray into electoral politics didn't help one bit. Only the supremely deluded would think they could spend five years in Sydney—where Smith was busy getting the GMA's Cape Breton operations up and running—and honestly suppose that he could win a by-election for a new legislative riding encompassing the entire island. My guess is that Smith saw the contest as a cakewalk for someone with the GMA's financial clout behind him. A single image demonstrates how badly he misread his audience: Smith parading into the open houses he threw throughout the Sydney area accompanied by his 40-man band, each member resplendent in a green scarf and white apron. Smith's opponent, William Young, was a showy, well-connected Halifax lawyer advocating responsible government for the colony. The pair were virtually deadlocked late in the race. Historian Brian Cuthbertson recounts what happened next: how Smith brought his Sydney miners to the Acadian community of Cheticamp for the final poll. There they were met by 150 of Young's supporters, Cape Breton Highlanders still grateful to Young for helping them find decent land when they arrived from Scotland. Armed with cudgels,

Young's supporters surrounded him as he seized the hustings. Smith's miners tried to fight their way onto the platform, then gave up. The sheriff, "in connivance with Young," closed the poll and declared Young the victor.

The story wasn't quite finished; Smith's men waited in a bog to ambush Young's victory party. Only a last-minute plea by a clergyman stopped them from opening fire. From Halifax, the honourable members of the Nova Scotia House of Assembly watched the events unfold in horror. Then, believing that Young had at the very least sanctioned the chaos, they overturned the result and gave the seat to the GMA head. They needn't have bothered. Smith headed back to England after a single session in the House.

By then, the ground was surely shifting. The push for responsible government in Canada began in Nova Scotia. Within that context, Samson writes, the GMA was increasingly viewed as an enemy of competition, an adversary of individual freedom and the other liberal virtues then catching fire in the province. At this point the GMA had other troubles. In the United States the Reading Railroad had been completed, connecting Pennsylvania's anthracite coalfields with the eastern seaboard. The cost of shipping a ton of American coal east therefore fell at the same time as Congress placed a duty of $1.75 per ton on imported coal. For Nova Scotia the impact was immediate: shipments of Cape Breton coal to the United States plummeted by nearly 50 percent between 1841 and 1842. All of this left the GMA managers scrambling to reduce costs. One way was to cut wages—but when the GMA tried that in 1840, the Albion miners struck and the company quickly relented.

Two years later the company tried again, this time cutting miners' pay by fourpence per cubic yard of coal. What happened a few days later is noteworthy in that it set the tone for labour relations in the coal industry well into the next century. The mine's general manager, Henry Poole—a humourless-looking burgher with judgmental eyes and a chanterelle mushroom beard—cut off the mining families' coal and supplies. At that point a crowd of a hundred women and children descended upon Mount Rundell, where they smashed the kitchen windows and heaped abuse on Poole. He took it for a while, then agreed to start up the coal supplies again. The catch was that the price of their coal would be 400 percent higher than the pre-strike level. The miners stood fast. There were no more threats against Poole, James Cameron wrote, although a small riot broke out in an Albion Mines grog shop. It took another three months before the company agreed to the employees' compromise terms—ten shillings a day—and the men returned to work.

Another way to boost profits was to put a gun to the head of the provincial government. The argument made in December 1842 by Samuel Cunard, who had emerged as the GMA's main agent in Nova Scotia, was simple: despite what everyone might think, "no interest or return" had been paid to the GMA on its huge investments in the province. On the contrary, all those capital expenditures had been made in expectation of almost unlimited demand for coal in the United States, now being flooded with American anthracite. The GMA needed an immediate break on its royalties. "Without this aid," Cunard declared, "the Association will be compelled to close the Pictou Mines and to dismiss the Colliers, and others employed there." The message got through. Royalties were immediately reduced, and the annual rent of £3,000 waived. Did anyone notice two years later, when the GMA opened a new mine nearby Cumberland County—a decision that seemed to undercut its entire economic argument? Hard to say. But the threat of extortion would be a common one during the remainder of the GMA regime.

The year 1848 was the turning point. Joe Howe's Reform party took power in Nova Scotia, forming the first colonial government within the British Empire to be popularly elected. They had a somewhat different attitude toward Nova Scotians' inherent right to control their own resources. Democracy, remember, was the spirit of the day—making it hard to live by a far-off decision to flog the title to the province's underground mineral rights to cover some spendthrift English nobleman's gambling debts. The GMA must have sensed that its day was done. Later in 1848, it was forced to open a small mine in Joggins to prevent Abraham Gesner and some associates from sinking a shaft there. Just months later, Joe Howe— he of the epic battles for freedom of the press and responsible government—introduced a bill in the legislature. It had a dull name (*An Act respecting Casual and Territorial Revenue*) but a huge impact. The legislation provided, amongst other things, that the right and title of Her Majesty respecting all mines, minerals and oil and all rents and profits from them were "assigned to the disposal of the General Assembly of the Province." Translation: Nova Scotia had repatriated its coal.

Henry Whitney started out as just a kid with a comfortable life in Conway, Massachusetts. After graduating from good old Williston Seminary, his prep school—"Sammy, my Sammy," went the school song, "My heart yearns for thee/ Yearns for your campus and your old elm tree"—he went home and worked in his father's store, then spent a few years kicking around the banking business before forming a New York shipping company. During the Civil War, he headed south to speculate in cotton and to dream up a scheme to raise sunken vessels. When those plans flopped, he returned to Boston and joined his dad's steamship company. He married. When his father, the General, died in 1878, Whitney took over the company, which grew more prosperous. Historian Don MacGillivray says that Whitney somehow got control of the Hancock Inspirator Co., "another flourishing concern," and also emerged with power over the "much criticized" Boston Water Power Company.

It was that kind of age in America: anyone could become a Rockefeller, Carnegie, Morgan, Astor, Mellon or Vanderbilt. An age when the rich built palaces and the poor went shoeless. Nova Scotia looked like everywhere else, just more so. Great fortunes were being built: by Cunard, the future steamship magnate, and his Halifax associate, Enos Collins, the ex-privateer who had started the first bank in North America, and had reputedly built the greatest fortune in the British Commonwealth by the time he died, in 1872, at ninety-seven.

Yet there was grim poverty too, particularly in rural Cape Breton, still reeling from the potato blight that had hit in 1845, reducing entire settlements to "poverty, wretchedness and misery," in the words of an emergency legislative committee struck to deal with the crisis. A woman from Loch Lomond recalled one of the food-seeking expeditions that could be glimpsed on Cape Breton roads during those awful years:

A group of men and women started for L'Ardoise by foot over blazed roads, following the lake and river down as far as Grand River then taking a blazed trail over L'Ardoise Highlands, for some of us were thirty miles from our homes. The poor women were barefooted and each woman took her knitting along with her and knitted away as they walked over and around the hills, by windfalls and swamps until they reached the shore, hungry and tired. Each man and woman was supplied with a half a barrel of Indian meal, then they cried for something to eat. Mr. Bremner rolled out a barrel of meal and they rolled it to a brook, opened it and poured the water from the brook into the barrel and made raw cakes and passed it around to each person. All ate heartily then each man and woman took their half-barrel on their backs and sang "Ben Dorian" as they left for their homes over the blazed roads.

All over the island, starving settlers begged for food. "The general destitution," wrote the "Reverend" Norman McLeod, a charismatic Scottish clergyman who had led a group of his parishioners to settle in Cape Breton, "has made it impossible for the most saving to shut their ears and eyes from the alarming claims and craving of those around them, running continually from door to door, with the ghastly features of death on their very faces." The blight was in his view payback for his neighbours' "unthriftiness, and offensive indolence," and their ability to "well feed and flutter, dress and dandle, and carelessly chafe away with toddy and tobacco."

Then again, McLeod, tall and sinewy, with the despot's unblinking eye, had a tendency to see everything as holy retribution. Born in Scotland, he was a fire-and-brimstone Presbyterian who couldn't follow church doctrine enough to be granted a preacher's licence. He taught, fished and then, in 1817, with a shipload of adherents in tow, headed for Pictou. Mister Fun he was not. The Reverend George Patterson wrote in *History of the County of Pictou:*

> He was not only not connected with any religious body, but denounced them all, even going so far as to say there was not a minister of Christ in the whole establishment. Those who have heard him at this time, describe his preaching as consisting

of torrents of abuse against all religious bodies, and even against individuals, the like of which they had never heard, and which were perfectly indescribable. He had never been licensed or ordained, but regarded himself as under higher influences than the ministers of any church. "I am so full of the Holy Ghost, that my coat will not button on me," he said once in a sermon.

Unhappy with the sinning at Pictou, in 1820 McLeod boarded a ship called *The Ark* bound for Ohio, along with dozens of his flock, but stopped and settled in St. Anns Harbour, Cape Breton, instead. There he set himself up as a "moral dictator," according to historians, "imposing severe punishments for trivial 'sins.'" Despite his fanaticism, when the potato blight hit, more than eight hundred of his followers obeyed his command to migrate to Australia, where one of his sons lived. McLeod was over seventy by then, but the Aussie penchant for strong drink was too much for him to abide. So he decamped again, this time to Waipu, New Zealand, where his word was again law amongst his followers. Historians there described him "as independent, self-reliant, and autocratic," and "unwilling to suffer any interference or restraint from any human source. If any men attempted to dictate to him he flung defiance in their faces and followed his own course. His word was law in church and state."

Just how bad were things in Cape Breton, if someone like McLeod couldn't cut it? With famine threatening, the government intervened, sending food to the island for distribution to the needy. Few died but many lost everything. Many backland farmers sold their few animals to buy meal and seed potatoes; when the blight reappeared the following year, they had no food and no livestock to sell for supplies. Some were forced to hand over their land to merchants to avoid starvation. Many decided to leave rather than stay and starve; in 1851 alone, five hundred passengers boarded vessels in Sydney for Quebec City.

Others made their weary, dispirited way to the coal towns, where something was happening. The GMA's stranglehold ended in 1858. Though it was granted new thirty-year leases in any area in which it was already operating, the door was now open to anyone with the capital and ambition to sink a shaft elsewhere in the province. The provincial government, not some far-off foreign power, decided who got access to the coal seams, where and for how long. Since the province had no clear policies for granting leases, it was a giddy, wide-open time—"a period," as economic geographer Hugh Millward put it, "of rampant speculation and enterprise."

People and companies sussed out prospects, scrambled to acquire leases, then raised capital. In Cumberland County, in the northern part of the province near the New Brunswick border, a number of American capitalists—looking to meet the increase in demand for coal because of the Civil War—picked up rights. New mines opened in Maccan, Chignecto, St. George, Minudie, Lawson, Victoria and River Hebert. In Joggins, the ascendant mining community in the area, existing mines were improved and lucrative new coal seams were discovered. In 1864 the first major mine in the Springhill area began operation. In Pictou County, local operators with the fee—and, undoubtedly, an in with the new government—lined up for leases. In the two years after the GMA's blanket lease was broken, the George MacKay mine, John Douglas mine, John Wilson and Carmichael MacKay mines opened up on one side of the East River, running through the Pictou field. Across the water, as Cameron recounts, the New Glasgow Coal Company sank a pit. A mine in the Barton area began operation.

Once the shallow reserves were depleted, the economies changed.

Serious money was needed to sink deeper shafts. Little local operators were forced to sell to outsiders. They, in turn, had to amalgamate or be swallowed by even bigger fish. The rush was biggest in Cape Breton, still largely a pre-industrial economy, which meant that few locals had the capital needed to extract enough coal to gain economies of scale. A few homegrown speculators—Millward mentions Simon Gotreau, Marshall Bourinot and a couple of guys named Roach and McInnis most frequently—gobbled up strategically located leases in the hope that the bigger operating companies would one day need to extend their underground workings. Mostly, outside capital poured in, and partnerships were formed or the locals were simply bought out. New Yorkers picked up Marshall Bourinot's Blockhouse mine. Two locals named Archibald and Moren joined hands with investors from Halifax and New England and incorporated the Little Glace Bay Mining Company. New York interests acquired the Cadougan and McLeod property. American investors, via the Caledonia Company, bought a lease in the area. So did the London-based Glasgow and Cape Breton Coal Company.

Brown estimates that during the next five years, more than forty exploration licences were issued for tracts in the Sydney coalfield. Several more were granted for the western shore of the island between Port Hood and Margaree. Some enterprising souls asked for and received licences for tracts under the sea floor, along the coast from Mira Bay to Point Aconi. "One enthusiastic adventurer" even took out a licence for a "submarine area" accessible only by sinking a shaft on a little rock called Flint Island, located more than a mile from the mainland. By Brown's reckoning, many of the licences were taken out by speculators lacking the cash to work them, with the expectation of flipping them later on for a neat profit—"Some of these were fortunate enough to realise their expectations." For others, including those who had taken out licences on the edge of the Sydney coalfield, no buyers could be found. In the end, they just swallowed the cost and surrendered their leases.

It may have been their lucky day.

CHAPTER SIX

Let There Be a Town

When a locomotive pulled out of Springhill en route to Parrsboro, when it chugged along from Schooner Pond to Sydney Harbour, when it steamed from Broad Cove toward the strait, it farted and wheezed like an old man. From the top of a hill in any coal community a passerby could watch it meander its way through the firs, maples, oaks, birch, pines and spruce, weave past the lakes and along the barrens, skirt the lush hills and the hard headlands. Today a boy on a skateboard would leave it in the dust. But it still filled a person with wonder to see the smoke-spewing metal mastodon bisect the wilderness, and to know that coal, which ran the trains and filled their cars, was responsible for the spectacle.

In 1839 the Albion Mines Railway, the second in Canada, opened, connecting the Albion collieries to a wharf on the East River. With time other rail lines began to vein the Nova Scotia landscape. Some were pre-Confederation public works projects like the provincial line that ran from Halifax to Truro, later adding spurs to the commercial centre of Windsor and the coal towns of

Pictou County. Others were projects that thrilled a nation, like the Intercolonial Railroad linking Nova Scotia to the rest of Canada, which connected first to the coal workings around Springhill, then pushed through to Cape Breton.

The new coal mines that materialized after the abolition of the GMA's lease did their bit to fill in the network. By 1871, twenty-six mines, employing a total of 2,469 men and boys and 286 pit ponies, were in operation. That year's report from the Commissioner of Mines also lists sixty-nine locomotives running on coal company rail lines throughout the province. A rail line brought the rest of the world—whether the latest fashions or the newest consumer goods—suddenly nearby. Existing industries thrived; new ones had a chance to bloom. Older communities blossomed into mini–boom towns.

By 1835 a man named Lodewick (Ludwig) Hunter was operating a small mine on a spring by a hill in central Cumberland County, near the Nova Scotia–New Brunswick border. Thirty years later, a man named Nathan Parks started another mine in the area after his wife kicked a piece of coal during a stroll through the woods. Coal was plentiful; in this out-of-the-way part of the province, access was the issue. When the GMA's lease was abrogated its compensation included a four-square-mile property near the Parks mine. But digging for coal in a place without a railway to move the product to market made no sense. So the GMA sat on the lease—until, that is, construction of a nearby rail line triggered a scramble for mineral rights in the area. Thanks to the railways, Springhill saw its population grow fivefold in a single decade; nearby Joggins swelled by 700 percent in thirty years.

When trains arrived, new places were coaxed into being. First, a number of factors had to coalesce: abundance of coal, for sure, but also the pitch of the seam and the stability of the ground beneath. The most easily reachable reserves were always exploited first; only when they were exhausted would operators try to develop deeper, more capital-intensive reserves. So with time, the shallower, smaller shafts were abandoned and the mines grew bigger and deeper. Throughout its life the Sydney coalfield was honeycombed with over seventy mines—some producing for only a few years, others for more than a century—only half of which, according to Saint Mary's University geography professor Hugh Millward, met the lifetime production level of 500,000 tons necessary to qualify them as "major."

Those with longevity in them were accompanied by rough buildings and sheds slapped up quickly to handle mine-related activities. Every one of them brought men to work the mines and housing for them to live in. If the mines were big enough or there were enough congregated closely together, a village materialized: first a cluster of houses and a general store, both owned by the coal company; eventually, a school, a church, a stable, and structures housing the purveyors of the other necessities of frontier life. Many of the places had Indian or French names long before the collieries arrived, but the places were rechristened with new handles rooted in the name of the seam, or some long-forgotten colliery manager, or the company that mined them. Sometimes they had no name at all. It was as if the miners understood the precarious nature of their existence. An accident of geology was all that stood between these places and nothingness. They were leaps of imagination. On some level the people who lived there must have understood that.

Why else, for example, would William Penn Hussey, big enough to blot out the sun, come moseying up the west coast of Cape Breton on his white steed one day in early 1888? Did he insist on dressing as a cowboy and wearing a pair of six-guns back in Boston, where he carried on business as a coal merchant? We can only speculate. What we do know is that the locals were mesmerized by this apparition from the moment he rode into town. "The native people, frozen by the isolation of the past, could lend him no inspiring hope," J.L. MacDougall wrote in *The History of Inverness County* in 1922. "A more timid man would have taken to the tall timbers instanter: but William Penn Hussey was not built that way. He loved to dance on difficulties."

They were considerable. The Scottish pioneers in the area had been hacking coal from the outcrops with pick and shovel from the moment they arrived. The fact that there was no harbour, railroad or market didn't seem to worry the big man one bit. He paid $62,500 for a property, then headed for Europe to round up investors. By all accounts Hussey was a persuasive fellow; somehow he talked his way onto the floor of the British House of Lords to tell them about his Broad Cove plan. Soon wealthy capitalists from Britain, France and Switzerland ponied up cash. When a Swiss moneyman resisted his blandishments, Hussey came up with one of the greatest confidence tricks I've ever encountered: Back in Cape Breton he painted the walls of rock facing the sea black. Sitting in a boat some distance offshore, the investor, probably, had never seen coal reserves as large as the ones he thought he now beheld. In any event, he was in. The Broad Cove Coal Company was up and running.

By the time of Confederation, new settlements were materializing at intervals of surprisingly short duration around the great harbour on the eastern end of Cape Breton. Think of Sydney, the island's largest centre, as the main reference point. The north side of the harbour housed the oldest mining areas: Sydney Mines, which we shall hear much more about later, and North Sydney, by 1870 the fourth-busiest port in Canada, thanks to the coal shipping piers built there and the steamships arriving daily from around the world to take on loads of bunker coal.

The south side was a newer, more dynamic work-in-progress. Cow Bay—yet to be renamed Port Morien—was the site of the original French mine that had supplied the fortress of Louisbourg. In 1837 its population had consisted of 187 people, mostly British loyalists and Scottish emigrants. Thirty-five years later, the Gowrie Mine was going. So were the Blockhouse Colliery—the scene of the first coal miners' strike in Canadian history—and the South Head/Cow Bay Colliery. The settlements of Dominion and Reserve Mines were still to come. But the opening of the Lingan colliery pushed the population in those parts to 3,500.

Glace Bay—named for the jagged sea ice that the French found filling the harbour during winter—was also just starting to hit its stride. When the 1871 census was taken, Glace Bay was just a bleak collection of four collieries at the far end of the island, the province, the continent. A wave that started at Glace Bay's rugged headland wouldn't make land until it hit Europe. Twenty years later, though, 2,459 people lived there. A decade from then the population had swelled by nearly 7,000, and it was officially a town.

One of the appendixes in the 1871 census is a list of occupations held by the citizens of industrial Cape Breton (Lingan, Cow Bay and Glace Bay). It goes without saying that there were clergymen (16), lawyers (10), doctors (10), teachers (39), butchers (10), telegraphers (18), tanners (18), fishermen (75), sailors (141) and cabmen (10). I'm not sure what to make of the fact that these three towns still boasted a startling number of farmers—783—along with 99 shoemakers, 369 servants and 43 barkeeps, but only one barber, machinist, druggist or mechanic, along with a single member in each of the "showman," shop boy, cordwainer (leather worker) and confectioner categories. Mostly, people worked in or around the collieries—miners (783), labourers (487), blacksmiths (97), carpenters (197), engineers (69), clerks (67), coal cutters (23), brakemen (13), foundry men (11), firemen (6), mine agents (5) and mining engineers (2).

There still weren't enough of them. Workers were being siphoned off to build railways. Strikes caused temporary dislocations. Miners moved from coalfield to coalfield. The GMA's internal correspondence burst with complaints about labour shortages. An 1864 report by the province's immigration agent is indicative: "There are many new mines now opening," he wrote of Cape Breton County, "and several companies will require hundreds of mechanics and laborers in the Spring." In relation to nearby Victoria County, he declared, "in consequence of so many young men being now employed at the coal mines opening, there is good demand for farm servants. Mechanics and miners will find profitable employment."

Since the Nova Scotia government seemed unenthusiastic about immigrants, the industry depended upon emptying out the rural areas, the marginal fishing and farming communities, the thin band of humanity that seldom extended more than a mile or two from the coastline. In Cape Breton, which accounted for roughly two-thirds of the province's coal production, the influx during the last quarter of the nineteenth century was truly epic: between 1871 and 1911, the population of the industrial part of the island grew from 12,246 to 57,263. It was, pointed out historian Del Muise, as if the earlier migration from the Scottish highlands to backwoods Nova Scotia was being replicated in the new migration to the coal towns.

The McKeen clan, which had actually fled Scotland for Northern Ireland in the late 1600s, would have understood precisely what Muise meant. A pair of them—brothers, John and James—had planned to emigrate in 1718. But John died before the ship cast off, leaving James to sail to North America with his brother's widow and her four children. One of her boys, also named John, married late in life and eventually moved his family to Truro, in the absolute centre of Nova Scotia. In 1811 one of his grandchildren, William, moved to the isolated settlement of Mabou, on the western coast of Cape Breton. There he prospered—in part, it's said, by foreclosing on the properties of settlers who owed him money during the mid-1840s famine. In 1849, according to historian Robert Morgan, McKeen received "for nominal sums, 1,100 acres and continued accumulating settlers properties until 1855."

William and his first wife had twelve children. When she died, he remarried and had another twelve kids, the third of whom was named David. Why am I telling you all this? Because David, who may have changed his surname to MacKeen, made his way to Glace Bay in the early 1860s to find work in the nascent mines. So impressed was Caledonia Colliery manager Henry Poole that he sent MacKeen to the Massachusetts Institute of Technology to study engineering. By 1867 David MacKeen had married Poole's daughter Isabelle, who died in childbirth. MacKeen devoted himself to prayer and hard work, before long moving up the ladder until he controlled the mine.

MacKeen became a local councillor, then a Member of Parliament in John A. Macdonald's 1884 caucus. He married again, and this wife also died in childbirth. Then, in Halifax, he met Jane Crerar, who came from a family of buccaneer Pictou lumbermen. It's said that her grandfather, on the verge of financial collapse, had bought a leaky schooner, loaded it with lumber, placed a sign on the stern reading "Liverpool or Hell," and taken his cargo to England to save the family business. The couple eloped in 1888. At fifty, MacKeen became a father.

Here a little executive summary–style background is helpful: demand for Nova Scotia coal streaked into the ionosphere during the Civil War with the Reciprocity Treaty between Canada and the United States in place. By the end of the war in 1865 two-thirds of Nova Scotia's coal production was heading for the American market. Demand started to drop with the end of hostilities. The export trade collapsed even further when the Reciprocity deal was abrogated in 1866. (The prospect of free trade with the United States was partly responsible for the decisions by Nova Scotia, New Brunswick, Ontario and Quebec to join Confederation a year later.) What's more, the American market was again closed off by higher tariffs and a series of freight rebates that were designed to help coal producers in Pennsylvania and Virginia.

Thus began a flurry of failures and amalgamations throughout the province's coalfields; independent coal companies had just a one-in-four chance of surviving in Cape Breton during the 1860s and 1870s. Thank God, then, for John A. Macdonald's 1879 National Policy—launched to create a strong manufacturing base in Canada—which established a fifty-cent-per-ton duty on coal imports into Canada. Sales of Nova Scotia coal to Quebec soared. The exploding Maritimes market—which grew by 200 percent during the same period—also bolstered demand.

All of which is to say that by 1893 the black stuff was back; mines everywhere were changing hands at a ridiculous pace and crazy prices. Family lore has it that one Saturday night some men came calling at David MacKeen's home. He knew what they wanted: the Caledonia mine. So he had his maid tell the men he was praying. That was fine, they said; they would wait. They waited for hours. Finally, just after midnight, MacKeen emerged. They wanted to make an offer for his mine. He was flattered, he said. Unfortunately it was now the Sabbath and, being a God-fearing man, he couldn't do business on the holy day. They left empty-handed. Early Monday morning the news broke: most of the mines in Cape Breton were being merged to create a new entity. The value of the Caledonia Mine soared. David MacKeen was a rich man.

Henry Whitney—who now controlled every mine in Cape Breton but one—had gall, give the man that. His emergence as president of the Boston-based West End Street Railway Company in 1887 may have been fraught with scandal, but it gave him credibility and clout in dog-eat-dog America. The largest street railway system in America ran on horses. Until, that is, someone introduced Whitney to a Virginian named Frank J. Sprague, "the father of electric traction." Whitney awarded Sprague the contract to adopt his electric trolley system for the Boston line—a move that cemented Whitney's reputation as a corporate visionary.

No one's precisely sure how Whitney came to strut across the stage in Sydney. One scenario has Nova Scotia premier William Fielding off to Boston in a scramble for new capital to invest in the province's expanding coal industry. Somehow, the story goes, he meets up with Whitney, who, as president of the West End Street Railway and owner of the Metropolitan Steamship Company, controlled two large consumers of coal. Then the boom began. All historian Donald MacGillivray, upon whom I lean heavily for the account of the events that follow, is sure about is that in the winter of 1891–92 two business associates of Whitney's—a Halifax lawyer and promoter named B.F. Pearson, and J.A. Grant, a Boston power plant contractor—bought the moribund Ontario Colliery in Glace Bay for $80,000. About the same time, Premier Fielding received word that "influential capitalists" in Boston were mighty displeased by his government's decision to raise the coal royalty from 7½ cents to 10 cents per ton in a bid to increase provincial revenues. On April 23, 1892—a Saturday—Whitney paid the premier a little visit.

The next Monday, Fielding introduced two pieces of legislation in the House of Assembly. One capped the coal royalties the government could charge. The other proposed that, if a company paid a higher royalty—or did something to ensure that provincial royalties increased even at the same royalty—a new lease with new conditions could be authorized. Both amendments easily passed. A few weeks later, in his report to his executive council, Fielding wrote, "It was particularly desirable that influential capitalists in the United States should be induced to make an investment in our coal-mining operations."

Those influential capitalists were already busy. Five years earlier, the provincial government had laid down the law: in future, the only coal leases renewed would be those being actively worked by their operators. The outcome was a free-for-all: leases opening up for the first time in years and being gobbled up by speculators and legitimate operators; companies amalgamating. The timing was impeccable for Whitney and the members of his shadowy cadre known as "the Boston Syndicate." In the months ahead, they picked up the options to every mine on the south side of Sydney harbour: the International, the Black Diamond, MacKeen's Caledonia, the Glace Bay, the Gowrie, the Gardiner and the Old Bridgeport. They obtained the Reserve property by buying control of the parent company on the London Stock Exchange. They took over the Victoria Colliery. The GMA still owned the old Sydney mines; otherwise, Whitney and his people held every significant mine lease on the island.

On January 19, 1893, the people of Nova Scotia discovered why. Fielding announced in the legislature that the Boston clique had been handed an unprecedented ninety-nine-year lease, renewable for an additional twenty years, at a fixed royalty rate of 12½ cents per ton. The Opposition howled in grief. The premier harkened back to an old election speech that Charles Tupper had delivered in which he had opined that "what nature intended was that the miners of Cape Breton should sell in the New England market; and . . . then would Sydney and Cape Breton flourish as never before."

Somebody was going to prosper, that much seemed certain. Within nine months the Whitney syndicate had broadened into the Dominion Coal Company, which officially incorporated on February 1, 1893, with an $18-million stock offering. The upshot: Whitney and his cronies had a near monopoly on the coal resources of Cape Breton without investing a cent of their own money. The first thing they did was consolidate, shutting down four of the eight local mines and centralizing production at the most efficient collieries. By so doing they hoped to cut management fat, streamline the transportation system and reduce duplication in everything from storage facilities to office help. Some of the decisions were head-spinners; the mine with the best-quality coal was shut, while another with the cheapest production costs was abandoned. Mostly, they spent. The ever-critical transportation system—a rat's nest of small, decrepit rail lines and antiquated wharfs—was improved, enlarged and centralized. Existing shafts were extended farther under the ocean. They sank expensive new mines. Everywhere, they added the latest appliances and equipment.

To what end, it was hard to say. "It is not our business to surmise as to whose shoulders the blame of these failures and delays should rest upon," said a nameless writer from the *Canadian Mining Review,* after visiting Dominion Coal's Cape Breton operations a year after the consolidation,

> . . . but we do no one an injustice in hazarding the conjecture that a great deal of the new work was somewhat too

experimental in character, and that the new management made the mistake of presuming that the change they had planned could be effected with as much ease in Cape Breton as in America; and mindful of the facts that materials had to be imported from great distances, that the climate in winter renders work very difficult and uncertain and finally that the local mechanics, good and reliable men as they undoubtedly are, could hardly be expected to adopt themselves immediately to revolutionary ideas and methods.

Progress was the ethos of the day, prosperity the blinding light which illuminated all things. Success transformed—especially success of the sudden kind. So if the government and business people and ordinary citizens had lingering concerns they ignored them. A decade later production from the Dominion Coal mines would have quadrupled. Whitney would be musing in the *New York Times* about using his Cape Breton businesses to—get this—control the price of iron and steel throughout the world.

Before that could happen, it was necessary for there to be workers. So many workers that even the flood of humanity from the countryside—many of them Scottish Gaelic speakers who knew hardly a word of English—couldn't fill the void. Dominion Coal and the GMA tried; they sent word north to Dingwall and Bay St. Lawrence, and south to L'Ardoise and Petit-de-Grat. In the hayfields of the Margarees men leaned on their pitchforks and shook their heads in wonder at the extraordinary possibilities life would hold if they just moved to the other side of the island.

By then, the Canadian government's ambitious campaign to attract immigrants was in full swing. Dominion Coal's overseas recruitment campaign met with full approval. Its agents, who were paid by the head, beelined to British, European and pre-Confederation Newfoundland ports, spreading the gospel about the opportunities available in Nova Scotia—which, according to the literature, was on the verge of becoming the manufacturing centre of Canada, now that the intercontinental railway was completed and the province had access to markets as well as raw materials. The ad seen in many European countries read like this:

> The Dominion Coal Company of Sidney [*sic*] Canada North America undertakes to furnish employment which will pay you $2.00 to $5.00 per day. Emigrants would have to go via Thieste (Austria) and there sign contracts concerning their future employment and wages. The steamship fare is $50.00 paid in advance.

Soon, the Nova Scotia government had also seen the light about immigration—the best and maybe only way to develop the province's natural resources. The first piece of propaganda rolling off the printing presses in Halifax in 1870 made Nova Scotia sound like some kind of muscular, northern Arcadia: "Nova Scotia surpasses every country of the same extent in the world in the variety and supply of material resources," it said. "All that an emigrant need supply himself with before leaving Europe is money."

You can almost hear their hearts pounding in their chests as they read those words half a world away. Envision the men—maybe freshly scrubbed after a day in the Lancashire pits, the dust of the pit perhaps still coating the insides of their nostrils and throats, infiltrating every crack or crease—perched formally in neat rows of chairs under the moonlight as the Dominion Coal Company agent pushed the glass slide into the Victorian magic lantern. Maybe there's an audible gasp—as from Berbers staring up into the Saharan sky and glimpsing their first airplane—as the images of mounties, glaciers, majestic waterways and impossibly long railroads appear on the whitewashed side of the building. And all the time, the agent's voice fills the night air, singing the praises of this rough-hewn paradise, this land rather like home, yet so enticingly different.

It would be hard to resist if, say, you were a middle-aged, fourth-generation miner who understood what life in the British mines promised. The images would appear like revelations. Everyone looking so prosperous and healthy—not like your uncle hawking his insides out with black lung, or the bloke across the street bent double from all those years working in tunnels no wider than a rain barrel. There, at the very least, was a new start in a place where a person's position in the world wasn't something permanent and beyond his control. There was the dream, of a better future, they'd say to themselves as the light from the primitive slide projector glinted off their wistful faces.

CHAPTER SEVEN

Lazytown

It's a mug's game to stand in a burial ground and try to channel an ancestor's thoughts and feelings from a century earlier. But here I am, on one of those Emily Carr fall days, wondering what it would have been like for my great-grandfather as he saw for the first time where his aspirant dreams had led.

It was September 1902. He was alone; Margaret and the four children would come two years later, as was often the way for turn-of-the-century immigrants. John William Briers had boarded the *Siberian* in Liverpool, along with a boatful of other Lancashire miners, London labourers and British domestics and farmers. There were even two other Chorley men aboard—Robert Iddon, twenty, single, who used to live with his parents at the far end of Charnock Richard, and Thomas Hart, a married father of one who made his home not far from the Rigby family grocery store—also bound for the Cape Breton mines. The North Atlantic can be a terror at that time of year, so the nine-day crossing to St. John's, Newfoundland, and on to Halifax was likely a hard one. There, John W. and the sixty-six other adults, fourteen children and four infants went through immigration. Eventually, he hopped on another steamship heading east along the province's jagged coastline.

It would have seemed so arbitrary to him, the way settlements materialized for no obvious reason along the Cape Breton shoreline: Port Morien giving way to what would become Glace Bay, followed by communities that in time would be christened Dominion, New Waterford and New Victoria. Then his steamer would enter the great harbour of Sydney, and he would taste the coal dust in the air, and see the silhouettes of the iron towers rising from the land, signalling that he had reached the place the locals simply called "the mines."

I walk out to the end of the antique cemetery on Shore Road and look back in the weak fall sunlight to see what he would have seen: a carpet of leaves, the land sloping gently upward above low cliffs, the rocks beneath striped with ancient plants and animals. I've dug up some old photographs from around the time he arrived. Nobody smiles in pictures like those. I take a short walk to where one of them was taken—the corner of Main Street and Shore Road, a spot known as Sutherland's Corner. Today, with its spacious lawns and comfortable bungalows, it's the epitome of small-town contentment. The November 26, 1902 shot out-and-out gives me the creeps: muddy, wheel-rutted roads, thinly dispersed wooden buildings, dilapidated fences with missing slats, naked poles lining the street like crucifixes, windblown clothing on the line, a lone, dark, blurred figure fleeing up Main Street.

Moustaches shaped liked push brooms and bicycle handlebars adorned the faces of the men who walked the primitive streets of Sydney Mines. Wide-brimmed fedoras, bulging derbies and cloth miner's caps sat atop their heads or were pulled down low over their eyes. Though they were workingmen the new-world informality of the twentieth century was strange to them, and they sported waist-coats, ties, suit jackets and long coats that dragged in the mire.

I'm assuming that John W. Briers's first accommodations were in one of the company row houses erected near the mines. Space was tight even if the coal companies slapped up housing as quickly as the lumber arrived. Foreign experience mattered in the local labour pool hierarchy, and Briers was one of those seasoned miners brought in to fill the turn-of-the-century skills shortage in Nova Scotia's collieries. When the rest of family arrived, they ended up in a house on Forest Street, a short walk from the Princess Mine, Cape Breton's biggest, which would operate for a full century after it opened in 1875.

John Briers was a pick-and-shovel man, which meant that he would work right at the coal face, in a seventeen-foot-square room separated from the next chamber by a sixty-foot pillar of coal. The seams were five to six feet in thickness there, allowing the men to mostly work standing up. His duties were clear: cut, shoot and load the coal, all the time keeping an ear tuned to the creaking timbers that held the shale and stone of the roof in place. He was thirty-one, which made him, by local standards, a veteran in a green, inexperienced industry. To this day I don't know if he had ever been out of England before boarding the ship to Canada. But I seriously doubt it.

A Cape Breton map from 1863 identifies the area where my people settled as Lazytown. There's a story behind that: farmers, arriving to sell produce in the morning hours, found hardly anyone up and about. Coal mining was shift work. At that time in the morning, most of the men were at the mine, and their wives—after arising at dawn to get their husbands off to work—had returned to bed.

So Lazytown it was, even though this has always been a place of toil, enterprise and endeavour. When Joseph DesBarres, the Lieutenant Governor of Cape Breton, encouraged United Empire Loyalists to come to the island in 1784, a few settled here. A century before my great-grandfather arrived, a ship carrying Gaelic-speaking Scots made land in the vicinity, the area's first significant migration. After the GMA arrived, the pace picked up. The 1901 transfer of the last of its north-side leases to the Nova Scotia Steel and Coal Company—run, for a change, by homegrown business talent— signalled a new chapter in the Sydney Mines story.

By the time John Briers stepped off the boat, something else momentous had occurred: Whitney had folded his tent and decamped. It was the sort of thing that happened all the time during the Gilded Age, that post–Civil War period of robber barons, railroad tycoons and steel kings which somehow slopped over from the United States into Nova Scotia. A carpetbagger only interested in fleecing investors? A short-sighted opportunist who stumbled from one business mistake to another? After all this time, it's hard to say about Whitney. But I have my suspicions.

A few things are clear. As Donald MacGillivray has written, Dominion Coal's success was predicated on gaining access to the New England market. Things therefore looked good in 1894, when the American House of Representatives erased the duty of seventy-five cents per ton on imported coal. But within two years the duty was almost back to its former level. The 1896 Smoke Nuisance Law further limited coal's use in the U.S. market. Even worse, production of bituminous coal in the United States was doubling every decade from 1840 to 1910.

The American market, therefore, was lost. Desperate to breathe life into the Dominion Coal stock price, Whitney and his partners tried to flog Nova Scotia coal in Britain and Germany,

two of the leading coal-producing nations in the world and exper-
imented with using coke on the New York, New Haven and Hartford
Railroad. (The latter endeavour led to a stupefying corporate shell
game and ended with Whitney and the others buying a moribund
penitentiary in Halifax as a pilot plant to convert coal into coke,
gas tar and ammonia.)

Somewhere along the line—by grand design or pure fluke—he
seems to have come up with a nifty little scheme: Dominion Coal
would sell its production to another Whitney company, the New
England Gas and Coke Company, which, in turn, would sell the
coal gas it produced to the Massachusetts Pipe Line Gas Company,
another firm in the Whitney stable, for distribution in the Boston
market. Also key to the arrangement were Whitney's plans to build
a large plant at Everett, Massachusetts, to convert Dominion coal
into coke and other by-products.

The whole thing was contingent upon Whitney getting a
charter to set up his new gas distribution company. Boston fin-
ancier Thomas Lawson had a first-hand view of what followed, in
1896. In his exposé on the world of Gilded Age finance, published
nine years later, Lawson wrote that Whitney employed an army
of operatives—bought-and-paid-for ex-senators, representatives
and local political bosses, lobbyists, detectives and "runners" who
"kept 'tabs'" on every move and deed, day and night, of the members of the Massachusetts legislature. Then he set up the head-
quarters for Massachusetts Pipe Line at Young's Hotel, where he
took over parlours 9, 10 and 11, along with rooms 6, 7 and 8 on the
second floor.

> In the morning the place was deserted, but at noon the parlors
> began to fill up with the different officers of the "Machine"
> and their friends, trustworthy members of the Legislature.

A little later an elaborate luncheon would be served, the supernumeraries eating in one room, Towle [Whitney's top lawyer] and his chiefs and the legislators in the other. At table the gossip of the morning session at the State House was exchanged and the work laid out for the afternoon legislative and committee sessions. Another interval of silence and peace until at 5:30 the real business of the day began. Mr. Patch [Towle's secretary] was generally on the ground first, carrying the books in which the bribery records were kept, for be it remembered that the efficiency of the Whitney machine was largely due to the thoroughly systematic manner in which its operations were conducted . . .

If any outsider could possibly have obtained the entry to the head-quarters of the Whitney Massachusetts Pipe Line, say at nine o'clock any evening during the session, he might easily have imagined himself at the Madison Square Garden or at Tattersall's on the evening of the first day of an international horse-sale. This is what he would have seen: In Parlor 10, seated at a long table a dozen of Mr. Towle's chiefs, all in their shirt-sleeves, smoking voluminously; before each a sheet of paper on which is printed a list of the members of the legislature; against every name a blank space for memoranda; at the head of the table Towle himself, frowning severely over a similar sheet having broader memoranda-spaces. One after another the chiefs call off the names of the legislators, reporting as they go along. The outsider would have heard droned monotonously: " . . . from . . . not my man; . . . from . . . my man and . . . 's man; seen to-day, stood same as yesterday; . . . from . . . , raised price, $20 making it $150; agreed; [$]10 paid on account, total of $90 due; raised because . . . told him that he had got $20 more from . . ."

As each man reports the other chiefs and Towle discuss the details, and when a decision on disputed points is arrived at, Towle makes a memorandum on his blank, and the chief concerned records the order in the little note-book which each carries. All reports at last in, Towle retires to Room 11 and speedily returns with the "stuff" consisting of cash, stocks, puts, calls or transportation tickets, which he deals out to the chiefs to make good their promises for the day. It would have been obvious to the outsider, as soon as he had learned what was being dealt in, that a large proportion of the members of the Great and General Court of Massachusetts had bargained with the different members of "the machine" to sell their votes not only in committee but in full session of the Legislature, and that the price was to be paid when the votes were cast, though something was invariably exacted on account, to tie the bargain. Payment was made in cash, calls on Bay State Gas or Dominion Coal, or transportation on any of the railroads in the United States or Canada. The latter appears to be a class of remuneration Towle favored, probably because it cost nothing.

The legislative committee approved the charter. But when the governor vetoed the bill, shares in Dominion Coal and the other related Whitney outfits "began to sink in price like pigs of lead from a capsized boat." Then, wrote Lawson, who spent the entire episode in the back rooms with Whitney and his cronies, "Fate . . . let fly another of her quiver's contents." Word got out that in a previous campaign much like this one, Towle had gone back on his promise at the last minute and forced the bribees—if such a word exists—to accept fifty cents on the dollar of what they had been promised. A messenger showed up at Young's Hotel with the "ultimatum of the Great and General Court of the dear old

Commonwealth: 'Money in advance or no bill!'" Whitney et al., who had been heavily buying to support share prices, thought they had averted financial disaster by persuading the state's "able and fearless" governor to approve the charter by writing in an amendment that put a sixty-cent ceiling on the price for which it could sell its gas. Dominion Coal and New England Gas shares upticked briefly—then ploughed steeply and irrevocably downward on news that the charter had been amended and "was not worth the parchment upon which it was embossed."

Lawson, who was there, recounted the mob scene as the ruined investors and bought politicians descended upon Young's Hotel "swearing desperate consequences to Whitney and Towle regardless of the effect upon themselves." The next morning a "desperate," "wild-eyed" Towle and Patch—who sound like a pair right out of *Nicholas Nickleby*—showed up at Lawson's office with a suitcase of documents, cash, a $10,000 cheque and orders from Whitney to disappear. Lawson gave Towle gold for the cash and he, Patch and the evidence "faded out of my life and into the gray mist of eternity." When the members of the Great and Good Court of the old Commonwealth of Massachusetts showed up looking for their payola, they learned that their "stuff" had been delivered to Towle, who had high-tailed with it to foreign shores "where he was living in luxury with Mr. Patch."

Which wasn't quite true, according to Lawson's account:

A few days after; a vessel dropped anchor off the island of Jamaica; George Towle's body was carried ashore and buried, and Mr. Patch was escorted back to the ship. A few days later, with weights of lead to carry it to its last resting-place at the ocean's bottom, the latter's dead body was dropped over the vessel's side. And somewhere floating the high seas are a venturesome sailor-captain and a crew, who when in their cups tell, 'is said, strange tales of bags of gold and mysterious documents.

Lawson sent two police officials to Jamaica to photograph the contents of a coffin marked "George H. Towle." Regretfully he wrote, "I could not photograph the contents of the ocean's depths."

All this chicanery didn't do much for Cape Breton. The Boston contracts took every bit of Dominion coal production. The trouble was the price—$2.25 per ton, even though it could have fetched $4.00 on the open market. The arrangement nearly bankrupted the Cape Breton mines. Whitney's attention was elsewhere: keeping New England Gas and Coke afloat by providing it with a stable, cheap supply of coal. At roughly the same time, his most overreaching vision of all came into being: establishing an iron and steel industry in Cape Breton. Not just a run-of-the-mill metal concern—"A Pittsburgh in Canada," trumpeted the *New York Times* on February 17, 1901.

The piece was datelined St. John's, Newfoundland. And no stock promoter could have asked for a better shill job:

> Even in these days, when a billion-dollar steel plant is projected in the United States, the capitalist who moves with the times cannot afford to disregard the smelting enterprise that has just sprung into being at Sydney, Cape Breton, and which has been rendered possible by the existence of immense deposits of hematite iron at Belleisle, Newfoundland, the most remarkable ore formation of its kind in the world. This Sydney smelter is operated by the Dominion Iron and Steel

Company, commonly known as the Whitney Syndicate, because at its head is H.M. Whitney of Boston. Almeric H. Paget of New York is one of the Directors, so that, although the enterprise is located in Canada, it owes its existence to Yankee brains and capital, and is therefore all the more important on that account.

Let's leave the last thought alone for a second and concede that it was probably hard not to get caught up in the excitement of the moment. Canadians, as the century dawned, lived in a young country at a moment of endless possibility: a transcontinental railway was opening the west and providing a new home for the flood of immigrants pouring into the country; the national policy of industrial protection meant new industries got a foothold; the prices of wheat, newsprint and base metals headed skyward as exports soared and our trade balance shifted.

The end of the nineteenth century marked the close of the age of wood, wind and water in the Maritimes. From here on in, Nova Scotia would be transformed by coal, steam, iron and steel. Prime Minister Wilfrid Laurier, on a swing through Sydney in 1900, prophesied that Sydney "would become not only the Pittsburgh of Canada, but the Glasgow and Belfast of Canada." Pictou County's New Glasgow, to give another memorable example, was on the way to becoming "the Birmingham of the Country." The Canadian government helped pave the way with tariffs that protected domestic iron from foreign imports and forced most Canadian rolling mills to use Nova Scotia–made bar iron as a raw material. The end result: by the late nineteenth century New Glasgow and its surrounding towns had evolved into the equivalent of a modern-day business hub. Pictou County even had its own industrial behemoth ready to take on the world: the Nova Scotia Steel Company, which, according to historian T.W. Acheson, "represented the most fully integrated industrial complex in the country" at that time. Based in Trenton and New Glasgow, it had open-hearth and blast furnaces, forges, foundries and machine shops as well as large Newfoundland iron ore deposits. If there was any question about Nova Scotia Steel's clout, that changed in 1900, when it acquired the Sydney coal mines from the GMA and started building coke ovens and a blast furnace in Sydney Mines to turn all that nearby coal into steel.

Whitney? To develop his steel complex he struck a typical deal with a desperate Nova Scotia government: a 50 percent royalty cut, a reduction in federal bounties, a thirty-year municipal tax exemption and a grant of 480 acres right on Sydney Harbour. Naturally, the linchpin of the arrangement—alongside the government largesse—was a deal that required Dominion Coal to supply the steel plant with product at a below-market rate at a time when prices were climbing. Once the contract was in place, Whitney and his partners hit the market with $25 million worth of stock—$15.5 million of which went to Whitney and his cronies for their efforts in putting the deal together.

Two years later he had vamoosed. Control of both Dominion Coal and Dominion Iron and Steel lay in the hands of James Ross, who had helped build the Canadian Pacific Railway (and a sizable personal fortune) from his base in Montreal. After all this time it's hard to know whether Whitney sold out willingly, or whether Ross just bought control on the stock market. It didn't much matter. Though it was a mess, Cape Breton's steel industry survived. As 1902 closed, 30 percent of coal production was bound for Sydney's coke ovens and blast furnaces and the new mill that had just been built in Sydney Mines.

One day I took a walk to see where John William Briers, Margaret, and their children Harold, John, Amy and Norman, came to permanently settle. By then, more kin had joined them: one of Margaret's sisters, Amelia, had emigrated with her husband, Robert Hodgson—variously described as a labourer in a wagonworks and a blacksmith before he became a shop merchant in the nearby Cape Breton town of Little Bras d'Or. Margaret and Amelia's eldest brother, Samuel, also made the crossing to Cape Breton, and settled in Sydney Mines in 1905. According to the 1911 census he was a "labourer in a coal mine" and had previously been a teamster.

Clyde Avenue is only a few blocks over from Forest Street where they first lived. In 2007 at least it's leafier, the overall vibe a bit more settled. My mother remembers the house as white, but number 12 Clyde is painted burgundy now, and its three levels are topped by a peak roof shaded by oaks, elms and birch trees. A green recycling bin stands resolutely on the front lawn. I walk past it, up the few front steps to the wooden door, and push the bell. When there's no answer I cup my hand over my eyes and peer into a small sunporch filled to bursting with tennis trophies. Then I walk out to the sidewalk and snap a picture with my cellphone to show to my mom.

My guess is that when John William Briers walked out that door he headed south on Clyde, along the muddy rutted road, before taking a quick right and walking two more blocks along King Street. Since the day the GMA arrived, Sydney Mines had been a one-company town. It's still easy to glimpse the early outlines of the community created in the image of the coal company masters. The nicest homes, owned by the executives, lined Shore Road and extended up the hill where Richard Brown's abode, the first in Sydney Mines, today stands festooned with Halloween decorations. The rows of company housing stretched out along

Pitt, Crescent, Main and Forest streets so that workers were close to the mines. Infiltrating the town like catacombs were the mine works, which are now "greenfield sites"—big chunks of vacant land, overgrown with heather and brush, that have morphed into nature trails and venues for teenage drinking, dope-smoking and nookie.

All told, it should have taken only a few minutes for him to walk to the Princess Mine. He would have company, loads of it. According to the 1901 census, all but two of Nova Scotia's counties had seen their population decline in the previous decade; the area around Halifax, the biggest urban centre east of Montreal, had grown slightly. The population of Cape Breton County—the newly industrialized eastern chunk of the island—had climbed by nearly 50 percent during that period. The head count of Glace Bay, the destination of coal miners and labourers from Scotland, Ireland, Germany, Italy, Russia and Eastern Europe, had tripled in a decade. Sydney's population had doubled almost overnight as Dominion Iron and Steel imported Poles, Lebanese, Syrians and Austrians to work the steel mills. Brand new neighbourhoods—complete with company houses, streets and stores—materialized around Dominion Coal's No. 2 and No. 4 collieries in the area that would come to be known as simply Dominion.

In Sydney Mines, which also doubled in size from 1901 to 1911, not quite everyone was a miner or steelworker. When I perused the lists of occupations in the 1901 census I also found teachers, store clerks, servants, locomotive engineers, horse drivers, moulders, stable-men, carpenters, teachers, blacksmiths and a pair of female Salvation Army preachers. I saw a dressmaker (Florence MacKinnon, thirty-seven, who still lived with her parents), a barber (John H. Boutilier), one insurance agent (a Newfoundlander named Joseph White), a tailor (James MacKinnon), a tin merchant (John McCormick), a tinsmith (Amable Bernard), a diver (James Cann), a typewriter (Daniel Harrigan), a policeman (Stephen McLean), a shoemaker (John McIsaac), a barrister (Blowers Archibald), a doctor (Bernard Francis) and a Roman Catholic priest (C.F. MacKinnon).

Most working people, though, were bound for the steel mill or the mines. When John William Briers headed toward the pit-head he was joined by a hodgepodge of humanity: Scottish, Irish and English, but also French, Spaniards, Dutch and even a few Swedes, Norwegians and Germans. A surprising number of them were Newfoundlanders with names like Tobin, Cashin and Hurley. Historian Ron Crawley has a logical explanation: between 1890 and 1914 Newfoundland's ailing fishery was in a state of crisis. The opportunity to work in Cape Breton's burgeoning steel and coal industries produced what he calls "one of the most dramatic movements of people in Newfoundland history." When the Briers family arrived in Nova Scotia, about half the Newfoundlanders living in Canada made their home in the province. Of that number, 57 percent—or nearly 3,700—lived in Cape Breton. And *The Daily News* (St. John's, Newfoundland) would see fit to carry the following ditty on July 7, 1903:

Come pack your duds and get away,
We are not wanted here,
We'll go where hundreds go every day
From hunger and despair.
We will seek a country
Where both milk and honey flow,
So pack your "duds" for Sydney,
For Ned Morris told me so.

When John and Margaret arrived in Sydney Mines, the first vestiges of civilization were just beginning to appear: hotels (the Jubilee and Old King Edward, both on Main Street); the red sandstone federal post office, a few privately owned stores, now that the province had passed a bill ensuring that the miners were paid in "coin of the realm" rather than scrip redeemable only in the company-owned "pluck me" stores. The town was still poorly equipped for newcomers no matter what their origin. Water came from wells until 1900. It took another three years before the town's first chief of police was appointed. That same year the first electric street lights went on, and an electric street railway began running. But it was 1907 before the town got its first plank sidewalk, and 1928 before the first automobile groaned through the streets.

Which, through the most convoluted of thinking, brings me to Arthur Lismer, the painter. It's not beyond the realm of possibility that it was Lismer, from 1916 to 1919 principal of the precursor to the Nova Scotia College of Art and Design in Halifax, who suggested that his pal Lawren Harris come east for a visit. In 1921—the year after the two took part in the founding of the Group of Seven, which impressed on Canadians the majesty of their own wilderness—Harris spent time in Halifax, then headed to Cape Breton.

Harris was always drawn to impoverished urban places. What he saw in Halifax shocked him enough to put brush to canvas to depict the poverty in the city's harbour tenements. His impressions from his trip to industrial Cape Breton had to gestate longer. A black-and-white Harris ink published in the July 1925 edition of the *Canadian Forum,* entitled *Glace Bay,* shows an emaciated woman clutching a couple of urchins to her chest in front of a nightmare collection of shacks and colliery buildings. It's like a prelude to *The Scream,* drawn moments before the subject howls in existential horror.

When I lived in Toronto back in the late eighties, I went to the Art Gallery of Ontario and found myself staring at *Miners' Houses, Glace Bay,* an oil painting that Harris also completed in 1925. A string of identical steepled houses—dark brown in the shade, ochre in the light—punches the sky. The hard terrain bucks and rolls. A gaping picket fence anchors the frame. Everything is a bit childish, off-kilter. The effect—and when I look at a painting the only thing I know how to do is squint hard and trust my first hazy impression—is stark and sombre but with a little something. The brightening sky leads my eye from right to left across the canvas. Every object seems to yearn for the warming glow in the distance. Up there, it seems to say. Up there is sunlight. Up there is hope.

Everything about coal mining lends itself to the easiest kind of symbolism: iron towers climbing mercilessly into the sky; railway tracks descending into the dark void. Anonymous, soot-faced miners digging their own graves miles below the light and air. Something about their houses, in particular, arrests the artist's eye and heart. "Between the bridge and the colliery, for a distance of two hundred and fifty yards, crowded so close together they looked like a single down-ward slanting building with a single downward-slanting roof, were the houses of the miners' row," is how Glace Bay–born novelist Hugh MacLennan introduces them in *Each Man's Son.* Half a century later, Ann-Marie MacDonald—father from Sydney and mother from New Waterford—considers the bleak vista in her novel *Fall on Your Knees,* and writes about how "spreading away from the collieries and coal heaps are the peaked roofs of the miners' houses built row on row by the coal company. Company houses. Company town."

They're still worth seeing; in many places, with the old mine workings eroding and disappearing, the company homes are the last best relic of Nova Scotia's coal age. Finding somewhere, anywhere, to lay your head was a serious challenge in turn-of-the-century colliery districts. The GMA built the first company homes—rough structures made of logs or brick—in Pictou County soon after its arrival. In the 1830s and 1840s, it started erecting wooden houses, shingled outside and plastered within, in the area. It wasn't necessarily a humanitarian gesture. As the industry grew, the coal companies erected housing pell-mell as part of their recruitment and retention program. The Sydney Mines experience was emblematic. In the English style, they built a dozen or so connected homes—which somehow acquired names like King William, Cahill's, Scalping, Blue and Maedon's rows—near the mine workings. When I went tooling around Sydney Mines one afternoon, the only company-built row houses still visible were so utilitarian-looking that I thought any second a door could open and a member of one of the dozen families living there in 1900— a Cunliff, say, a Westhead, Strickland or Birmingham—could step out, carrying his miner's lamp and tin lunch box.

Those who didn't inhabit the miners' tenements—in 1901 Dominion Coal alone owned a thousand of them—bunked in the boarding houses, or "shacks," as they were known locally. Each shack held seventy-two men who slept two to a bed. (Cooks were hired by the company to feed the men, although the price of each meal was deducted from their pay envelopes at the end of the week.) Thousands of others squatted in crude homemade board-and-tarpaper shanties, or somehow gained entrance to one of the private homes where as many as twenty boarders lived in a single tiny house.

I've seen variations on the Sydney Mines company cottages through-out every colliery town in the province: rough little two-storey, semi-detached, wood-framed boxes arranged in linear fashion along the road. They were meant to be cheap, not elegant or interesting. If you went to sleep in one on Crescent Street in Sydney Mines and magically awoke in another on Foord Street in Stellarton, it might be a couple of hours before you realized teleportation had taken place. The single one I entered, preserved from *circa* 1930 as part of the Glace Bay Miners' Museum, was a bleak collection of tiny rooms: a parlour, kitchen and pantry downstairs, and a pair of bedrooms—one for the parents, the other where the kids slept several to the bed—up the rickety stairs. Nothing but bare essentials throughout: plain, unpainted floorboards; hard homemade furniture; thin, unforgiving straw beds; a small coal stove as the single source of heat; maybe a photo or painting of some dour ancestor adorning the walls.

The backyard probably once contained a small garden; according to historian Robert McIntosh, the companies encouraged mining families to grow vegetables to avoid famine during the bad years, and also as a way to justify keeping wages low. Bathing took place in a tin tub in the backyard during the summer months, and for the rest of the year, in a tub in the kitchen. A privately published history of Sydney Mines reported that women would sometimes steal a peek at the brawny colliery men. On the other hand, maybe they were just killing time; their baths didn't happen until late Saturday night, while the men were asleep. When John William Briers happened on the scene, most everyone in Sydney Mines still thought of the toilet as an outhouse in the backyard. According to the same history of the town, that primitive facility was an uninviting prospect in the middle of a cold February night, so the chamber pot was used "to good advantage." In the case of the men, "a nearby window would also turn the trick."

Only after 1900, when Nova Scotia Steel and Coal took over

the mines, were residents permitted to purchase the homes and begin improving them. Yet there were clear advantages to living in a company house: rent was cheap; tenants often received preference when work was scarce. If production and wages were low, they could continue to live in the house and buy at the company store. "But," cautioned historian Ralph Ripley, "the rent mounted and such indebtedness effectively tied the tenant to the company."

And that kind of uneven relationship left the miners open to all kinds of abuse. The coal companies were brutal when it came to quelling outbreaks of independence among their working folk. We'll hear soon about the goon squads brought in to use fists, sticks and guns to control striking miners, how the miners were ridden down in the streets by mounted provincial constabulary, and gunned down by company police. CBC broadcaster Bill McNeil could have been referring to just about any Cape Breton coal mining family when he described the one in which he grew up:

> My mother's own family was evicted from a company-owned house in the dead of winter, and her sick father was carried out, bed and all, and placed on the sidewalk among the tangle of tables and chairs. That was his folly and crime because he was a striker. Mother, who was fourteen years old when this happened, never could forget that terrible day, and she could never, even in her old age, tell the story without breaking down in tears.

The coal company's influence, particularly at the beginning, was all-pervasive. The company not only built and owned the houses in the town, but supplied the coal that heated them and, later, the power plant that lit them. It supplied the water the miners and their families drank and—through its stores—the food they ate. It wouldn't be long before independent proprietors arrived and the first co-operative stores appeared. But in the first few decades of the twentieth century, only the company stores could offer credit. And so, when a Princess miner got his weekly pay packet, it would include a long list of deductions already taken: rent, coal, electricity, water and anything bought on credit at the company store. Later the list of deductions known as check-off evolved to include the cost of providing church, hospital, sanitation and physician services.

It was 1888 when Alexander McGillivray, a miner at the Little Glace Bay Mine, testified before a Royal Commission appointed by Sir John A. Macdonald to consider the relationship between labour and capital in Canada. Not much would change in the intervening years.

Q: Look at this (memorandum handed to witness). That is the statement of your account for the month of July, 1877?
A: Yes.
Q: You cut 66 [tons] and a half of coal?
A: Yes.
Q: For which you were credited $33.53.
A: Yes
Q: And you cut two cubic yards for which you were credited $1.60.
A: Yes.
Q: Making a total of $35.13?
A: Yes.
Q: Against this you were charged rent $1.50, coal 1.25¢
A: Yes.
Q: How much coal did you receive for that?
A: About two loads.

Q: You are charged for the hauling end not for the coal?
A: I think so.
Q: You are charged with oil 80¢?
A: Yes

. . . . .

Q: You are charged with powder $3.24?
A: Yes.

. . . . .

Q: You are charged for school 15¢?
A: Yes.
Q: Doctor 40¢?
A: Yes.
Q: For tally 30¢?
A: Yes.
Q: That is for the man miners employ to watch the tally?
A: Yes.
Q: You are charged for store account $28.49?
A: Yes.
Q: Would you run that much every month?
A: No.
Q: This would probably include some book account?
A: Yes
Q: So the credits and the debits for the month exactly balance, each making $35.13?
A: Yes.
Q: You received that month no cash?
A: No.
Q: Is it generally the case that at the end of the month, no cash is coming to you?
A: On many occasions.

One day I went looking for the old coal company store—the symbol, as Bill McNeil once put it, "of everything that was wrong in a system where the company had it all and the workers had nothing." By the early 1900s the miners were at least paid in real money rather than scrip. "I knew week in, week out, fellows who never drew a red cent," recalled Gordon MacGregor of Glace Bay. "To my mother there was a kind of blight, in a way, for everyone to deal there. She had a fear of it. Lots of women did." Choice was the issue; the few privately owned stores were small and poorly stocked. When the coal companies doled out a job or a house it was usually with the understanding that the recipients would do all their shopping at the company stores. Duncan MacIntyre, a miner in Glace Bay's Caledonia Mine, told the 1888 Royal Commission on the Relations of Labour and Capital that he didn't think "there are half a dozen families at the colliery but deal at the store."

A pizzeria, convenience store and lumberyard now fill the real estate where the Sydney Mines store once stood. So it takes some imagination to picture what an early-twentieth-century coal miner's wife would have seen when she stopped to peer in the front windows and then, passing underneath the Nova Scotia Steel and Coal sign, entered. Inside, ornate fifteen-foot ceilings, gleaming wooden floors, dark, polished counters and white-coated clerks. And the merchandise . . . Lord, the merchandise. I defer to John Mellor's description. "Butter—fine quality creamery butter—was sold in large square wooden boxes. Cheddar cheese in huge rounds was just as delicious," he wrote. "Bacon, cheese and plug tobacco were sliced, weighed, and wrapped expertly on the countertops by clerks who were well-trained, efficient and for the most part pleasant to deal with." The flour was kept in big barrels, for loading into cotton bags of such "excellent quality" that, during strikes or slowdowns, the material could be used by miners' wives for underwear and daughters for dresses. Hanging in the cool basement were sides of beef and mutton and whole carcasses of pork. "Stacked up to the low ceiling were hundreds of bags of flour, barrels of wet salted cod, turbot, mackerel, and herring, boxes of apples and biscuits, hogsheads of pure molasses, crates of eggs, and a great multitude of foodstuffs." There were clothes and bolts of cloth, sewing gear, hardware, clay pipes and "a hundred and one knickknacks of every description." At the back of the store stood a shed containing "bales of hay and foodstuffs for horses, cattle and pigs for those fortunate enough to own livestock." The upper floor contained "boots and shoes, house furnishings, furniture, bedding, linoleum, cutlery, crockery and hundreds of other household items."

You can see how it would have been hard to resist. How mining wives would have been reeled in like poor bingo addicts entering a casino for the first time, blowing their available credit on candy and useless doodads until there wasn't enough for groceries in the end. You don't have to be able to recite *Das Kapital* by heart to conclude that the "pluck me" stores—so named, legend has it, because a Cape Breton miner, discovering one week that after all the deductions he hadn't made a cent, turned to his buddies and shouted, "Christ, they've plucked me!"—represented one of the worst aspects of industrialization. The credit system kept the miners and their families in perpetual servitude; once a miner was in hock at one colliery, there was an agreement that he couldn't move to another mine, or even get credit at another company store. Mellor says the situation was perpetuated by the rhythm of the town. During the winter months the mines stopped operation. The workers' families had to depend upon the largesse of the company stores for food and clothing during those periods, running up large debts that could only be worked off when the mines reopened. In the end the store credit system was simply another weapon the

coal companies could use on the miners, when they needed to battle a union drive or to end a strike.

One thing the miners somehow found money for was churches.
In Sydney Mines the world view was almost exclusively Christian.
(The 1901 census counted Roman Catholics (1,716), Presbyterians
(905), Anglicans (309), Methodists (161), Baptists (42), Lutherans
(72), Salvation Army (44), Adventists (22) and Congregationalists
(16).) The novelist Ann-Marie MacDonald was talking about
nearby New Waterford when she told Oprah Winfrey that her
home was the kind of community where "all the beauty, imagination and aesthetic yearning would be expressed by the church." That
statement, though, applied equally all around the harbour.

A Prince Edward Island architect named William C. Harris
was most responsible for brightening the view throughout Cape
Breton. He built a gothic revival gem for the Anglican call to worship in Sydney Mines. He also built Anglican churches in the
Whitney Pier area of Sydney and in North Sydney. Probably his
work on the north side of the harbour brought Harris to the attention of officials of the Cape Breton Coal, Iron and Railway
Company. In 1904 they hired him for his most ambitious commission to date: a ten-thousand-person town planned for the middle
of the Cape Breton forest.

They called it Broughton, after the English country seat of
Horace Mayhew, the company's president. And all the hope and
ambition of that time and place is visible in the original plans for
the town, which I one day unfurled at Cape Breton University's
Beaton Institute in Sydney. The drawings were prepared by
M.G. Henniger, a local civil engineer, and dated April 20, 1905.
The miners' cottages—all 111 of them, by my count—are arranged

in geometrically straight streets, divided by the rail line into residential areas. The streets are numbered, or bear names such as
Lakeside Drive, Main Street or Broad Street. The margins of the
plans are adorned with precise drawings of the front and side views
of the office building, the assistant manager's house, the railway
station and the Broughton Arms Hotel. Each drawing carries
Harris's unmistakable style, "with hipped roofs and gables, round
towers and bartizans, and bargeboards decorated with lines of little holes," in the words of his biographer Robert C. Tuck.

Technically, the vision was that of another man: Thomas
Lancaster, an Englishman with a bit of mining experience who felt
certain that the Cape Breton coalfields extended some sixteen kilometres from Sydney. In 1904 he raised some seed capital from a collection of bankers, coal men and members of the venerable Gladstone
family back in England. Then he bought the land and won the go-
ahead to develop ninety-two square miles of their holdings.

What did he foresee? A modern town hacked out of the wilderness. Progress, yes, but a more humane version than the kind taking
root in the nearby coal towns. Early the next year, the Broughton
mine was up and working. A rail line connected the pithead with a
nearby Dominion Coal rail line so that building materials could be
brought in. Soon the foundations for a power plant were laid. Italian
labourers arrived and started clearing the site for the town that
would follow.

"Architecturally," Tuck wrote, "Broughton had unity but not
uniformity." The Anglican chapel was furnished with an altar and
pews made of birch logs (even the covers of the prayer books were
made of birchbark). The Cape Breton Coal, Iron and Railway general office boasted "massive dormers and decorative buttresses on
single storey round towers." Even the assistant manager's house was
decorated with "hipped gables, buttresses and an umbrage at the

front entrance." The hotels, by all accounts, gave the fullest display of "the abundance" of Harris's creative imagination. The Crown Hotel, where the workers stayed, was less imposing. The three-storey Broughton Arms, with its "spacious basement and attics, round topped by conical roofs, and encircled by a veranda," made jaws drop. "Out in the calm hushed solitude of its country fastness," wrote an anonymous scribbler at the time, "on a remorseful blueberry patch, and near the sacred precinct of an old and venerable swamp is built and equipped a superb hotel—nothing better east of Montreal."

In 2008, no signs that I could find showed the way to the site of Broughton Mines, which had even managed to fall through the gaps in the ubiquitous MapQuest grid. So I just headed south from Sydney until I hit something called Morrison Road, where I took a right and drove until the blacktop ended. I chugged back and forth on the sparsely populated dirt road and pulled over to ask directions from a skinny guy gathering bottles from the culverts. He'd never heard of Broughton Mines. A farmer a few miles the other way had; he directed me past the swamp I'd read about in some of Harris's letters until I saw a break in the woods, and yellow "no trespassing" tape stuck to the trees.

I went in anyway, and walked around piles of dirt, rock and rubble and over a couple of small craters. About a hundred yards in, I stopped by a mossy concrete foundation, probably twenty feet by thirty, in the process of being reclaimed by the undergrowth. I have to confess: I've always had a soft spot for ruins. I know I'm not alone in this regard; the Japanese have a whole aesthetic—known as *wabi sabi*—that cherishes the weathered and transient. Which is certainly one way of thinking about what's left of Broughton. The money ran out. The company, it turned out, didn't even have clear title to all of the land. Out of the blue, Lancaster quit. Mayhew visited the premier and asked for subsidies to finance the construction of a rail line to carry the coal to Sydney. When that didn't work, he sailed for England on May 17, 1906, leaving his son, Horace Jr.—a melancholy-looking fellow, from the one photo I've seen—in charge of Broughton. Mayhew promised to be back in six weeks, but never set foot in Cape Breton again. One Sunday morning that summer, Horace Jr. took his life in the Broughton Arms Hotel.

Some new managers tried to reboot the enterprise. In 1915 the mine closed, more or less for good. The Broughton Arms, which had claimed to be the location of North America's first set of revolving doors, burned down a year later, not long after being taken over by the officers and men of the 185th Battalion Cape Breton Highlanders as they assembled to head overseas. After the First World War, the remaining buildings fell into neglect and decay. Some of the miners' cottages were hauled away to Sydney or Glace Bay to be turned into private homes. Eventually, a few foundations were all that was left. Nothing lasts. Not even the most expansive of dreams. The coal-mining communities were already discovering that.

CHAPTER EIGHT

He Was That Young

Youth, you will recall, lasts a very long time. Minutes meander, hours creep, days expand. My grandfather—earnest, blue-eyed, sandy-haired—never said a word about the eternal dark, the dust coating his throat, the rats dancing across his boots. But when you are eleven years old, time unspools at a sluggish pace. On a summer afternoon at a beach that slowed-down, dreamy state is a gift. Alone in a hole in the ground—listening to the eerie creak of the roof, the incessant drip of the water—it had to be agony pure.

He didn't have a choice, not really. When you came from coal-mining stock, when your father was a coal miner and his father before him—all the way back to the days before false teeth, the photograph and shampoo—your path in the early twentieth century was as clear in Sydney Mines as it would have been back in Britain. John Briers Jr., who went by Jack, had at least completed grade five, which made him an intellectual compared to the boys of nine or ten whose parents said the hell with the rules and sentenced them to Nova Scotia's Victorian coal mines. In 1906, when my grandfather entered the Florence colliery, another nine hundred or so boys already toiled in Nova Scotia coal mines. In Sydney Mines—according to the 1901 census—60 percent of families with working-age boys had sent one of their children off to the pit.

We blanch in horror now at the thought of it: the youngest boys—so small they could only make the long trek to the pithead in their fathers' arms, so scared they cried on the way to work each day, so young they still believed in Santa Claus—working as trappers, opening and closing the doors that ventilated the mine. Yet by 1906 people were just starting to see these children as victims. Historian Robert McIntosh points out that a tour of the colliery was a must for any visiting journalist or travel writer in the late 1800s. The scribes thought the mines were exotic, macabre and scary. Nobody batted an eye at the soot-faced children in the workforce. "The youngest 'imps' were 'cheerful,'" he wrote, summarizing the coverage. "Older boys were 'happy,' 'bright,' 'interesting' and 'animated.' Mine visitors agreed that the colliery boy was colourful; he was content with his work. His place was in the mine."

I don't have any pictures of Jack Briers from around this time. I doubt that he'd look much different from the other pit boys captured on the photographic page during that period. Playful adjectives really aren't the ones that come to mind. A smile flickers at the occasional angelic face. A few of them look perplexed. Posed in their peaked miner's caps, dark, thick coats and beat-up boots, they mostly look cocky, hard and weary—trying with an insolent stare or a nonchalant posture to make the photographer believe they are tough enough for some task which, in a better world, they wouldn't need to perform.

The Beaton Institute possesses one photo taken in 1900 at Glace Bay's Caledonia Mine. Shift's over. A few of the boys have been dragooned to sit for a shot. The ones seated in the front row—among them Fred Wadden, a hulking guy with a clay pipe in his mouth, and Tius Tutty, who I discover is twenty and has already put in six years at the Bridgeport and Dominion mines—look older, tougher and worldlier. The eye, though, is drawn to the left of the picture. There Allie MacKenzie—who later became a legend on the rugby field and baseball diamond, before dying during a mustard-gas attack in the First World War—stands uncertainly. He's shorter than the other miners, even though they're seated. Which, I suppose, isn't overly surprising. MacKenzie was nine years old. At that point he had already worked three months as a trapper boy in the Caledonia colliery.

School, to many of them, seemed boring and pointless, in part thanks to the poorly trained teachers the colliery towns tended to attract at the turn of the century. To malinger too long in the classroom was viewed as downright effeminate in a place where manliness was the ultimate aim. The very air felt different when the colliers—role models, heroes, elders, all in one—strode down the streets. Songs were written about men like these. Who could cut the most coal? Who was the strongest? Who could stand the gaff—endure whatever the company threw at them—when the animosity between the miners and their employers boiled over? Legends were born in these young places searching for their own unifying stories.

When I started to sift through the words of the miners, I discovered that tradition was part of what drew them. "My father was here as a blacksmith," said Edgar Bonnar, who started working in the Princess mine in 1925 at the age of sixteen. His story is typical. "My brother was here, all the family worked here." When George Dooley, who rose to become the manager of the fabled Drummond Mine in Westville, tried to figure out what to do with his life, the fact that his grandfather had worked there for forty years and his father for fifty-eight heavily influenced his decision-making. Lybison MacKay, who worked a number of Cape Breton mines, felt the same weight of precedent: "My father worked 50 years in the Inverness Mines. . . . I kind of graduated into coal mining myself. He took me underground when I was just seven. It was quite an experience. Yes, I think that had quite a bit to do with it."

That and the fact that they didn't really have a say anyway. "It was every young lad's ambition to get into the mines. That was the only thing here in this area," recalled Ray MacNeil, who went into No. 12 colliery in Scotchtown in 1925. "I had an old suit—dear God there were 1,000 patches on it—and after the seventeenth visit to the mine office in my suit, I got hired." Bob Hachey, who spent forty-four years in the mines around Joggins and River Hebert, was just thirteen when he entered the Bayview Mine: "I had no choice and neither did my brother." Springhill miner Joe E. Tabor also quit school at a young age: "My father said, 'If you're going to quit school you'll have to come work with me in the coal mines.' So that's what I did." And Jimmy Johnson, who started working at the Allan Shaft in Stellarton in 1930, experienced the same kind of familial pressure: "My mother said, 'I don't know what we're going to do,'" he remembered years later. "At the time I couldn't get a job nowhere. So there was no other place to go but the coalmines. She said, 'I don't know what we're going to do, we ain't got nothing to eat.'"

Childhood was hard. Yet it's a mistake to think of the boy colliers as simply underaged casualties of industrialization. Queen's University historian Ian MacKay writes that going into the pit "was a declaration of independence" for the juvenile miners. So they put on extra overcoats and lied about their age. Or one day they just signed up without their parents knowing. Suddenly, bewilderingly, they were men. At home, their status changed; they received adult-sized portions of food and got a place at the table along with the men, while their sisters and even their mothers stood so the breadwinners could dine. "It was a big day when I went to the mine," recalled Archie MacDonald, who was fourteen when he started working in the Scotia Colliery in Sydney Mines. "It was the first job in which I made money. In other words, it meant I had my foot in the threshold of being a man—I would be somebody. I would be something on my own."

There they did real men's work. When their rights were being trampled, they revelled in the adults' ability to shut down the entire coal mine by walking off the job over job security, wages and safety. Back in the light and fresh air—where they earned a reputation as underaged drinkers and rowdies with a liking for scrapping with their sworn enemies the "school boys"—there was a new swagger to their gait. Being a coal miner meant you were more than pure sinew and animal labour. Other people, even other workingmen, might look down on you, with your sooty face and your work that meant going into a dark hole in the ground. You knew, though, that going into the pit meant being part of something bigger than yourself—part of a community, brothers in arms with your own distinctive skill set, worries and joys, even your own distinctive language. It was more than just shared pain. It was sharing an intense experience that only the wise could understand. Going into the pit was no place for someone hell-bent on the twentieth-century be-all and end-all of bettering yourself. Tell you this, though: you knew you were alive, every second of the way.

The mine companies liked the pit boys because they worked for a lot less than adults. (In 1880, the average boy working in a Nova Scotia colliery made just half of what an adult labourer took home; by 1920 a Sydney Mines mineworker classified as a boy still made only 60 to 70 percent of a man's pay.) They also liked the boys because they had a pulse, they could do a day's work. Canada's rapid industrialization powered a fourfold increase in production from Nova Scotia's collieries from 1880 to 1910, which translated into an unlimited appetite for cheap, skilled boy miners, particularly those who would take on jobs that older men couldn't do.

With time their pay envelopes grew. So did their value to the rest of the family. In Sydney Mines and the rest of Nova Scotia's mining towns, most men and women lived with their families until they were married. As a result, a household's peak earning years were that brief period when the unattached sons were living at home and the father was still working. The extra income, McIntosh points out, likely made the difference between mere subsistence and a level of comfort. All the more reason for miners to push their children into the pit rather than see them choose a line of work that might require them to leave home in quest of a job.

By 1908, owing to the industry's tremendous expansion, 36 percent of Nova Scotia mineworkers were under the age of twenty and fully 67 percent were under the age of thirty. John William was thirty-seven, and no cushy retirement with a pension plan awaited. The Sydney Mines Friendly Society—whose chief object was to raise funds "by the subscriptions from the members, contributions from the Nova Scotia Steel & Coal Co., Ltd., and the Local Government, and by donations from parties who are not members, to make provision for the support of ordinary members, their widows, children or other relatives in the case of sickness or other accidental injury, of old age, or of sickness or injury"—didn't come into being until 1909. The "friendlies" were dirt poor, but they were the miners' only safeguard against infirmity, illness and disease. Nova Scotia's Workmen's Compensation Act came along in 1915 but, as a report for the federal Department of Mines pointed out a year later, it made "no provision for loss of earning power due to sickness, except in the rather obscure and debatable field of occupational diseases."

The year before Jack Briers went underground, twenty-two people lost their lives in Nova Scotia mines. In 1906, thirty-four males—twenty-one of them in Cape Breton—died from rockfalls and explosions, from being crushed by runaway trolleys, jammed by boxes and flattened by hoppers. As the pace quickened in the coalfields, the collateral damage continued to mount in Nova Scotia mines: thirty-six dead in 1907; another fifty in 1908. "In those days, if the head of the household died there was no such thing as widow's allowance. No such thing as relief," Gordon McGregor, a retired miner, told *Cape Breton's Magazine*. Often it fell on the shoulders of the oldest boy, no matter what his age, to go to work.

> My cousin Peter had to go to work. He was so young that when he'd start early in the morning in the winter, between their house and the mine there was a cemetery. And he was so young, and so many ghost stories told in those days he was scared to walk past the graveyard in the dark. And his mother used to have to take him by the hand to get past the graveyard, to go to work. He was that young.

Jack Briers was compact and sturdy in old age So let's assume he was the same way as a preteen. Imagine him arising in the dark—awakened by the colliery steam whistle—and gulping down some breakfast before donning his pit clothes, described by a newspaper of the day as "a pair of indifferent-fitting duck trousers, generously patched, an old coat, and with a lighted tin lamp on the front of his cap, his tea and dinner can securely fastened on his back." At the mine he wouldn't see much as he moved down the narrow passageways. But he'd taste the smoke and dust, hear the dripping water and feel the cold rush of air when the doors opened.

The job of a trapper boy wasn't strenuous: open the doors when carts or miners approached, then close them afterwards. The stress of waiting for hour after hour alone in the dark, listening for the sounds of the coal cars, was what got you. That and the rats. Sydney Mines–born Johnny Miles, who stunned the sporting world when he won the Boston Marathon as a complete unknown in 1926, started as a trapper in the Princess Mine a few years after my grandfather. After his death in 2003, the *Boston Globe* reported that he had depended upon the sounds of rats to know that no poisonous gases had accumulated in his compartment before opening the door.

New Waterford miner Sid Timmons was ten and a half when he went underground.

> I had a dog. He was what they call a badger hound. And he'd tackle anything—didn't matter how big it was—anything.... I was on the back shift all alone. So I decided to take him to the pit with me. You know—good company. So I took him. And the first night he got a rat. He grabbed the rat by the head—like that. And when he grabbed the rat, the rat grabbed his tongue. I had to kill the rat in his mouth—you know. But he never made that mistake after.

You grew up fast in the coal mine. Dan J. McDonald, whose father, uncles and grandfathers all spent their lives underground, was fourteen in 1917 when he got a job as a trapper boy in the Dominion mine. His first day was an eye-opener:

Another young fellow and myself started work on the same day, I on the day shift and he on the night. The second day when I went out to work I heard a group of the drivers talking in subdued tones.

"Wasn't it too bad about that boy last night?"

I asked what was wrong.

"That young fellow was killed."

"Who was he," I asked. And when I heard his name I tingled all over and didn't think mining was such a good thing then. I didn't want to go down, I was so frightened.

"Make up an excuse for me," I said to the boys. "I don't think I'll go down today."

"You're yellow! You're cowardly! We know why you're leaving," they shouted.

"I'll show you if I'm yellow," I said. And I went back. But I went through a thousand deaths that day while I was underground.

Boys like my grandfather entered a world that hadn't changed much since the coming of the steam engine. Vertical shafts were still used to reach the coal; from there, the coal ended up in cars hauled by ponies across rails laid along the mine floor, and the cars were then coupled together into a train, or rake, that carried coal, men and equipment to and from the surface.

The Cape Breton coalfields presented an extra challenge: most of them lay under the ocean. The shaft of the Princess Colliery, where John William still worked, was sunk on land in 1873, but the miners were under salt water almost from the moment they walked through the entrance. By the time the colliery closed in 1975 the workings were two thousand feet under the ocean floor and extended three and a half miles from the shoreline. These, then, were no ordinary coal mines. Splitting open dry land and digging out coal was hard enough. When the seams were underwater, the sea had an unnerving tendency to break in and flood the shaft. Furthermore, the longer the shaft, the harder it is to pump air down to the men and to move coal to the surface.

So the trapper boys, who controlled the airflow, remained as important as ever. Not that anyone wanted to stay stuck in that lowly job. The colliery offered a surprising amount of workplace mobility. The next move up the pecking order might be as a loader, filling the boxes with freshly cut coal. Or as a driver, riding herd on the pit ponies that moved the boxes of coal from the seam to the bottom of the slope for transportation to the surface. With time, they might graduate to become breaker boys (removing stone and other impurities on the service) or other "company hands"—everything from the chain runners who kept the underground railway running, to the timber men who built and demolished the roof supports.

But the romance, along with the good money, was down at the coal face, where the miners toiled in teams who were mutually responsible for their "room" or "bord." The hand pick was still the tool of choice in the early days of the twentieth century, recalled Sydney Mines collier Gordon MacGregor:

> An old handpick miner he'd . . . lie on his side. He'd have to lie under a cut of coal. He'd dig a trench in the bottom of the seam. There could perhaps be seven feet above him. And he'd work his way until all you could see sticking out from under the mining, as they called it, was his heels. Solid coal was above him. He was taking a chance of being crushed. But the good miners would timber themselves—put timber up and they'd just pick away.

Once he'd hand-picked in far enough, recalled Tius Tutty, the miner used an auger to bore a hole in the coal above the cut. Then he stuffed the hole full of blasting powder in preparation for the blasting, or "shooting."

> When you had it all stemmed up you pulled the needle out and at that time you used what they called squibs—powder done up in paper, you know? You'd open up the end of it and tear a little piece off and you'd stick that in the hole. It would go right in the hole where you pulled the needle out. And you'd light it—with your lamp. Then you'd take off. You'd duck down. There was always an opening you could run to, because they had places for air to travel, you know? You'd sing out, "Fire!" There'd be only two men in the place anyhow. . . . You'd wait a few moments after that goes off in case there'd be some coal loose that'd fall and then after the smoke would drive out you'd go up and start loading your coal.

After the drivers and pit ponies took over, a miner might stop to drink tea and eat lunch from his can. Maybe he'd have a chew of Pictou Twist, a blackish strong tobacco popular in the mines, where no matches could be used to light a pipe or cigarette. Then he started all over again. Eight to ten tons of coal were considered a good day's work. Someone working in a Pictou County mine in the early 1900s received forty-five cents per tonne. That worked out to $4.50 per day minus sixty cents to pay the loader, as well as the cost of the powder and sharpening the picks. For the same kind of shift a trapper boy would receive forty-five cents. A loader, who usually worked for two miners, was paid $1.20 in return for loading between fifteen and twenty 1,100-pound boxes.

Yet the miners stuck it out. They stuck out the tedium. They stuck out the loneliness. They stuck out the darkness. (If a man's lamp went out—and a breath of air would be enough to make that happen—he had to roam around in the dark to borrow another man's light to get it relit.) They stuck out having to urinate and defecate wherever they worked, and having to eat their coal-tinged sandwiches and drink tea with grimy hands—washing before meals was unheard of—sitting on a pile of coal. The youngsters stuck out the harassment from the older workers, who painted the boy miners' faces in the Springhill mines, and in the Pictou collieries jumped the youngsters and kicked and punched them. They stuck out the choking coal dust, the wetness, the cold and the heat.

They stuck out the fear of death and dismemberment. Let your attention wander—look away to talk to a co-worker, take a wrong turn and end up in the path of an oncoming balance box, fail to notice a coal chute—and just like that, life changed forever. Riding rakes would detach; coal boxes would run away; coal, stone, wooden pillars and even fossilized trees fell from the ceiling. The lucky ones were maimed. "Everything came down and I got caught," recalled Huey D. MacIsaac, a promising baseball player before he entered the Inverness Mines. "I was the only one. I lost my arm and I got $57 a month for two years. . . . They couldn't figure out how I was able to live. After that accident I couldn't even carry a bucket of coal to throw on a fire."

Vigilance alone wasn't enough. So much of it was plain luck. The Cape Breton fields were nothing like the gassy Pictou County fields where, in 1873, 60 men died in a terrible explosion at the Drummond Mine. Mercifully, Cape Breton mines had little in common with the upheaval-prone Springhill Mines, also shot through with dangerous amounts of gas. There, on February 21, 1891, a pocket of airborne coal dust ignited and 125 men died from the explosion or the poisonous gases it released, the highest body count in nineteenth-century Canadian mining history. "Sorrowful mothers and wives were to be seen everywhere, weeping and lamenting for those near and dear to them," said a newspaper account the next day. "The majority of the bodies bear no marks of violence, death having apparently been caused by firedamp. Others are horribly mutilated and almost unrecognizable." Of the 125 victims, 21 were under eighteen years of age. The youngest was twelve, and two were thirteen.

That same sort of grim ratio existed in the Cape Breton mines. In 1878 six men died in Sydney Mines when a naked light ignited gas, causing an explosion. Seventeen years later two workers died roughly the same way in the Dominion No. 1 mine. In 1899, eleven men lost their lives in the Caledonia colliery following an explosion and fire. Another five men died in 1903, after a gas explosion in the French slope of the No. 5 mine in Reserve. Four years later a coal box got loose in the Scotia No. 4 mine, a mile from the colliery town of Florence, crushing three men. Three more were scalded to death when a surface boiler exploded at one of the Glace Bay mines in 1907.

Con Hogan said there was nothing out of the ordinary when he went down for work in Dominion's No. 12 colliery in New Waterford on July 25, 1917:

> All of a sudden everything got right quiet and right hot. We heard a big bang, just like a big bump. And she let go with a bang. Well, she fired everything as far as she could fire. I was fired right through the trap door, the trap door on the lee. I didn't know any more till they got me to the surface. I was still in a daze. My legs were broken. My head was broken. I had both eyelids cut right off, my whole face just hanging right down.

Mount Rundell (photographed circa 1880) was the Stellarton, Nova Scotia, residence where the manager of the General Mining Association and his wife entertained visiting dignitaries.

By the 1940s, mining families, like this one from Florence, Cape Breton, still lived in poverty.

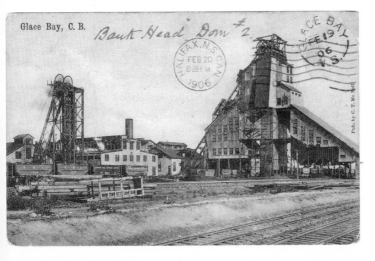

This postcard was sent in 1906 by a Mr. Brown to his daughter, "to show you a Colliery Bank Head at No. 2 [Glace Bay] where I worked."

Thousands of children (as young as four) and women toiled in slave-like conditions in coal mines in Victorian Britain. These drawings are from the Report of the Children's Employment Commission in 1842.

In Nova Scotia's mines adolescent boys and pit ponies rarely saw the light of day. This picture is dated 1905.

Boys young enough to still believe in Santa Claus worked in mines like the Caledonia in turn-of-the-century Glace Bay. Allie MacKenzie, off to the left, is nine years old.

Jack Briers took a break from the mines to experience some of the fiercest fighting in World War One.

Clarie Demont, not long before he died, with his grandson and this book's author (one of the upper-case-M DeMonts).

Eric and Russell DeMont and Earl Demont on a bridge on the Mira River in Cape Breton.

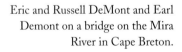

Clarie "Flash" Demont was once the fastest
Canadian to run the 100-yard dash.

Russ DeMont and Bill
"Shaky" Stewart entertaining
the students at
Acadia University with
a little soft shoe.

Mabel Demont, in the kitchen at York Street
in Glace Bay, has a rare quiet moment

Army officers stationed at Glace Bay during the 1909 coal strike.

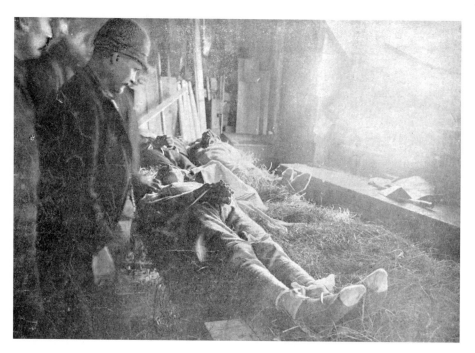

In the morgue, a victim of the 1891 Springhill colliery explosion awaits identification.

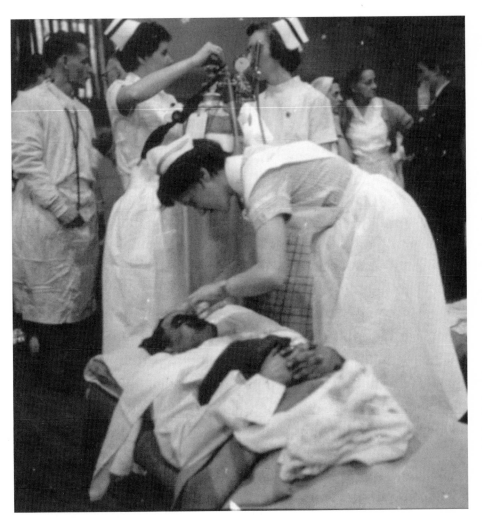

Nurses tend to a survivor of the 1956 Springhill disaster. Eighty-eight miners were rescued after the explosion, which killed 39 men.

The fabled union leader J.B. McLachlan fought for miners' rights in Cape Breton.

Richard Smith, the General Mining Association's imperious manager, helped bring the industrial revolution to Nova Scotia.

He spent a year in the hospital. His name at one point was added to the memorial for the sixty-five who died in the explosion. Later it was refinished, and his name removed.

The hearses even lined up on the western side of the island, where, a century later, subterranean death is the last thing on a traveller's mind. Route 19 winds past cliffs, beaches and wide-open ocean, beyond rolling farmland and hills thick with hardwoods, along hamlets bearing two-hundred-year-old names traceable straight to the Scottish Highlands. I've spent a lot of time here, taking in the soaring old-country fiddle music, casting for salmon in the picture-perfect rivers, just ogling the spirit-lifting scenery. It took me ages to realize that coal had once ruled here too. Yet once I understood where to look, the signs were everywhere: in the ancient peatlands that burst through the coastal cliffs in Mabou; along the main drag of the seaside town of Inverness, where the coal company cottages still stand and William Penn Hussey once swaggered.

After the start-up capital was in place, Hussey rolled up his sleeves and got busy making the mine at the Big River seam commercially viable. According to J.L. MacDougall's history, that involved dredging a channel to let the coal boats in, then building piers and a narrow-gauge railway to the harbour. Hussey imported a steam engine to pull the coal cars. He built houses for the miners, who numbered three hundred by 1899, when he decided to dissolve the company. "It is said," wrote MacDougall, "that Hussey screened a cool million out of Broad Cove."

The yarn wasn't over yet. William Mackenzie and Donald Mann, two of the greatest names in Canada's great age of rail, somehow heard about Broad Cove's seams. They built a rail line from Broad Cove to the coastline in a place called Point Tupper, near the Strait of Canso. Then they incorporated the Inverness Railway and Coal Company and proceeded to open new mines.

More housing—duplexes known as the Red Rows, and stand-alone houses for management—followed, to accommodate the miners flocking to Inverness, as the town was christened in 1904.

At one point there were so many newcomers arriving that a section of town became known as Belgium Town, in honour of the three to four hundred families from that country who had shown up to work the seams. From a standing start, Inverness ballooned to three thousand people—mostly Scots, but also French, Irish and a smattering of Russians to go with the Belgians—in a few short years. By the time MacDougall sat down to put pen to paper the town had electric lighting, an "excellent" water system and a "competent" fire brigade. It boasted three large hotels, two barbershops, at least two butchers, a "flourishing branch of the Royal Bank of Canada," a "moving pictures theatre," a town hall and labour temple—both described as "imposing"—a "commodious" brick building that served as post office, customs house and telegraph office, and six school buildings. There were bands and sports fields, including a cricket pitch, to give the miners a bit of good clean fun after a week of twelve-hour shifts with just a single day off.

Other outlets materialized for the men. It was estimated that some forty saloons ran along the road leading to the No. 2 mine, which immensely displeased MacDougall: "Liquor is the deadly enemy of all men engaged in deep thinking or perilous practical pursuits," he wrote.

Take the miner for example. . . . He is lowered in a rake through a yawning artificial passage into the deep, dark, and rumbling bowels of the earth. He has to work with pick and shovel, and with dangerous explosives. For him there is no liberty, no air, no room, no moon, no sun, no day: all is one weird, long and lingering night. For him no birds are singing; no flowers are blooming, no glad voices of innocent children to cheer his burdened soul. Every moment he is under ground his life is in jeopardy. When he returns again to light the reaction is so severe and sudden that it is dangerous for him to expose himself to the ordinary influence of the streets. He must avoid all incentives to violent excitement. What he needs is fresh air, wholesome food, comfortable rest, and the kind care of a well-kept home. The same is true also, of sailors, soldiers, intensive farmers, and strenuous mental toilers whose work presses acutely on mind or body, or on both. These are the men who carry the world on their shoulders.

A few kilometres south of there, Port Hood, with a population of about one thousand—215 of them miners—was smaller and not quite as raucous. In 1906, when a company called the Port Hood and Richmond Railway Coal Company bought the area's defunct mine, it exhibited all the characteristics of the textbook boom town—new houses and stores appeared, doctor and lawyer shingles materialized and "a general prosperity took place throughout the district," according to one account. How depressingly short it was. Two years later, on February 7, 1908, an explosion shot through the Port Hood mine. Ten men died, their skulls crushed and their bodies so burned and broken that they were unidentifiable. The funeral procession was nearly two kilometres long. Inside the church, the caskets formed a line from the front to the back of the room. "Never before in the history of Port Hood has a spectacle so sad been witnessed," declared the *Sydney Daily Post* after the funeral. Four of the dead were Bulgarians, so fresh to the province that no one even knew their first names. If that wasn't pathetic enough, on June 22, 1911, a mine on the main seam flooded with ocean water. Just like that, Port Hood's run of luck was over. The miners left, searching for work elsewhere. Soon the town was destitute enough that its electricity was cut off, not to be reconnected until 1938.

To me that's a sorrowful story. I feel the same way about those horses, intended by nature to canter across green fields, being forced instead to work underground in the cavernous gloom of the mines. Pit ponies had been hauling coal in British mines since the early 1700s, which made it inevitable that the pattern would repeat itself in the English-dominated Nova Scotian collieries. By 1916 horses cost between $180 and $200 but were still in short supply. Not just any horse would do. The tunnels were low and steep, so the ponies had to be short and sturdy. Size was important because of the heavy loads, but so was sure-footedness, since the roads were rocky, uneven and full of debris. A pit pony also had to be even-tempered; shy ones took too long to break, and ornery ponies were a danger to everyone around.

At one point as many as eighty ponies were at work in the Princess mine, pulling coal to the shaft and equipment from the shaft to the wall. Their masters tried to make life tolerable. It was mandated that the height of the roof in the underground stable had to be seven feet for a five-foot horse—the average size of a pit pony working the Nova Scotia mines in 1917 was between 4'8" and 5'6"—so it could raise its head and relax its neck muscles after stooping throughout the workday. The stables were meant to be temperate, clean and adequately drained. The horses were supposed to be well shod; if the job was unusually difficult, a ferrier would go into the mine, take the measurements and hammer the shoes into shape on the surface. The ponies were fed ample amounts of hay and grain. In a perfect world each animal would have one driver, and the roof carefully brushed to rid it of protruding rocks that might injure the horse.

Alas, this world was not perfect. The hauling was hard, the shifts often twice what the men worked and the pony didn't always keep his head down. "Well he would scruff the top of his head, it would like scalp him," remembered Patrick McNeil, who assisted the first veterinarian in the Sterling Pit in Glace Bay. "When that horse would come in, that piece of flesh would be hanging like a flap over the top of his head. Well, that would have to be removed. Sometimes that would be scraped right to the bone."

In those days the horses never came out of the mine. (By McNeil's reckoning it was the 1940s before the miners started getting vacations, and took the horses up and put them out in big pastures next to the collieries.) Horses caught lockjaw. They broke their legs while pulling the coal boxes on the rails laid on the rock. When that happened they had to be put down. Time was when someone just pounded the animal's head in with an axe. Eventually a supposedly more humane way was found: slicing a vein inside the pony's rectum and letting it bleed to death. McNeil remembers times when the crew in his mine lost a horse every second day. No grand burial for these animals, he recalled:

> At the back of the hospital there was a big smokestack from some old colliery back of the Sterling Mine. And way back in the years it was closed. They left the big flue up and they built an incinerator there, and any horses that were destroyed or died, they would just take them down there and hoisted up and put them in this incinerator and burned. There was no need of digging holes and burying them out in the ground: just burn them right up and there'd only be an ash left. They'd burn them with old wood.

CHAPTER NINE

I'm Only a Broken-Down Mucker

According to his war records, Private 715959 of the Canadian Expeditionary Force was 5'8¾" tall. His chest, when fully expanded, was 38½ inches, his complexion was "fresh," his eyes were blue, his hair was medium brown and he had a pair of vaccination marks on his left arm. Jack Briers was twenty-three years old on March 7, 1916, when he walked into a recruiting station and volunteered for the CEF. His unit—36 officers and 1,009 soldiers—took ten days to make the crossing from Halifax to Liverpool aboard the *Empress of Britain*. They spent eleven days in Shorncliffe before leaving for France. There they joined the 14th Infantry Battalion, a unit of the 3rd brigade of the 1st Canadian Division.

The 14th Battalion arrived too late for the horrors of the second battle of Ypres. But the action that followed, according to a Department of Defence letter that accompanied my grandfather's war records, was also "difficult." The 14th Battalion marched across the corpse-littered muck of the Somme, bolstered the assault on Vimy Ridge, sacrificed themselves at Passchendaele and Hill 70 and

trudged on through the Hundred Days Campaign. By my calcula-
tions more than 34,000 Canadian soldiers fell during those engage-
ments, some of the bloodiest and most pivotal of the Great War.

Somehow, John Briers avoided being one of them. When he
was discharged in Montreal in April 1919, he discovered that things
had changed mightily during the three years he was away. Women
had the vote. Spanish flu had killed as many Canadians at home as
the war had overseas. Working people, after years of self-sacrifice,
had grown angry and resentful at their place in society. In 1919
alone, 150,000 Canadians would hit the bricks, as workers came
back from overseas unwilling to accept pre-war working conditions.
After years of labour shortages, with factories cranking out arms
for the military and Western farmers worked to exhaustion export-
ing wheat to England, the economy had come to a screeching halt.

The coal industry was hit harder than most. On the eve of the
First World War, America produced more coal than any nation on
earth. The British industry—which, by 1913 employed 10 percent of
the male British workforce and, in the previous five years, had
accounted for one-quarter of the earth's coal production—was, to
borrow a phrase, "one of the economic wonders of the world."

In Nova Scotia, coal production hit eight million tons by 1913,
a fivefold increase over the previous thirty years. There was a perfectly logical explanation, actually several of them, for that rip-
roaring expansion. A countrywide railway boom pushed demand
for coal to run the locomotives sharply higher. Quebec's rapidly
expanding industries were also big buyers of Nova Scotia coal. With
the steel mills of Sydney, Sydney Mines and Trenton turning out 41
percent of all Canada's pig iron, there was also a large homegrown
coal market. But the Nova Scotian heart still swelled to note that
by 1913 the coal mines of Cape Breton, Pictou and Cumberland
counties accounted for half of Canada's total coal production.

When the war ended, so did the country's insatiable need for coal. Suddenly no one was laying rail. The Quebec market found new suppliers. A subsequent federal Royal Commission on the economy of the Maritimes said that Nova Scotia's steelmakers would have prospered if they had capitalized on the growing demand for structural steel and for lighter materials for new industries like the motor car. They hadn't, in part because they lacked the capital to change over to completely new equipment. By the end of 1920 the Sydney steel plant's coal consumption had fallen from a peak of 100,000 tons per month to just 40,000. In the Sydney coal field, production had fallen to 4.5 million tons by 1920, compared to 6.3 million seven years earlier.

Shell-shocked veterans wandered the streets of Sydney Mines and every other Canadian town or city. Yet everything I have heard indicates that my grandfather came out the other end intact; maybe life in the pits was the only real preparation for the trenches, with their knee-high mud and biblical infestations of lice and rats. He was twenty-three, a decorated war veteran who had spent nine years in the pits and another three in the midst of some of the worst carnage the world had ever witnessed. But he did what every dutiful unmarried son did when he returned home, moving back in with his parents, his twenty-six-year-old brother Harold and his sister Amy, now twenty. His old room was waiting for him. So was the Florence mine.

Every now and then, when the spirit seizes me, I grab the handle of a scuffed and beaten rectangular case, lay it down on the kitchen table and unsnap the clasps. Twenty years ago I received the best Christmas present of my life: Jack Briers's alto saxophone, which my aunt sent up from Sydney Mines and my wife had refurbished.

It's a Chu Berry model (named after the American saxophone player Leon "Chu" Berry), made in the late 1920s by the legendary C.G. Conn Ltd. of Elkhart, Indiana. I've been playing it on and off for more than twenty years now, with, it must be acknowledged, little discernible improvement. Sometimes when I'm doing this my mind stops on one of the nagging mysteries in the Briers family saga. Music is at the centre of the riddle. John William, by all accounts, had a tin ear. His oldest son, Harold, on the other hand, went to study music at McGill University in Montreal, an almost unheard-of leap for a collier's son in that day and age. In Sydney Mines, where Harold set up shop teaching music, he was known as Professor Briers. Which has always left me wondering: how come he got to make his living sitting in a drawing room, grimacing as little Angus journeyed up and down the piano scale, while my grandfather had to go underground at age eleven?

I've asked every living relative I can find for some kind of explanation. They're as baffled as I am—particularly since Jack Briers surely had a musical aptitude. I used to meet older ladies who would close their eyes in rapture as they recalled my grandfather's alto at dances at the North Sydney Yacht Club. He also played the clarinet, violin, tuba, French horn and piano. My mother remembers him as a middle-aged man coming home from a day in the mines, taking a short nap, having an old-fashioned English dinner and then retreating to the living room and filling the house with music.

I used to take comfort in that image because so much of his life sounded hard. The fallout from the First World War led to more consolidation in Nova Scotia's steel and coal industries. In 1921, after a head-snapping series of bids and counterbids, shareholder revolts and boardroom battles, a British syndicate called the British Empire Steel Corporation (Besco) finally took Dominion Steel—which owned the Sydney steel operations and Dominion Coal, along with Nova Scotia Steel and Coal, which controlled steel mills in New Glasgow and Sydney Mines, where it also owned the GMA's old coal interests. It was the GMA redux, except that one company now controlled the steel mills along with the collieries. The deal Roy Wolvin and J.W. Norcross, a couple of operators from Montreal, put together to finance the arrangement was so complex it makes my brain hurt nearly a century later. Along the way Besco issued millions' worth of preferred stock, which not only watered down the value of the existing common shares but also placed immense pressure on them to cover the dividends. (Wolvin had a history of doing that sort of thing. Paul MacEwan, a former Nova Scotia MLA from Cape Breton, writes about how he merged three steamship companies to form Canada Steamship Lines in 1913. Total capitalization was $16.2 million. But Wolvin "turned the water hose into the stock bucket, poured in $16.8-million worth of paper" and, voila, the company's capitalization stood at a cool $33 million.)

Situations like that just never pan out for the guys actually doing the work. The problem was a straightforward one. In the early 1920s—before the downturn really took hold—the coal company was more profitable than the steel arm, but virtually every red cent of profits was going out the door in the form of dividends. That left little money for reinvestment; economist David Schwartzman has calculated that from 1920 to 1924 Besco spent a stingy $2 million on upgrade and upkeep in the collieries and steel plant, at a time when both dearly needed both. There was also understandable consternation in early 1922 when Besco announced that workers' pay packets would be slashed by one-third—a sizable reduction, considering that the Dominion Bureau of Statistics estimated at that point that it cost a miner 90 percent of his earnings just to pay rent and feed his family.

Wolvin had to know how the miners would react. From 1901 to 1914 there were twenty strikes in the Glace Bay mines, another nineteen in Springhill and eighteen more in the Joggins area. Coal miners accounted for about three-quarters of the strike days in the Maritime provinces during that period.

Miners were pushing back in other ways, too. They elected labour-sympathetic men to town council, the mayor's office and even the provincial legislature—in the 1920 provincial election, Farmer-Labour candidates swept the four seats in Cape Breton county—to cancel out the immense political clout of the coal company officials. The mining communities were even starting to assert their independence from the loathed company store. Soon after arriving from England, John William Briers had joined a group of British émigrés to form the British Canadian Co-operative Society. In the years that followed, co-op stores, owned by working people, had opened in Dominion, Glace Bay, Sydney and Sydney Mines. Every member family got a co-op number. John William had number 7, which he later passed on to his son.

By then, Jack Briers's life was rolling along in other ways. For one thing, Margaret Brown had made her entrance. Her family were Scots who had arrived in British Columbia in the last years of the nineteenth century, hoping to make their fortune in the Klondike gold rush. When that failed to happen, James, the coal miner patriarch, moved his family to Sydney Mines, where they took up residence in a wooden house on Cranberry Head, a spit of land riddled with collieries that juts into the Atlantic Ocean. Somehow she and Jack met. Margaret was stunning and full of life; he was taciturn, but solid and starting to move up the ladder at the Florence colliery. When they married in 1924, they first moved into the Clyde Avenue residence. Then they relocated a couple of blocks away, to Brighton Avenue, to a brown two-storey house with a sun porch, comfortable parlour and immaculate lawns.

Naturally, the immigrants stuck together. Distinct neighbourhoods— in some places little more than ghettos—began to emerge, and gave towns their own taste, smell and feel, along with a cosmopolitan sheen that seemed way out of whack with their small size and bottom-rung economic status. The French and Irish flocked to Reserve Mines and New Waterford, named after Waterford, Ireland, from which many of the immigrants hailed. In places like Dominion, Italians played bocce and *scopa* and sang lugubrious old-country songs. In Glace Bay, the smells of West Indian food wafted out of open windows over the heads of yarmulke-wearing Jews piously making their way down the streets to the island's oldest synagogue.

The waves of arrivals rubbed up against each other. Black furnacemen recruited from the United States to work in the Sydney steel mills experienced the same sort of racism and inequality they felt in their old country. Italian immigrants were beaten and robbed routinely enough by Sydney toughs that they began to travel in packs for protection. Eventually, they had had enough. One Saturday morning they marched to the front of their church carrying guns, pitchforks and "anything else suitable to serve as a weapon," Esperanza Maria Razzolini Crook recalled. The priest defused the situation and things got better for a time, but the tensions between nationalities boiled over when Mussolini joined Hitler in the Second World War, making Italy an enemy of Canada. A few Italians from Cape Breton were sent to internment camps. For those allowed to stay, the hassles increased.

The earliest Jewish settlers came after spying advertisements offering free passage—and a chance to escape the European pogroms—in return for labour in a coal mine. Instead, most became peddlers, moving on to open retail businesses in competition with the company stores. David Epstein, whose existence I discovered in an old issue of a local historical newsletter, was one of them. He arrived in 1907, at age sixteen, unable to speak a word of English and without a cent in his pocket. He began to "peddle" for his Uncle Morris, who owned a general store in the Whitney Pier area of Sydney. Epstein's turf was all of Victoria County. "I had a 75 pound pack on my back and fifty pound pack in front," he recalled years later. "I walked house to house from [Cape] Smokey to Bay St. Lawrence." That's a good half-day drive in 2008; a century earlier, on foot, it must have taken weeks.

Sydney was a particular magnet. That's why I want to take a minute to consider the three-square-mile, triangle-shaped area around the steel mill known as Whitney (as in Henry Melville) Pier when it was in its prime. Once it was an all but empty expanse of scrub land with a few scattered homes housing folk who lived off the ocean and subsistence farms. With the coming of the steelworks and the coal-shipping piers, the area filled up. What emerged was a community of communities: the Poles and Ukrainians settling in Bryan, Ferris and Roberts streets, an area known as Hunkytown; the Italians in "Shackville"; the black immigrants trying to escape the poverty of the West Indies in the "Coke Ovens."

The Pier—with its substandard housing, lack of amenities and services, poverty and crime—was as elemental as any turn-of-the-century frontier town. Overshadowing everything: the hulking coke ovens, open hearths and blast furnaces that spewed flame and noise, that tainted the sky with an orange chemical cloud noxious enough to strip houses of their paint.

Yet when I think of Whitney Pier in 1924—around the time Jack Briers and Margaret Brown were getting hitched—I'm elated, not depressed. In this apocalyptic setting, amongst this grab bag of humanity—which, within a few square blocks, seemed to contain more life than all of Halifax or any other Maritime industrial hub—some dazzling alchemy occurred. You didn't have to look far. Walk down the street and you'd hear the exotic tongues of the Syrians and Lebanese, and the Italians who'd arrived to build the steel mills and never left. You'd hear the drawl of the black steelworkers from Alabama, Pennsylvania and Tennessee who showed up to supply experience and expertise in the early days of the steelplant. You might see a middle-aged Chinese man who came for the steel mill but discovered that he was only allowed to work in laundries and restaurants. (Between 1903 and 1923, ten laundries and two restaurants owned by Chinese families operated in the Pier.)

In the Pier the different nationalities and groups had their own places of worship, like the Adath Israel Synagogue, St. Phillip's African Orthodox Church, the African Methodist Episcopal Church, St. Mary's Polish Church and St. Stephen's Hungarian Church. They had their own community centres and clubs, like the West Indian Cricket Club, the Croatian Club and the Italian Club. Benevolent societies, created to address the spiritual, cultural, social and financial needs of new immigrants, abounded: the Daughters of Jacob Aid Society (for Jewish women over eighteen), the St. Rita Society (for members of the St. Nicholas Italian Church), the Brotherhood of the Holy Ghost (Polish), the St. Michael's Polish Benefit Society, the Knights of Columbus (Catholic), the Protestant Society of United Fishermen, the Universal Negro Improvement Association, the African Community League and the Menelik Ethiopian Hall (named after Emperor Menelik II), where Marcus Garvey one night extolled his vision of Africa for Africans, before a packed house.

Using a local history as my guide, I like to imagine walking through the Whitney Pier commercial district when the older Celtic business names from Cape Breton and Newfoundland were suddenly mixed with handles like Rosenbloom, Lubchansky, Bonavitsky, Lee and Wong. Victoria Road was lined with photography shops, drugstores, livery stables, laundries, restaurants and other businesses supplying groceries, clothing, hardware and the other necessities of a burgeoning working-class population. The rest of the community was expanding too: a French shoemaker, a blacksmith named Manchevsky. Lebanese folks ran grocery stores and barbershops. Up Lingan Road, Gallivan's store stood between the Mendelbaums' and Eli Hirsh. West Indians owned a bookstore, a jewellery store, a tailor's shop, a shoe repair and a bakery. The Oriental bakery on Tupper Street was owned by the DiPentas. There were also bakeries owned by Bernie Kokowska, the Martinellos and a man named Sappatalonia.

Strolling through the Whitney Pier streets—past the golden Byzantine globes of the Holy Ghost Ukrainian Church, and the descendants of Caribbean slaves marching through the streets with their brass bands and "Back to Africa" banners—you'd have to wonder if you were really in some scruffy steel and coal community on the edge of the continent. In those days you could walk through your own front door and not know precisely what was in store for you. You could pay a nickel and see a silent picture at MacLeod's Building. You could visit one of the pool halls, an outdoor bowling alley (two cents a string), or the Mt. Pleasant Turkish bath (five cents a bath). There might be a concert, dance or vaudeville show at one of the church halls or community centres. There could be a play at the outdoor amphitheatre on the Maclennan estate. If it was fight night, you might climb the stairs above Mike Martinello's store to where boxing matches were held. Though women were in relatively short supply in the early days of the Pier, a trio of dance halls thrived on Victoria Road.

Time was, after Prohibition ended in Nova Scotia in 1930, a fellow could start drinking before dusk and still have somewhere new to go for a round when the sun was climbing over the steel plant. He could make a detour through the private men's clubs. He could move on to the taverns, and when they closed he could hit one of the bootlegger joints at just about every corner. "Bootlegging was the same kind of enterprise as running a corner store to augment the wages of the house," recalled Ron DiPenta, born in the Pier in the 1930s. "If you had six or seven kids to support, and earned only 45 or 60 cents an hour at the plant, that wasn't very much money." Eventually, a fellow might even slink up to Curry's Lane, to a bar once run by one of the few black American steelworkers who stuck around in Whitney Pier, which for a while became a combination bar and brothel.

Places like that, where the proprietors packed pistols on their hips, were like Wild West saloons, according to old men who remembered them, with card games and fights and raucous goings-on. Sometimes on Saturday nights the ethnic divisions and old-country rivalries would bubble to the surface in brawls that ended up outside and went up one street and down the other. All the same, "an almost tribal pride grew up from within," Whitney Pier native Mayann Francis, the first Afro-Canadian lieutenant governor of Nova Scotia, recalled on her website. "A sense of place was born, a place of connection, a place of reaching out and of looking out. The many 'I's' had become a singular 'we.'"

In Sydney Mines today it's still easy to see the settlement patterns: the Italians (Legatto Street), the Irish (Tobin Road), the Newfoundlanders

(Bugden Street). English folk like the Brierses tended to make their homes near the centre of town. They were inclined to stick to themselves—eating their meat pies and bangers and mash, going to Sunday services at Trinity Anglican, playing English football on the church grounds, visiting the Sons of the British Isles Social, Literary, and Provident Society and the Old Country Club to mark special occasions. In particular they liked to make music, which was deeply imbedded in this immigrant coal-mining community. The churches and community centres rang with it. Come Saturday night, so did the speakeasies, blind pigs and kitchen parties. There were jigs and reels from Ireland, calypso from the West Indies—music that just grew more mournful and intense, the farther geographically it got from its source.

Judging by their love of doleful old country songs and the mawk-ish Great War tunes sung in the parlour with their countrymen, the Briers family were just as sentimental about their old lives. The Sydney Mines brass band would have provided a little solace. By 1900 there were said to be twenty thousand amateur brass bands in the United Kingdom sponsored by enlightened mill, colliery and foundry owners interested in providing good, healthy recreation and entertainment for their workers. Naturally, the immigrant labourers brought the tradition with them. Cape Breton's first brass band was organized in Sydney Mines in 1862 by Robert Wilson, the manager of the Low Point mine, who later formed community bands in Victoria Mines and Sydney. In time, brass bands spread to all major centres of the newly industrialized region. Religion didn't count. Age didn't matter. All that was needed was an ability to play an instrument, or at least a willingness to try to learn.

The immigrants wouldn't be the first people to realize that music—particularly music played with large groups of people—has the ability to transcend, uplift and transport. My grandfather played the church organ on Sundays. As a member of the Blue and White Serenaders he blew alto sax and clarinet for a little extra cash at local dances and during intermissions at the Strand Theatre in Sydney Mines, where he always played "Annie Laurie" just for my grandmother when she was in attendance. He played in the brass band, at picnics and store openings, civic holidays and special celebrations. Whenever called upon, the band would play. Even at funerals, where they would lead the procession to the cemetery playing "Abide With Me," then—once the ceremony was complete—break into a jaunty "Yes Sir, That's My Baby" on the way back.

Sometimes musicians played old-country coal-mining songs, because those tunes caused a nostalgic pang right there in a person's solar plexus, but also because those tunes took their history and lives and distilled them into narrative form. Stories are our memory; songs are the recreation of that memory. Those coal-mining songs travelled seamlessly from place to place and culture to culture because they spoke of an experience that's as true in the collieries of Wales and the coal mines of Poland as in the deeps of Cape Breton. Coal-mining songs, with their everyday language and simple melodies, called attention to injustice. They gave the poor and disenfranchised a voice. They communicated the hopes, sorrows and beliefs of working lives. "A coal miner is no ordinary man," Nina Cohen, a Glace Bay native who started a miners' folk society and the miners' museum there, once told Professor John O'Donnell. "His story has a heartbeat. It should not be allowed to die."

Sometimes it seems there are more songs about coal mining than about love, cars and death combined. Sometimes it seems that songs about coal miners are more popular than the miners themselves. Once, O'Donnell tried to come up with a list of Canadian coal-mining songs to provide material for the Men of the Deeps, the Cape Breton miners' chorus that he directed. He ended up with

150 titles, even though his list includes no French and only a few Gaelic songs.

One day I sat down and read the words to every one of them. A lot of them had "Caledonia" in their title—"Caledonia," "Farewell to Caledonia," "When I First Went to Caledonia"—which seems perfectly fitting since, along with being the name of a mine in Glace Bay, Caledonia is the name by which Scotland was known until the tenth century. A lot of them were about disasters ("The Miracle at Springhill," "New Waterford's Fatal Day," "Disaster at No. 1 B," "Unknown Miner's Grave"). There were loads of protest songs ("Arise Ye Nova Scotia Slaves," "The Pluck Me Store," "The 1925 Strike Song," "Black Is the Coaldust"). There were union songs ("Roll Along, United Miners"), songs about scabs ("The Honest Working Man"), trains ("Little Pinkie Engine") and individual coal mines ("No. 26," "One Million Ton"). Some of the songs I knew well enough to sing along: "The Ballad of Springhill" (recorded by Pete Seeger and U2), "Sixteen Tons" (Tennessee Ernie Ford), "Dark as a Dungeon" (Merle Travis). A few—"I'm Only a Broken-Down Mucker," "Jolly Wee Miner Men"—just made me want to laugh.

There weren't many of those, though. Miners—with the exception of Dopey, Grumpy and Sneezy—seldom sang while they worked. They saved singing for the kitchen, the parlour, the union hall and the tavern. The old songs, passed down from parent to child, and the new ones, reflecting the changing reality of their lives, were like a collective moan. If I were to try to distill all of these songs down to a single theme, it would be this: life is hard and ends badly, but it's all we have. It's difficult not to reach for the Paxil after hearing stanzas like this: "I work in the pit, it's a terrible hole/ Getting paid by the comp'ny for hauling the coal/ By dodging this trip it's queer I'm alive/ For each day I work I get three sixty-five." Or this: "I gave my best to Besco/ They gave me their worst/ Faceless men have sucked my blood/ What can I do but curse?/ The British Vampire Company/ Sunk its teeth into my veins/ Broke my back, starved my kids/ Drove me half insane." And doesn't a fellow's spirit lift to read the following, chosen at random from O'Donnell's collection? "Deep down in the earth where we take out the coal/ The chill of the mine will soon enter your soul/ Though you long to be up where the warm sun can shine/ You just gotta be down, down, down deep in the mine."

I picture each and every one of these songs being sung by the same bony old coot with hands like tree roots and a voice hollow and ravaged as a banshee's. Songs about George Alfred Beckett from "Old Perl'can," who "landed in Glace Bay," ends up killing a taxi driver and hanging for it. Or Archie MacInnis, who was born in New Waterford in 1916 and ends up fleeing for the mainland after his buddy dies in an underground rockfall. They're all laments—at least, the memorable coal-mining songs. The harshness of life transformed into simple, direct, powerful expression. The more stripped-down and unadorned, the better. Music isn't even necessary. It's all in the words:

> His name was Eddie Crimmins
> And he came from Port aux Basques
> Besides a chance to live and work
> He had nothing much to ask;
> No, not a dream he ever had
> That he might work and save—
> Was quite content to live and die
> And be a working slave.
> And yet, he starved, he starved, I tell you,
> Back in nineteen twenty-four,
> And before he died he suffered
> As many have before.

When the mines closed down that winter
He had nothing left to eat,
And he starved, he starved, I tell you,
On your dirty, damned street.

A guy right out of the pages of Jack London wrote those words: Dawn Fraser, who was at various times a male nurse, pharmacist, labourer in the lumber and construction camps, gravedigger, circus barker, copywriter and salesman, before joining the Canadian infantry in the First World War. He immediately sailed off to Siberia in an ill-fated attempt to quell the Bolshevik Revolution, got wounded, then returned to Glace Bay, his birthplace, to sell aluminum pots and pans door to door. Along the way, he would stop people on the street and read them a verse, and perhaps even try to sell them a book of poetry. Robert Service was his literary model. At first Fraser wrote about hoboes, seamen, labourers and card players (Fraser, according to historian Donald MacGillivray, was a self-professed drifter, drinker and gambler). His sympathies lay with the workingman. And since he came to live in Cape Breton during the 1920s, his later poems read like fragments of a dark age told in rhyming couplets.

Many of them were about the events of 1922, when the miners—led by a radical leadership that had swept the recent union executive elections—went out on strike to resist a one-third wage cut ordered by Besco. Wolvin begged Prime Minister William Lyon Mackenzie King for military intervention. Dan Willie Morrison, the mayor of Glace Bay, refused to send a requisition for troops. But a sympathetic judge was found, and the first troop train left Halifax a day later.

Within days, with Prime Minister King promising that "full protection" would be accorded the strike areas, "practically the whole Canadian army" was en route to Glace Bay. The province formed a special thousand-man provincial police force to go into the coal-fields and patrol the mines. Two Canadian destroyers, the *Patriot* and the *Patrician,* received orders to proceed to Sydney to render assistance. The general in charge in Sydney requested that airplanes from Dartmouth, Nova Scotia, be deployed, and also tried to dragoon some British battleships then in Newfoundland waters into service. Mercifully the fighter planes and warships never arrived, but Fraser's poems still burst with admiration for how the miners and their families persevered.

Fraser also wrote about the events that occurred the following year, after the Sydney steelworkers went out against Besco in an attempt to win union recognition and the coal miners also walked off the job in support and to protest the military rule in Cape Breton's industrial area. One of Fraser's favourite subjects was the arrest and jailing of union secretary-treasurer James Bryson McLachlan and miners' president Dan Livingstone for their part in promoting the sympathetic strike. "Merry Christmas to you, Jim," Fraser wrote of McLachlan on the "smooth board unpainted wall" of a flophouse where he was staying. "In your prison dungeon dim/ What although the bars are cold/ They have sheltered hearts of gold/ Fit companions they for you—/ Steel is strong and steel is true."

I'm told he was right on about the prison being "dim" and the bars "cold." At least, so said Eva MacKeigan, the union's secretary. My great-aunt's duties, it's reported, included delivering McLachlan's supper while he was in jail in Halifax, along with smuggled messages from his union buddies. Later on, if memory serves me right, she would gather up the dirty dishes, along with any hidden correspondence headed the other way, and leave the jailhouse. They told that story at her funeral in Halifax more than sixty years later. People shook their heads, as if it was the most amazing thing they had ever heard.

CHAPTER TEN

Jimmy and the Wolf

We are not stupid people. At least no stupider than most. Nonetheless, most of the Demonts and DeMonts I know grew up thinking their family was French. Some of us—well, at least one of us—spent long decades bragging about a shared kinship with the Huguenot nobleman Pierre Du Gua, Sieur de Monts, who was given the original charter to settle "the countries, territories, coasts and confines of La Cadie" and put up the cash for Champlain's 1604 voyage to New France. It was the kind of thing that made a person feel mighty important in grade six history class. And deeply mortified to discover, forty years later, that I was almost certainly descended from a stocking weaver—an occupation that doesn't exactly conjure up images of derring-do—hailing from some unknown canton in German-speaking Switzerland.

My ancestor's main virtue was that he was Protestant at a time when the French and English were still bitterly contesting dominion over what would become Nova Scotia. The English, wanting to counteract the Roman Catholic presence throughout French-speaking

Acadia, recruited "foreign Protestants" from southern and central Germany, Switzerland and the Montbéliard region of France. One August day in 1751, the *Gale* made port in Halifax. The 205 passengers included a thirty-one-year-old male, first names Frantz and Joseph, with a surname that has variously been translated as Demone, Dimon, Timming, Timon or Timmon, depending upon which source you consult. (The confusion over how to spell the last name continues to this day: my grandfather, one of my uncle's families and even my brother spell it Demont, while my father and I, along with another uncle and his people, choose DeMont.) Chances are that he spent time working on the fortifications in Halifax to pay off the cost of the voyage. Then, in 1753, he headed south until he reached a place named Lunenburg where they were handing out land grants.

From there it's the usual story: his offspring put down roots in the area and became farmers, fishermen, sea captains and businessmen. By the mid-1800s it seems that one of them—quite possibly because he was illiterate or, at the very least, a bad speller—had changed the name to Demont. The family still didn't stray too far. In 1855 my great-great-grandfather, Jacob Demont, and his new wife, the former Leah Vaughn, migrated north to the Annapolis Valley. When Jacob died at thirty-two, after being crushed by a molasses barrel, Leah and the seven kids moved across the Avon River to a farmhouse in a place called Wile Settlement. Eventually her second son, Edward—Ned—moved to Windsor, a bigger centre nearby.

I haven't been able to discover much about Ned's early life there. But while he was out cutting wood one day his young wife, Eva, died of a ruptured appendix, after just six months of marriage. Four years later Ned married Elizabeth May Armstrong, age twenty-three, also of Lunenburg County. For all anybody knows, things were good in Windsor at the end of the nineteenth century. Then on the morning of October 17, 1897, a fire started near the riverfront. It spread down King Street to Park Street and continued to the crest of a hill. For a brief moment the blaze seemed almost under control. Then the wind shifted and increased to hurricane force and the flames began leaping from rooftop to rooftop. Soon the whole downtown was ablaze, the flames so bright that they were visible in Halifax, sixty miles away, the heat intense enough that the town's railway tracks buckled.

No one died. Yet most people lost everything—damage was estimated at $2 million, of which only $600,000 was insured—and were left homeless and destitute. Money, food and supplies came from as far away as Boston. The military arrived with tents and supplies and erected a small tent city to provide shelter for families as the rebuilding began. A year later, 150 new buildings were standing. The *Halifax Herald* trumpeted, "she [Windsor] has been rebuilt more beautiful and more imposing and more substantial than ever."

Ned and May Demont weren't willing to wait around to see whether the town could really rebound. For a change, there were other opportunities in Nova Scotia. One of Edward's brothers, Harding, left for Pictou County, where he found work in the rolling mills. Edward, at forty-one, decided to take his wife and four kids to Sydney, where he understood they were hiring at the steel plant.

Ned and May bought a house on Fairview in Sydney's North End where, at night, they could peer out the window and see the orange plumes from the Dosco steel plant inflame the sky. The children went to school, courted, got jobs, eventually left home. Blanche, the baby, married a car dealer and set up house in Sydney. Gordon, the second-youngest, started working as a teller for the Bank of Montreal; in 1916 he went overseas with the 36th Field Battery. Three years later he returned to Sydney, joined Imperial Oil and started moving up the ranks. Florence, born in 1894, was widowed after only two years of marriage. Six years later she remarried; a dozen years after that, she was widowed again.

Her twin brother, Clarence—my grandfather—had sandy hair, gentle eyes and a heart-shaped face that narrowed to a pointy chin. He was a dreamy, amiable fellow possessing one remarkable thing: an extraordinary set of legs. By that I mean legs strong enough to outrun racehorses, to chase down enough outfield balls to single-handedly account for seventeen of twenty-seven possible outs during a single baseball game, to clamp leg scissors on any opponent in the wrestling ring and be assured of victory.

They called him Flash. He wasn't just fast. When he ran in road races it was as if some kind of trick photography was making his legs move in a blur, like Neo in *The Matrix*. Once he false-started at the beginning of a hundred-yard dash, his specialty, which meant he was forced to start ten yards behind the other runners. He jumped the gun again and was pushed back another ten yards. The other competitors closed ranks in front of him.

"Hey," said Clarie Demont.

When they looked back at him, he motioned for them to push to the left and right so that he could see the finish line up ahead. Around the seventy-yard mark he shot the gap, and won the race by a comfortable couple of lengths.

In my mind—amongst eyewitness accounts of him outstriding a thoroughbred horse, newspaper stories about how, at 170 pounds, he wrestled the heavyweight champion of the Canadian Expeditionary Forces to a draw, tales of his exploits on the ball field and in the hockey rink—the thing that lingers longest is a black-and-white photograph of some long-ago race on the streets of Glace Bay. Another hundred-yard sprint. The runners are clumped together somewhere in the first third of the picture. Unless you look closely you miss him. But there, so far to the right that he's almost out of frame, is Flash Demont, apparently running in some other race.

In 1913—according to his obituary in the *Toronto Star*—he ran the hundred-yard dash in 9.6 seconds, which, had it occurred with the proper timing device and on a regulation track, would have tied the world record. By rights the 1916 Summer Olympics, slated for Berlin, would have been his moment. They were cancelled, though, because of the Great War. Family legend has it that he could have made the team for the 1920 games in Antwerp. But that would have meant losing his job, something a young man just starting out didn't do lightly in industrial Cape Breton.

Two years later he was living in Glace Bay, married to Mabel MacKeigan, a coal miner's daughter who worked for the United Mine Workers of America (UMWA) union before their first child was born. By this time, Clarie Demont was a pressman at the *Glace Bay Gazette*. Its pages carried the usual stuff of life in a Nova Scotia town of the day: rum-running boats going down in flames, steamers missing at sea, detectives arriving to bring back wealthy Montreal girls who had eloped with young miners, big truckloads of beer mysteriously disappearing on the highway. On January 19, 1923, readers could peruse ads for dentures ("$9 for a regular $15 plate"), a class at the Savoy Dancing Academy ("55¢ admission/8:30 to 12"), fish at MacKenzie's Market (salt July Herring/salt flat mackerel/pickled cod/kippers and digbys) and movies at the Savoy (Tom Mix in *Just Tony*) and the Capitol (William S. Hart in *Three Word Brand*). They could scan the timetable for the tramway, which left from "Senator's Corner for Sydney Bay and points around the loop," the schedule for the Sydney and Louisbourg Railway and last night's score from the colliery hockey league (5–4 for Sydney). Elsewhere, they would learn that the best way to darken hair was to steep a cup of sage tea and apply it directly to the follicles.

A.D. MacNeill, the *Gazette's* managing editor, understood what his readers wanted. So any wire story that dealt with coal mining half a world away would make the paper, and maybe even the front page. It would be joined by perhaps the first thing readers turned to when they picked up their *Gazette:* yesterday's production tally for the Glace Bay mines—15,634 tons on January 19, 1923—broken down by individual colliery. Inside, they'd read items about new rail orders for Sydney Steel, a missing iron-ore boat bound for Wabana, Newfoundland, and announcements that "12 horses 5'0" in height not under 1,000 lbs" as well as "35 horses not over 4'4" to 4'5" not under 500 lbs." were required at once for pit work.

Mostly there would be stories about the relationship between the mineworkers and the owners. It was no romance. After the First World War, the ordinary Cape Breton mine-worker—like the ordinary miner in the coalfields of Pictou County, the Appalachian mountains of West Virginia or the colliery towns of Alberta—existed in the same state of servitude as had their parents and grandparents. During the Roaring Twenties, the standard of living of most Canadians improved. Not in Cape Breton, though, where many families had to raise chickens, cows and pigs to keep the children fed. In 1921 the national infant mortality rate was 88.1 per 1,000 babies born. The rates in Sydney Mines (140.0), New Waterford (148.1), Sydney (175.9) and Glace Bay (an incomprehensible 305.9) speak to the level of sanitation and poverty in Cape Breton's coal towns.

Inside the mines, life was as dicey as ever. On July 27, 1917, a horrific explosion ripped through the No. 12 colliery in New

Waterford. The final tally: sixty-five dead including twenty-two Newfoundlanders, seven of them from one small fishing village where their bodies were returned for burial. The union found enough violations of the Coal Mines Regulation Act to take the company to court over the deaths. The company was found not guilty. It was the kind of decision that wouldn't stand scrutiny today. Humphrey Mellish had been preparing Dominion Coal's defence in the case. Before the trial began, he was appointed a Nova Scotia Supreme Court judge. His first case: the charges against the Dominion Coal Company, in which he heard his former law partner present a defence that Mellish himself had crafted. He directed a not-guilty decision from the jury—a rare ruling, particularly for a newly-minted judge.

Miners and their families were getting tired of it all. A strike was one way to make their displeasure known. As Canada industrialized, union membership soared, and coal miners realized they held some sway in a world in which most everything of any commercial value—factories, mills, railways and steamships—depended upon coal. Some of the strikes ended happily for the Nova Scotia miners; many of them didn't. All in all, coal miners won 35 percent of their strikes outright, and clearly lost 23 percent, during the period from 1900 to 1914.

By the 1920s, the relationship between labour and capitalism was realigning itself around the world, and miners everywhere were fighting for their rights. The most fabled battle occurred in Matewan, West Virginia, in May 1920, when the coal companies hired private detectives to evict miners from their company-owned homes after they joined the United Mine Workers of America (UMWA). The locals rushed into town toting guns to confront the detectives. The mayor and the police chief, a former miner—both of whom had openly co-operated with the union drive and protected the miners as they held organizing meetings—showed up to side with the collierymen. What ensued was the bloodiest gunfight in U.S. history. When the smoke had cleared, ten men were dead, including seven detectives and the mayor.

It wasn't over yet; fifteen months later, the private detectives retaliated by killing the police chief on the steps of the courthouse, in a murder so brutal that it touched off an armed rebellion of 10,000 West Virginia coal miners in the largest insurrection the U.S. had experienced since the Civil War. Miners from across the state gathered in Charleston, West Virginia, and began a march south to organize the coalfields. Thousands of miners joined them along the way. At Blair Mountain, a natural barrier before the town of Logan, they were met by a reviled local sheriff and his army of deputies, mine guards, store clerks and state police. The battle that followed went on for four days. At the governor's request, 2,100 federal troops showed up as reinforcements. So did a chemical warfare unit, a bomber and fighter planes. The miners eventually surrendered. During the fighting, at least twelve miners and four men from the sheriff's army were killed. Special grand juries handed down 1,217 indictments, including 325 for murder and 24 for treason against the state.

Cape Breton was isolated. The new thinking seeped in anyway, through editorials in the *Maritime Labour Herald* with its overheated language of class struggle, via recruiters from the Communist Party of Canada and organizers for the UMWA. The deplorable working and living conditions and the shrinking Besco pay envelopes made action an easy sell. Between 1920 and 1925 Cape Breton coal miners struck fifty-eight times. Most of those were localized demonstrations of workplace power: a few miners walking off the job at a single pit for a day or two. The long, district-wide strikes, though, were part of a bigger, broader strategy of organized resistance. These weren't strikes as we know them today in Canada: nice, safe, rotating picket-line duty, a sympathetic press and a protective social welfare net to ensure nobody goes hungry. Going off the job in the first part of the twentieth century more than likely meant a cracked skull from a strikebreaker's sap, being denounced from the pulpits and the front page, maybe the kids going without food and even shelter, summer or winter.

Downing tools required grit—or, at the very least, the desperate knowledge that your back was to the wall and only drastic measures would do. Communal purpose required a common enemy. His name was Roy the Wolf, and it was said that he dined on young flesh and groaned in pleasure at the thought of a miner's family starving in the cold. Thank God, parents whispered to their children, there was one man who was man enough to do battle with this moustache-twirling villain. And they would tell them about J.B.

His office was painted red, my great-aunt Eva told me, the one time I asked her about James Bryson McLachlan. Understandable for a man who went into the Scottish coal mines at the age of ten, found guidance in the writings of his countryman Thomas Carlyle, the great critic of industrial capitalism, and discovered his calling at eighteen, when the newly minted Scottish Miners' National Federation stood up to the big coal companies of Lanarkshire for the first time. "Out of his own experience in the coal mines and the influence of socialists such as Keir Hardie, he came to support public ownership as the only reasonable way of fairly sharing the wealth of the coal industry," says his biographer David Frank. "His 'economic gospel' looked for practical solutions, which to him meant a transfer of control to the working class, first through better conditions and then through a better world."

McLachlan's involvement in the Great Strike of 1894—when tens of thousands of Scottish coal miners went out over a one-shilling reduction in wages—got him blackballed by the bigger coal and iron companies. Consequently, he had to seek work at smaller and smaller independent mines. Then, at thirty-three—tired of being used as dumb-animal labour by the companies, weary of the continual search for work—he headed for Sydney Mines with his wife and four children.

It was 1902, the same year John William Briers arrived from Lancashire, which meant that McLachlan and my great-grandfather entered the Princess Colliery for the first time within months of each other. As an experienced cutter in an industry filled with rookies, McLachlan would have been working at the face. His words, in a newspaper letter to the editor about state-sponsored old age pensions, a fixed minimum wage or an eight-hour workday, carried weight. On the stump—where, to be better heard, he would take out his false teeth, fold them in a handkerchief and place them in his pocket for safekeeping, and where his Scottish brogue thickened the more excited he became—this bantam rooster seemed "a mile high," in the words of his daughter-in-law Nellie McLachlan. "The greatest political question of this century," he declared six years after his arrival in Sydney Mines, "is how to distribute the enormous wealth that the ingenuity of the last century enables the world now to produce." In 1925 he told a Royal Commission, "I believe in education for action. I believe in telling children the truth about the history of the world. That it does not consist in the history of Kings. Or Lords or Cabinets. It consists of the history of the mass of workers. A thing that is not taught in the schools."

In between, he had other things to say. Often they were about the deficiencies of the existing miners' union, the Provincial

Workmen's Association. The PWA had been spawned by adversity: the Springhill Mining Company's 1879 bid to cut miners' wages at a time when it was showering handsome dividends on shareholders. One man saw the move for what it was: Robert Drummond, a grocer's son who had immigrated from Scotland in 1865 and spent the next few years shuttling back and forth from one dangerous, poorly paid Cape Breton pit to another. Eventually Drummond moved to Pictou County and took a management job at the fast-growing Springhill mine in Cumberland County. That left him in an enviable position to examine the merits of the company's case for demanding the 1879 wage cut. His decision to publish his discoveries under a *nom de plume* in a Halifax newspaper led to his sudden termination as an employee of Springhill Mining. Instead, Drummond had a new job—salaried grand secretary of the newly formed Provincial Miners' Association, the precursor to the PWA—and a new purpose: to be the miners' voice in a perilous, backwards industry. "Drummond upheld the values of a classical liberal individualism," historian Ian MacKay wrote in his entry on Drummond in the *Dictionary of Canadian Biography.* "'None cease to rise but those who cease to climb' was both the association's motto and his own cherished belief."

Under Drummond's leadership the PWA fought historic battles for better mine safety legislation and improved training for miners and managers. It also gained recognition of trade unions as a legitimate social and economic force. The seventy or so strikes that occurred while Drummond was grand secretary show that the PWA acted when it had to. But throughout his long reign he preached the importance of harmony between labour and capital—a view that was anathema to the more militant trade unionism of the UMWA, which mounted an unrelenting war for supremacy in the coalfields of Nova Scotia during the early 1900s.

This wasn't just some elevated battle for miners' hearts and minds. By 1909 it was a grinding war of attrition, fought against a backdrop of soaring profits by the colliery and steel plant owners. UMWA members were discriminated against in the pit, harassed by company police at lodge gatherings and unable to set up even cursory meetings with company officials. The mainstream newspapers assiduously printed the company line—the miners were thugs willing to murder, maim and sow disorder to reach their goals, the police were "heroic," the mine company officials and replacement workers "loyal" and "stoic"—no matter how far removed from reality. The facts, though, are clear: Dominion Coal, which had strung electrified barbed wire around its collieries and the bunkhouses erected for strikebreakers, was ready when a strike was called over its unwillingness to accept the union as legitimately representing the miners. "We're going to fight them," vice-president F.L. Wanklyn announced. "We have the right of the matter and we're not going to give in to a bunch of American agitators."

Within days, special trains with troops bearing machine guns and light artillery pulled out of the garrison in Halifax. As the strike dragged on, UMWA members filled the jails, their credit was cut off at the company stores, they were evicted from company houses and their property was confiscated for back rent. The UMWA threw up tents and built ramshackle buildings to house the homeless families. In a show of solidarity an estimated three thousand UMWA members one afternoon marched through Glace Bay toward Dominion, only to be turned back by a military machine-gun nest set up along the road. Through it all the PWA members, under military protection, remained on the job, along with scabs brought in from Newfoundland, Europe and Montreal, to keep the mine going.

The UMWA spent $1 million in Nova Scotia during the ten months. The strikes in Glace Bay, Inverness and Springhill failed anyway. Union president Dan McDougall was dragged out of bed and charged with publishing a criminal libel against Dominion Coal. As the case dragged on, McLachlan retaliated by charging a list of Dominion Coal executives with fixing coal prices. McDougall was eventually found not guilty. Still, McLachlan paid a price: he never worked in a colliery again. Which, given the events that followed, was probably just as well.

By 1923 Jim McLachlan was fifty-four. My great-aunt remembered him as short, straight-backed and bandy-legged. He had a well-used face, a red, bristly moustache, shaggy brows that overhung deep-set eyes. He was a serious teetotaller, with an unexpected sense of humour and the eccentric's distracted air. "He took no mind of what he was wearing," Nellie McLachlan, aged one hundred, recalled, when I went to see her. "He would wear one red sock and one black one. I remember one time his wife Kate putting these formal white gloves on him to keep his hands warm. He went on the bus—they never owned a car—and didn't care or seem to notice; his mind was always on other things."

To supplement his income as a union official, the family grew cabbages and potatoes on their six acres of land on Steele's Hill, toward the back end of town. They also raised cows, and sold the milk from a wagon going door to door. (They even kept a few geese, although that didn't work out; Nellie remembered the fowl once getting loose and nibbling the tops off all of his prized potato plants. McLachlan butchered them and gave them to his three daughters for Christmas.) Money, other than the necessities it could buy, meant little to him: his daughter-in-law remembered that he was forever hauling hungry strangers home for dinner. When his kids or grandchildren asked for money for a treat, he wouldn't even look up from the book he was reading while fishing a hand into a pocket and offering them whatever coins happened to be there.

McLachlan knew who he was and what he was about; he had a core set of beliefs and a true believer's honesty that left working people inclined to trust him. When this stumpy Lowlander took out his teeth and spoke, people would do the damnedest things. Not always "good" things, mind you. But under the circumstances, history seems able to forgive that. In 1923 Cape Breton's steelworkers walked out, ostensibly in protest over the firing of a union leader, but really over Besco's unwillingness to recognize their union. Wolvin's words a couple of days before the walkout gave little hope of a quick resolution: "The policy of the Dominion Iron and Steel Co. is to maintain the open shop . . . trade unionism is wrong in principle . . . and will not be tolerated by the company."

The first night, some one hundred strikers, mostly young men, made their way into the coke ovens and drove out the maintenance men who were keeping the furnace fires going. The chief of police arrived with sheriffs, deputies and the local magistrate in tow. "Surrounded by city and steel company officers," read the story in the *Sydney Post*, the local magistrate "started to read the Riot Act to the mob, where he was assailed by a shower of missiles from a dozen different directions, one of which hit him on the head, knocking him unconscious."

A similar scene ensued when thousands of men gathered at one of the boiler houses. The arriving police wagon was "greeted with a fusillade of stones." The *Post*'s reporter on the scene added, "Detective MacDonnell drew a revolver which only seemed to aggravate the strikers. Deputy chief Anthony was knocked down and his baton was taken. Sgt. Rannie Macdonald later reported that he was struck with stones several times during the fracas." The mob broke through, took the Besco loyalists who were working there and "paraded [them] up and down Victoria Road, amid the jeers of the mob." Mike Fedora, a "foreigner who often acted as an interpreter," was "subjected to many indignities at the hands of his fellow countrymen."

The next night the strikers were at it again; 1,500 of them massed outside the plant and then, using another "fusillade of rocks" as cover, rushed the gate. Inside, the *Post* reported on June 29, 1923, "they got a reception which made them wish they had never entered the plant"—an ambush by 400 strikebreakers armed with iron bars.

Two days later the first soldiers rumbled down the track from Halifax. A light engine arrived first to ensure that the railway spur into the steel plant hadn't been sabotaged. Then came the troop train with an armoured gondola—the sides piled high with sandbags, the car decorated with machine guns—as added protection. Soon after, provincial police set up tents on company property and erected machine guns and searchlights at the plant gates. That night, when the strikers showed up, the police fired over the heads of the angry rock-throwing crowd. The strikers stood their ground. Nobody budged when one of the machine guns was trained on the crowd. Only when an artilleryman took his position and prepared to fire did the miners' nerve fail and the crowd scatter.

"Armstrong's Army," the provincial police force mobilized by the new premier Ernest Armstrong, was ready when a mob of steelworkers gathered near the coke ovens the next night. "Provincial police read the riot act and asked them to disperse," said a story in the *Halifax Herald*, "when they didn't the Mounties appeared at the city end of Victoria Road and charged the mob, using their batons freely." What ensued was a chaotic blur: mounted police charging into the mob; steel-helmeted soldiers advancing with fixed bayonets; the strikers scattering, some of them heading up toward the Whitney Pier area, with mounted police in pursuit.

At that moment, Bernie Galloway Sr. and his wife were just coming back from evening service at the Polish church in the Pier. "When we got by the railroad we saw this bunch of horses coming," Galloway recalled more than half a century later. "Men on horseback—provincial police—with sticks, something like a baseball bat. I don't know how many of them there were. They lined up. They were coming down Victoria Road towards the Pier."

I'll leave it to Doane Curtis, now dead, whose voice survives on a tape kept at the Beaton Institute in Sydney, to explain what happened next.

> With four-foot batons . . . they went up and down the street hitting people on the sidewalk. Some of them were coming from church. They even hit a man was just out of the hospital and crippled with his wife leading him around the streets. Hit him on the head, spit his head open. Then they went to the Atlantic House [a hotel] and passing the Atlantic House, a fellow jumped up there and the proprietor sitting on the verandah who was an invalid—they jammed him up against the building, hit his brother-in-law over the head. And the marks of the horses' shoes was on that verandah for years.

The next day the *Herald* tallied up the carnage: dozens of broken heads, five rioters injured seriously enough to require medical attention, two steelworkers in jail and several wrecked automobiles.

If you lived in Cape Breton in 1923 you had to pick a side. The miners were with the steelworkers all the way. At midnight on

July 3, all ten thousand of them—including the maintenance men who kept the pumps working that stopped the mines from filling with water—went out in sympathy. The next morning, as more recruits were called for in Halifax to augment the thousand already patrolling the pit areas, picket lines formed around the collieries. The last ponies were led blinking from the mines. Coal was dumped on the tracks leading into the colliery yards. At last, I imagine McLachlan telling himself. At last it's under way.

CHAPTER ELEVEN

Silence Profound and Sinister

I visited Dorchester Penitentiary once, to talk to a murderer. It's the kind of place that sticks with you, rising as it does from the New Brunswick flatlands, its dark stone walls leaching the light from the sky. You expect to hear Gregorian chant as you walk up to the entranceway, perhaps be greeted by a cassocked hunchback when you pry open the heavy front door. Instead, a uniformed guard was inside. My heart still sank as the sliding doors slammed shut behind me. I hadn't spent much time inside prison. Then again, neither had Jim McLachlan.

The day after work stopped throughout the coalfields of Cape Breton, he sent a letter out to the union locals:

Brothers:
This office has been informed that the Waterford, Sydney Mines and Glace Bay sub-districts are on strike this morning as a protest against the importation of Provincial Police and Federal Troops into Sydney to intimidate the steel workers into continuing work at 32 cents per hour.

On Sunday night last these Provincial Police in the most brutal manner rode down the people at Whitney Pier who were on the street, most of whom were coming from Church. Neither age, sex or physical disabilities were proof against these brutes. One old woman over seventy years of age was beaten into insensibility and may die. A boy nine years old was trampled under the horses' feet and his breast bone crushed in. One woman, beaten over the head with a police club, gave premature birth to a child. The child is dead and the woman's life is despaired of. Men and women were beaten up inside their homes.

Against these brutes the miners are on strike. The government of Nova Scotia is the guilty and responsible party for this crime. No miner or mineworker can remain at work while this government turns Sydney into a jungle; to do so is to sink your manhood and allow Armstrong and his miserable bunch of grafting politicians to trample your last shred of freedom into the mud. Call a meeting of your local at once and decide to spread the fight against Armstrong to every mine in Nova Scotia. Act at once. Tomorrow may be too late.

Fraternally yours,
J.B. McLachlan, Sec. District no 26. U.M.W. of A.

Two days later, Sydney's chief of police and a deputy walked up the stairs into the UMWA offices on Union Street in Glace Bay and told McLachlan, the District 26 secretary-treasurer, and Dan Livingstone, the union president, to come with them. The charge: "unlawfully publishing false tales whereby injury or mischief was likely to be occasioned to a public interest, namely the government and provincial police of Nova Scotia, contrary to Sec. 136 of the criminal code." Expecting trouble, the chief had brought along a car full of deputies who waited outside. The two union leaders were surely surprised by the charges, but went along quietly anyway. Everything seemed cordial enough; along the way they stopped at McLachlan's house so he could tell his family what had happened. Since it was late they went to a restaurant for dinner. "On the way there," reported the *Sydney Record*, "Mr. McLachlan conversed with the chief of police and others in the car but confined himself to common place topics and made no reference to the charges against him."

McLachlan and Livingstone spent the next weeks in and out of jail as the lawyers argued. But obstacles could not dispirit this pair, nor hardship humble them. Somehow, in the midst of the objections, bail hearings and legal wrangling, they trudged forward trying to reach some resolution in the strike—which is how, on July 17, they found themselves at the Pictou train station being ushered into a vice-regal rail car. Inside the long drawing room, Julian (Bungo) Byng—who had commanded the Canadian Corps to victory at Vimy Ridge and was now governor general—sat in an overstuffed piece of furniture. Also there were Dan Willie Morrison, the labour MLA and mayor of Glace Bay, and Senator John MacDonald, a Shediac, New Brunswick, businessman who had brokered the meeting.

I depend upon historian David Frank for the account of what followed. Lord Byng and Morrison had a drink; the union men, both teetotallers, abstained. At the end, everyone shook hands. Then they went their separate ways, the train on to Cape Breton and McLachlan and Livingstone to tell the miners that they had a deal to end the strike. All they need do was agree to return to work, and Byng would advise the provincial and federal governments to withdraw their troops. And that's how it could have played out.

Except that Prime Minister King and the war hero would never exactly see eye to eye. Three years later a full-blown constitutional crisis erupted when Byng refused King's request to dissolve Parliament and call a general election to spare the Liberal government an embarrassing parliamentary vote. Instead, Byng invited the opposition Conservatives to form a government. Tory leader Arthur Meighen accepted, but a week later lost a vote of non-confidence. In the election that followed, King's Liberals won a clear majority. Once in power, they moved quickly to clearly define the role of the governor general.

King ignored Byng's guidance on the coal standoff. Further complicating matters was mine union strongman John L. Lewis, who didn't like UMWA District 26's truculently independent path, or the way the Nova Scotia strike undermined his credibility with other union locals. His displeasure with the radical ways of the district's leadership grew daily; a story in the *Sydney Record* a week after the arrest of McLachlan and Livingstone had him musing about ousting the pair "in an effort to purge district 26 of its vivid Red element." A week later, Lewis telegraphed a letter excommunicating McLachlan and Livingstone and any other District 26 officials. With their ouster, District 26 officially ceased to exist. It was being replaced by a provisional district run by a temporary president.

The jailing of McLachlan and Livingstone was a huge blow to the union side. Before the summer was over, the steelworkers' union had been broken and the coal miners were back to work. Still, the machinery of justice ground on. The trumped-up charges against McLachlan and Livingstone not only stuck but were upgraded from "publishing false news" to "seditious libel." Instead of a maximum penalty of a year in jail, the pair now faced up to twenty years.

Much was at stake, then, when McLachlan's trial, one of the most fabled in Nova Scotia's history, began in October 1923. It lasted two and a half days. The prosecution tried to establish a direct connection between the confrontations in Sydney and McLachlan's opinions, expressed in the July letter to the union membership, and, by implication, in a copy of the constitution of the Red International of Labour Unions seized from his home during a police raid. The defence countered that most of the allegations he made in his letter—including the assault on the pregnant woman—were true, and that he was only expressing the views of thousands of miners whom he was representing. (If McLachlan was "red," argued his lawyer, then the miners who elected him continually to office were also "red.")

Despite McLachlan's celebrated gift for oratory, his lawyers declined to put him on the witness stand. Chances are that it wouldn't have mattered. The trial, according to legal scholar Barry Cahill, "was a gross miscarriage of justice." One fact says it all: presiding over the case was Humphrey Mellish, whom you have already met, who was appointed to the Nova Scotia Supreme Court while preparing to defend Dominion Coal officials against manslaughter charges laid after the 1917 New Waterford mine disaster. Four years later he was again there for the people who had once retained him; in a clear violation of judicial ethics, he wrote a decision rejecting union arguments for a stay in wage reductions by Dominion Coal until a federally appointed board could consider the situation—even though a delay was clearly mandated by the existing laws.

During McLachlan's trial the old bias was evident. When the union leader's lawyer asked for a change of venue from Halifax to Sydney because, among other things, they didn't have the money to bring witnesses to the provincial capital, Mellish refused. A jury in Sydney, where McLachlan was actually charged, would have been unlikely to return a guilty verdict. Instead, the jury was out for less than ninety minutes—part of which, according to the *Morning Chronicle* (Halifax), was spent eating lunch. McLachlan was found guilty on all three counts and sentenced to two years on each offence, with the sentences to be served concurrently. Upon appeal, one of the convictions was set aside. Early in 1924 he began doing his time in Dorchester.

It's hard to think of him inside those grim walls: the indignities of the shaved head and upper lip, the prison uniform (he wore No. U-908), the cramped cell no bigger than the average bathroom. According to his biographer, he kept the books in the shoemaking shop, where he "learned something about the making and mending of shoes." He was fifty-five years old, but looked far older. And as this aging, unyielding man sat there in prison, his legend was burnished until it glowed with white heat. Once he had been Jim McLachlan, local hero to some men and their families whose rights and welfare he had tirelessly championed. Behind bars he became . . . J.B., the near-mythic labour warrior; the fighter of many principled, hopeless battles; the man willing to go to jail rather than surrender to the rapacious monopolists who once again controlled the only thing his poor community had to offer.

You could see it in the way they rose to his defence, the union men and communists, the politicians, even the ordinary citizens who asked for his sentence to be commuted. When he finally was set free—on March 5, 1924, through a form of conditional release that meant he had to report regularly to the local chief of police until his sentence formally ended on eighteen months later—he received a hero's welcome as his train chugged east. In New Glasgow the Pictou miners packed a concert hall where he described sedition as "when you protest against the wrongs inflicted on working men" and "when you protest against the resources of the province being put in the control of men like Roy Wolvin." In Sydney, huge crowds filled the railway station and poured into the steelworkers' hall on Charlotte Street.

He was warmed up by the time he stepped on the stage in New Waterford. There he accused the attorney general of railroading him to Dorchester, and declared Wolvin a prevaricator who couldn't be believed.

> I cannot keep peaceful when men have to work under such conditions to prevail in the mines of this province and would sooner fight, and go to Dorchester and die with a clean conscience than submit to the Roy Wolvins, who are murdering miners and creating widows and orphans in order that coal may be produced at a few cents a ton cheaper in order to make bigger dividends for the shareholders.

Then he left for Glace Bay, where throngs of thousands waited and cheering crowds followed him through the slush-filled streets into the Savoy Theatre, just blocks from where he had been arrested.

Like many people who visit industrial Cape Breton, I wanted to see the most famous shrine to the struggles of the island's coal miners. So I drove down frost-riven streets, past tired company homes and boarded-up stores, until I reached what was once the town of New Waterford's colliery lands. In February, the view is bleak and blasted across the frost-dusted, ice-puddled grass. I walked straight to one end of an abandoned rail line and stopped in front of some old cars, which looked freshly painted and were coupled together as if just waiting to take another load of miners underground.

Next thing you know, it's 1925 and you can almost see the emaciated faces—jaws set hard, eyes flinted with pain and anger—of the men, women and children moving like a gathering storm through the streets of New Waterford. The steelmaking slump after the First World War meant the Besco plant sat idle for long stretches, removing the coal industry's single largest market. American anthracite had displaced a big chunk of Nova Scotia coal in the Quebec market, where increased use of hydroelectric energy was also eating into sales. By 1925, Nova Scotia's coal production sat at just 3.8 million tons, a 40 percent drop from two years earlier. Some mines were hardly working. In the colliery towns, people were literally starving. And a fatalistic, aggrieved temper hung like smoke over everywhere where coal had once been king.

London, Ontario, businessman Hume Cronyn—father of the esteemed actor bearing the same name—summed up the mood in a personal appendix he attached to a report by a Royal Commission into the state of the Nova Scotia coal industry struck in 1925:

> We in Ontario are accustomed, if not hardened, to the accusation made in the Prairie Provinces that the East treats the West unfairly; but the sense of grievances unredressed which prompts this charge is as nothing to the depth of feeling which exists in the Maritimes against the Central Provinces of Ontario and Quebec. That resentment is of old standing and one of its causes is the belief that the Atlantic Provinces were more or less cajoled into Confederation by promises and alluring prospects which have failed of fulfillment. It is indeed not going too far to say that the tie of sentiment which binds Nova Scotia to the Dominion has worn very thin. . . . If then we of the Central Provinces are unwilling to sacrifice something of our prosperity on the altar of common citizenship to aid, perhaps indeed to save, the main industry of Nova Scotia we may witness an estrangement of far-reaching consequences.

When the latest union contract expired in January 1925, Besco demanded another wage reduction. "Coal must be produced cheaper in Cape Breton," Besco vice-president J.E. McLurg explained, "poor market conditions and increasing competition make this an absolute necessity." The company was already taking its share from the workers; in 1924, according to the report of Cronyn's Royal Commission, it deducted $176,055.59 from workers' pay for supplies, $228,548.07 for rent for company homes and $348,396.58 for coal. The company doctor cost workers $222,100.15, hospitals $118,126.68 and churches another $75,883.64. A grand total of $1,199,293.78 went to the hated company stores. (By comparison, $247,130.47 went to union dues and another $145,657.97 to the employees' benefit society.)

The miners—who were taking home a whopping $3.65 on the rare occasion they worked an entire day—had no more to give. Reports started appearing in the newspapers of housewives using flour bags for children's clothing and cement and feed bags for bedding. A Glace Bay health official sent a report to the prime minister stating that two thousand idle Cape Breton miners and their families were "on the verge of starvation." Prophetic words, it turned out, for it was about then that Dominion Coal posted notices at the Besco company stores in New Aberdeen, Caledonia and Dominion No. 6—known union hotbeds—announcing that all credit had been cut off to the unemployed miners.

It was, even viewed dispassionately eighty years later, an unconscionable act. Most of the miners and steelworkers had been living hand to mouth for the past six months. The company stores were the only source of food for many people. There was no strike fund. The March 7 front page of the *Sydney Post* explains what happened next:

At the appointed hour last night—11 o'clock—every miner in the employ of the British Empire Steel Corp in Cape Breton and on the mainland, "downed tools" and left the pits, as ordered by the executive of the United Mine Workers of District 26. . . . Rapidly the men were hoisted from the deeps and in little knots of from three to a dozen wended their way homeward without the slightest display in token of satisfaction or disapproval of the tragedy that had encompassed the country. By midnight not a wheel was turning below or above ground and a silence, profound, deep and sinister settled over those collieries, where previously there had been continuous din and bustle. Six thousand men came out of the pits and to these must be added a like number who were unemployed, making a total in all of 12,000 miners out of work today.

The "100 percent strike"—so called because even the maintenance men at the mines had walked—was a desperate measure; unless Besco decided to sit down and negotiate, the mines would fill with water until they were unusable. Could the miners outwait Besco? Even before the men walked off the job, relief committees were distributing supplies, and the hungry were lining up in food depots that had sprung up in church basements and the soup kitchens that opened in the offices of the British Canadian Co-operative Society. They hacked off coal from bootleg mines to heat their homes. They went fishing and ran rum to put bread on the table.

The destitution was just so overwhelming. Within days of the strike's start the mayor of Sydney Mines wrote to the prime minister that conditions were "very grave" and local resources "about exhausted." A clergyman told the *Sydney Post* about meeting entire families living on little more than black tea, molasses and soup bones. Agnes Macphail, the trailblazing reformer MP from Ontario, paid a visit in late March and seemed unprepared for what she encountered. "I called in homes that were homes only in the sense that shelter from the elements may be called a home," she told a reporter for the same paper. "Awful rooms, exquisitely ugly and barren of even the ordinary comforts of life. . . . In one an expectant mother with several other children, had had no bedding until a relief station gave one blanket and one quilt. Their only food comes from the relief and the rations reclaimed by this family . . . consisted of bread, milk and potatoes."

Archbishop Worrell, the head of the Anglican Church in Nova Scotia, also arrived to have a look-see. "There are many families, at least some 3,000 souls, mutely crying for food and clothing," he told people back in Halifax.

> Many of these mining family had had no coal for several weeks and no food for days at a time. . . . Many of the workers were earning such a small sum for weeks before the strike that they were compelled to spend all on necessary food and so had nothing for clothes. . . . The straits in which these people have found themselves are as desperate as those of shipwrecked men on a desert island and yet . . . they have restrained themselves and have kept law and order, notwithstanding the provocation of hunger and want.

Stories of the tragedy taking place in Cape Breton spread across the country, mobilizing do-gooders of every description. "This morning I saw 60 or 70 people picking over the garbage in the city dump getting a meager supply of half-spoiled food," wrote Randolph Paiton, special correspondent for the *Winnipeg Tribune*, in a particularly moving piece.

> One of the noticeable things throughout this mining district is the fact that both boys and girls of six and seven were selling

papers—and there were literally swarms of them. The way they beg one to buy a paper is so piteous that it is cruel torture to walk down the street. They don't make very much noise, they don't shout; they troop along with you for blocks even if you have a paper in your hand, quietly but desperately trying to persuade you to buy another.

Sara M. Gold, a research worker for the Canadian Brotherhood of Railway Employees, also made a trip to Glace Bay to see for herself. Even allowing for the pro-labour bias, her account, reprinted in a journal called *Social Welfare,* makes hard reading:

A Scottish miner who had served for eighteen years in the coal pit, and for four years at the front, I found living with his family of wife and 8 children in the usual half of a company "double" house. Two rooms upstairs could not be used because of bad disrepair. . . . The plaster from the kitchen walls and half of the ceiling was crumbling, the floor humpy, but covered bravely with a home-made ragmat; the woodwork dirty, and for years unpainted. The cesspool has overflown, and refuse flows into the street. There are, of course, no sanitary conveniences, but there is a wire cord for an electric light. . . . There is absolutely no bedding outside of two small pillows and a thin rag coverlet, and the mattresses are sagging and shedding cotton. For warmth the family go to bed in their clothing.

Not one of them have other clothing but what they wear. There is no change of underwear for anyone, and the children wear none at all; I found them in bed trying to keep warm, with thin cotton dresses against their little bare bodies. They had that winter not been to school or outdoors, for they had no boots or stockings. The miner his wife and older children have bad teeth and red defective eyes. The children have diseased throats and breathe badly. They all look undernourished; the children especially are wan, puny, with dark rings under their eyes. One little girl, three years of age, cannot yet walk—she still has rickets, and none for years have tasted cow's milk. It costs ten cents a pint in Glace Bay! The youngest boy, of 15, sells papers in the village in lieu of work in the mines. He has no boots; he was given that week a huge pair of lumberman's rubbers by the Relief Committee, together with an old coat.

It wasn't just the bleeding hearts who found the conditions wanting. The 1925 provincial Royal Commission, made up of Cronyn, a British coal expert and a clergyman from Antigonish, Nova Scotia, was equally appalled.

We have formed the very definite view . . . that so far as houses rented from the operators are concerned, the accommodation and state of their repair generally fall short of reasonable requirements. . . . Many of these houses are old—some of them being erected by the General Mining Association more than fifty years ago. Others were built for the purpose of housing men engaged on the erection of portions of the operators' plant or in opening up new mines; the latter are little better than temporary shelters and are known and properly described as "shacks. . . ." The houses generally have no kitchen or cellar, and in certain districts, in default of waterworks, water is either delivered by the operators or in carts or has to be carried from a distance. Where water is piped into the house, there is an almost total absence of bathrooms or waterclosets, due, we are informed, to the lack of sewers. . . . The badly rutted streets, the straggling fences, and the outside privies add to the unattractiveness of the general picture. . . . We find that the average total deducted in 1924 was between one-quarter and one-third of the average total earnings. In cases of men having irregular employment the deductions in a given week were sometimes 50% or even up to 100% of their earnings for the week.

So many were starving before the lockout. Now thousands were dependent upon relief agencies for even the barest sort of subsistence. An urgent appeal from the Citizens Relief Committee of Springhill, which appeared in the April 4 *Sydney Post*, underlined the depth of the woe: "At present, 170 families, about one-seventh of the town's entire population, have been forced to apply for food. . . . We are allowing for each person in these families only one dollar per week. This means about five cents a meal for each person . . . there is nothing between them and starvation save our generosity."

Relief poured in. The Red Cross sent money and supplies; so did town councils, individuals, churches and labour organizations across the country. The Legislative Assembly of Manitoba passed a resolution imploring the federal government to grant immediate relief to Cape Bretoners. A committee of men from Peterborough, Ontario, sent a train carload of food—flour, bags of potatoes, other vegetables and canned goods—to Nova Scotia. After much delay, John L. Lewis arrived on the scene, surveyed the conditions and authorized $10,000 from UMWA headquarters for the rest of the strike. Even Moscow—in the form of the All-Russian Miners' Union and the Red International of Labour Unions—offered to contribute $5,000. According to a newspaper story, a four-year-old boy walked into a bank branch in Quebec City and handed over sixty cents in pennies that he had saved in his bank, "for the little boys and girls down there," he said, waving his hand in what he considered the general direction of Cape Breton.

The outrage swelled higher after Besco cut off the sale of coal to the miners' homes and mounted a public relations campaign that, incredibly, tried to blame the miners for their own predicament. W.G. McQuarrie, a Conservative MP from New Westminster, B.C., stood up in the House of Commons and called federal Labour minister James Murdock "the most unpopular man in Canada" for his unwillingness to intervene in the Cape Breton trouble. The *Halifax Herald*, which raised $20,000 to aid the miners and their families, thundered from the front page,

> Immediate action must be taken by the responsible authorities to rush without further delay, clothing, food and other necessities of life to the wives and children of the men who have been unable to secure employment for months and who are now slowly starving to death in many sections of our province. IT PASSES UNDERSTANDING THAT THOSE IN AUTHORITY SHOULD ALLOW THIS SITUATION TO CONTINUE ANOTHER DAY.

The *Ottawa Citizen* accused Besco of having "the mentality and soul that looks upon labor as a chattel to be bartered for profit, as a mere something to be used, and, if necessary, broken, on the wheels of industry, for dividends," and described the Nova Scotia government as "notoriously friendly to the British Empire Steel" to the point where "men and women and little children starve" because the provincial government was either too weak or too much a Besco puppet to grapple with the situation.

Miners' families, labour groups, clergymen and all stripes of politicians urged the prime minister to act. King knew his way around a negotiating table; as a young deputy minister of Labour he had proved an adroit hand at reaching compromises in touchy negotiations, including one that settled the 1906 Lethbridge coal strike. Later, during a lull in his political life before becoming prime minister, he was called in by oil tycoon John D. Rockefeller after militia fired on strikers at a Rockefeller-controlled coal company in Colorado, resulting in seventeen deaths—an event known thereafter as the Ludlow Massacre. At the oilman's behest, King set up a plan that gave workers—who failed to win union recognition during the strike—representation on committees dealing with safety and working conditions. He also wrote a study on industrial relations for Rockefeller's foundation, which posited that labour, management and capital were partners. And that industrial peace could be restored only if the partners recognized their common interests. Apparently that wasn't the case in Nova Scotia—where the prime minister pleaded that he could only intervene at the request of the provincial government.

His plea had a decidedly hollow ring. In late May, as historian Donald MacGillivray points out, Ottawa was sending aid to help the Leeward Islands recover from a hurricane. Not a cent in federal aid, though, was sent to the Cape Breton miners, who by then were reduced to travelling around the island to take handouts of food—perhaps a bit of fish, some flour or a few potatoes—gathered by truck from farmers in a ritual called the Bag Parade. On April 3 the province of Nova Scotia finally acted, issuing a one-time grant of $20,000 to the Canadian Red Cross to maintain health standards in the area. Otherwise, Premier Armstrong stayed out of the strike except for threatening to call in the troops to protect Besco's property "should the union's policy of picketing the mines and alleged interference with maintenance men endanger the people's interests."

Besco's pockets, though, were deep, and its resolve infinite. Shortly after the walkout began, a Canadian Press reporter visited J.E. McLurg, Wolvin's Besco lieutenant. During the interview McLurg demonstrated an unexpected gift for metaphor by comparing the negotiations to a poker game. "We have all the cards. . . . Let them stay out two months or six months, it matters not; eventually they will have to come to us." Then, in a single phrase that seemed to sum up all the company's arrogance, greed and malice, he uttered five words that would echo through time as a war whoop for Cape Breton's coal miners: "They can't stand the gaff," he gloated, by which he meant that they lacked the guts to endure what Besco was about to do next.

Somehow the miners had hung on: but after weeks of struggle, out of desperation, they decided to escalate the strike rather than wait for public sympathy to sway the company. Pickets prevented company officials from entering the Glace Bay collieries. At New Aberdeen the miners dumped coal on the rail tracks, cutting off the delivery of coal to the power station. Then, on June 3, they withdrew the last of their maintenance men and drove off the remaining Besco employees at the Waterford Lake power station which supplied electricity and power to the town of New Waterford and its collieries.

I'm standing where the New Waterford miners started to mass: on a field where a sharp winter wind threatens to shear flesh from bone. My father—who played basketball for Glace Bay in the forties—hated playing the New Waterford Strands. For one thing, they were good enough to once win the Canadian juvenile championship. Even worse, the Waterford crowd was spirit-wiltingly tough; to dribble too close to the sidelines meant risking being poked with a stick, or even stuck with a hatpin.

The last bit was surely apocryphal. But you get the drift. Hard people, not prone to taking a backward step. When Besco ignored the town's requests for an emergency pumping station, miners formed a committee to keep the local hospital—according to press reports, filled with sick children—supplied with water from nearby wells. Meantime, vandalism picked up. On June 5 Besco police arrested seven New Waterford miners and jailed them in Sydney. A day later the handcuffs were slapped on eleven miners from Reserve Mines and Caledonia for shutting down the maintenance plant at No. 10 mine. Early on June 11 company police retook the power station at Waterford Lake.

At that point the miners had been out for fourteen weeks. They'd been starved, frozen. Governments had abandoned them. Their employer, Besco, had become the epitome of nineteenth-century corporate villainy. And so, on June 11, the crowd at the Waterford ball field began to swell.

I'm retracing their footsteps now, walking into the wind along what was known as the Old Green Road—a path, really—which runs along the rail line that heads west from New Waterford. Eighty-two years ago, between seven hundred and three thousand people, depending upon which source you consult, made their way through the forest. Today, the path is empty of all humanity. After twenty minutes, I emerge at a mostly-frozen lake ringed with a few institutional-looking buildings. There's one house in view, a couple of hundred yards away. I make for that, walk around back and knock.

"It's been twenty years since somebody came asking about Bill Davis," Lloyd (Muzzy) Hogan, seventy-four, says a moment later, inside his kitchen. Small, wiry and bouncing with energy, he shows little wear after a working life spent in the mines. At one time seventeen families made their homes on the north shore of Waterford Lake, working in the nearby colleries and keeping the power station going. Now he, his wife and their dog are the lone holdouts at the end of a dirt road down to the water.

He wasn't even born when the mob emerged from the woods that day in 1925. After all this time, questions remain about whether the horses bolted or the police just charged. Whatever the reason, before the union leadership even had a chance to state their demands, the police opened fire. Since many of the miners were veterans—at that time 5,352 Great War soldiers were on the Besco payroll in Cape Breton Island—they stood their ground as the police rode forward on horseback, brandishing nightsticks and firing their revolvers indiscriminately. Several miners were knocked down by horses. Others caught bullets and fell to the ground wounded. Then, though unarmed, the miners fought back, knocking the police from their saddles and pummelling them when they hit the ground.

Within ten minutes the police, who had fired more than three hundred bullets, were in full retreat. Some of them galloped to New Victoria. The ones knocked off their horses made for the woods. Woe to those who weren't fast enough to outrun the mob: "One policeman found in the woods was severely mauled . . . bleeding from half a dozen cuts from his face," said the *Sydney Post.* "Some of them returned where in New Waterford they were once again visited with the fury of the mob, who . . . after beating them and manhandling them severely dragged them to the town jail and demanded they be locked up."

The riot, in the words of the *Sydney Post,* was the "result of five months of government inaction, corporation obstinacy, and the accumulated desperation of hungry men. . . ." But it was no coal community victory, even if they recaptured the power plant and put thirty policemen in hospital. One miner had broken his back, another was shot in the arm. Gilbert Watson caught a bullet in the stomach. William Davis, all 5'2" of him, took one through the heart.

"We used to play over at the stump where they found him lying," Hogan explains as we walk down along the lake, past the town's new generating station. "There were three or four bullet holes in the wood. That's how we knew it happened there." At thirty-seven, Davis left behind nine children and a wife pregnant with a tenth. Also a legacy: from then on, every miner in Nova Scotia has downed tools on June 11 to commemorate Davis's death.

New Waterford had never seen anything like Davis's funeral. Some five thousand people—even more than at the burials of the sixty-five miners who had died in the 1917 disaster at the Dominion No. 12 mine—arrived from every colliery district in the area to pay their respects. "All were quiet and subdued and a feeling of tragedy seemed to envelop all," wrote the *Sydney Post*'s reporter. A clergyman stood on the veranda at the house where Davis's remains were laid out and counselled restraint and reason. The day after the Battle of Waterford Lake, a crowd of six or seven hundred men, women and children still descended on the Besco company store in Sydney Mines and smashed in the big picture windows. What happened next must have been cathartic, as well as the difference between survival and starvation. "Barrels of sugar, bags of flour, canned goods of every description . . . and clothing were carried out and carted away," recounted the next day's newspaper coverage. "Hardly anything of value was left in the main store or basement. . . . In many cases thieves took off their old clothing and donned new outfits, thus leaving with full cargoes and attired in brand new clothing." A police officer tried to interfere but was stoned by the crowd. Besco's wagons were stolen, loaded with goods and never seen again.

All told, more than $500,000 worth of company equipment and property was taken and destroyed in the days after Davis's death. More troops were dispatched, this time from Quebec City and Petawawa, Ontario to join those in the Sydney area. Miners pelted them with rocks when they arrived. They also promised swift retribution when Premier Armstrong sent out a telegram to churches in Saskatoon who were raising relief funds for Cape Breton, informing them the labour wars on the island had been exaggerated and no outside aid was needed.

On June 26, the day of the provincial election, the miners wreaked their revenge. The Tories took all but three of forty-three Nova Scotia seats, tossing the Liberals out of power for the first time in forty-seven years. Within weeks, Armstrong's army was disbanded. Edgar Rhodes, the premier-elect, put together a six-month deal that gave the miners the same wage package as in 1922, and gave Besco a rebate on coal royalties for the rest of the contract.

McLachlan watched the events unfold as if from afar. At fifty-six, he was noticeably aged: his UMWA days were over. His reformist zeal still burned bright through the editorials he wrote for the *Maritime Labour Herald* and on the stump during his repeated unsuccessful campaigns, under a variety of left-wing banners, for a seat in Parliament. But his daughter-in-law remembers him spending more and more time in the screened-in porch built onto the farmhouse as the bronchitis he had contracted in Dorchester deepened into tuberculosis. In time, he resigned from the Communist party over what he called its "sad march to the right." When he died there, on November 3, 1937, he was sixty-eight years old. Yet, his influence and legacy were still apparent in the enactment of the Nova Scotia Trade Union Act, during the same year as his death, which gave workers the right to union recognition, and three years later with the election of a coal miner,

Clarie Gillis, as the first Co-operative Commonwealth Federation member of Parliament east of Manitoba.

A funeral procession a mile long carried McLachlan from Steele's Hill through the centre of town, then up the hill to the Greenwood Cemetery. At the graveside stood five hundred miners, the scars on their faces livid from the November cold, their heavy clothes bulking their work-hardened bodies. It's possible that McLachlan's old co-worker John William Briers, by then sixty-six, made the sombre trek to the graveside. His son Jack, now living in a Sydney Mines two-storey with Margaret and their three girls, Mora, Norma and Joan, likely did not.

Yet I'm willing to bet real money that somewhere in the Glace Bay streets stood Clarence and Mabel Demont, there to say good-bye to her old boss. It's not even beyond the realm of possibility that their three offspring were there too: Earl, the youngest; Eric, the middle boy; and Russell, by then fourteen. And that when the procession passed, they walked together back to their two-storey house on York Street, just up the road from the Glace Bay brook.

CHAPTER TWELVE

Moore the Magnificent

The brook down near the bottom of York Street was maybe ten yards across and froze solid in the winter. During spring breakup, big chunks of ice would float there, suspended. My father, when he was just a kid, would jump from floe to floe, an activity known, for some undetermined reason, as "skooshing the clampers." The Glace Bay boys had other hobbies. They'd walk down to the harbour and throw a fishing line off the wharf. When snow fell, they'd grab onto the back of one of the town's few cars—an act known as "hooking a ride"—and let it haul them through the streets. When the ground was clear they'd pitch "glassies," or marbles—for "keepsies" or just for fun—into holes dug in the soil or off the wall at Central School, across the street from where they lived. They'd play foot'n' a half, a local version of leapfrog. They'd chew roofing tar still soft and malleable after falling to the street. They'd drink McKinley's Iron Brew—which looked like cola but tasted like nothing you'd ever encountered before—down at Senator's Corner, where the town's three commercial streets met. Occasionally, when the testosterone was really firing, they'd venture up to Chapel Hill, where the "Prods" would do manly battle with the "Katlicks." Improbably, no one ever seemed to be seriously maimed, even though some savage snot-nosed battlers strode through the unpaved streets of Glace Bay in their baggy corduroy pants, high-top sneakers and peaked miner's caps.

Some seventy-five years later, when I asked my father, Russell, to name the most feared of these street urchins he'd reply without hesitation "Donny MacInnis," who long ago lived on Brookside Street and went by the nickname of "Rugged." Then he'd invariably turn to one of his favourite subjects—Cape Breton nicknames— and within minutes I'd be laughing right alongside him. Since most of the people who settled Cape Breton came from a few places in a few countries, there was a shortage of names. A single fact, to me, illustrated the problem; at one point the Dominion Steel and Coal Corporation, which later took over from Besco, was said to have 650 MacDonalds on the payroll, 150 of whom were named John. A little ingenuity was the only way to keep all those John MacDonalds, those Alexander MacNeils, those James Macleans and Jim MacKinnons separate in a person's mind. So the DeMonts of York Street grew up near a family known as the Big Pay MacDonalds— so called because an earlier member of the clan had once emptied just two cents out of his pay envelope—and someone known as Horse Shit Dan because at one point he'd had the unenviable task of cleaning up after the pit ponies.

Sometimes the nickname referred to an occupation: the Borehole MacDonalds, or Danny the Bugler. Sometimes it had to do with geography: Art Swamp and his brother, who for some inexplicable reason was called Alec the Pond. Often it denoted a physical characteristic: the Pockmarked Donalds; the Big Archies; Black Angus; Duncan the Nose; Alex the Clock, for a miner with one arm shorter than the other. Many times, the origins of a name were an out-and-out mystery: the Bullsheep MacNeils, the Weasel MacDonalds, the Red Micks, the Bleeder Campbells. Just as often, names could be traced back to some piece of family history: the Stood the Heat MacNeils, who at some point had done something brave; the Pickle Arse Macleans, who had received that handle not because of a genetic deformity but because a family member had liked to while away the hours sitting on the pickle barrel at the company store.

Once you earned such a handle, it was yours for life—maybe longer. At least, so said Richard MacKinnon, director of the Centre for Cape Breton Studies at Cape Breton University, when I spoke with him one day. To make the point, he talked about a great-uncle living in Glace Bay who stormed the bastions of the company store during the 1925 riot and grabbed a barrel of biscuits during the looting that followed. Though it ended badly—the relative dropped the barrel on his foot, breaking a toe—MacKinnon thought the whole episode was ancient history. Until, that is, the day he arrived at Fredericton's University of New Brunswick to give a lecture on Highland names. Once the talk was finished, MacKinnon opened the floor for questions. A shaky hand went up in the back of the room.

"Excuse me, Mr. MacKinnon," said an ancient, quivery, disembodied voice, "but are ye one of the Biscuit Foot MacKinnons?"

In 1933, Stump, Poo Poo, Pick Handle Tony, Burnt Rory, Pudding Head, Cut Worm, Little Pope and every other Cape Breton man or woman was thinking about soup kitchens, work camps and breadlines. Mostly they wondered what the hell had happened. Before the thirties, Canada had supplied half the world's wheat and more than 60 percent of its newsprint. Exports of manufactured goods had boomed. So had shipments of minerals, including coal from Nova Scotia, which was making something of a comeback after the postwar slump. On the eve of the stock market crash, the province's annual coal output topped seven million tons—nearly 60 percent above what it had been four years earlier.

That turnaround was too late for Roy Wolvin. A careful reader of the financial pages would have watched the Besco saga unfolding with the inevitability of Greek tragedy: how the company suspended dividends in 1924 as losses mounted, and how, two years later, the banks denied it bridge financing. From there, Besco—"mighty in name but feeble in earnings," according to *Time* magazine—began to unravel. By 1927, unable to service its massive debt and with its once high-flying shares grounded, Besco was in receivership. Wolvin tried to reorganize the mess, but the banks wouldn't buy in. Enter Sir Herbert Samuel Holt, a Montrealer—president of the Royal Bank of Canada and Canada Power and Paper, among a slew of other companies, and reputedly the richest man in Canada. (Peter Newman wrote that around 1930 Montrealers complained, "We get up in the morning and switch on one of Holt's lights, cook breakfast on Holt's gas, smoke one of Holt's cigarettes, read the morning news printed on Holt's paper, ride to work on one of Holt's streetcars, sit in an office heated by Holt's coal, then at night go to a film in one of Holt's theatres.") Holt liked the idea of owning one of the largest industrial complexes in the British Empire. Along with James Gundy—a co-founder of the Toronto-based Wood Gundy brokerage house—and some associates at the Royal Bank, he bought out Wolvin and consolidated control over Besco. In 1928, with the support of some big British investors, they incorporated a new holding and operating company, the Dominion Steel and Coal Corporation (Dosco), which took over Besco's holdings.

Nowhere have I found a record of Holt's thoughts as he watched markets fail and global trade screech to a standstill. By 1932 stock prices were worth less than one-quarter of what they had been before the crash, and almost one in four Canadians who wanted to work couldn't find a job. On the·Saskatchewan prairie, men and women looked to the dust-darkened sky and cursed the day their parents had left the Carpathian Mountains of Ukraine or the fertile plains of Hungary. In the relief camps of Northern Ontario, single unemployed men who had been criss-crossing the country, looking for jobs that didn't exist, cleared bush, built roads and put up public buildings for pennies a day.

In the Maritimes, which had been in decline throughout the 1920s, misery blanketed the land. In 1933, the average Atlantic Canadian's per capita personal income of $185 was marginally over the $181 every resident of the devastated Prairies took home. When it came to federal relief programs, Atlantic Canadians—who struggled to come up with the money needed for cost-shared programs with the federal government—received just over a third of the national average on a per capita basis. The upshot, writes historian Ernest Forbes: "elderly and destitute refused assistance, deaf and blind cut off from schools, seriously ill denied hospitalization and moral offenders savagely punished."

Not everywhere, mind you. The mining towns of Springhill, Glace Bay and New Waterford did a better job than most municipalities when it came to supporting their needy. In part, that was because District 26 of the UMWA co-operated with Dosco to ration shifts in a way that spread the money around, and worked with the municipalities to find and distribute additional relief funds.

Alas, this was but a Band-Aid on a bullet hole. As the Depression deepened, railways and factories began to turn to oil, natural gas and even electricity as fuel sources, and demand for coal to heat homes plummeted. In Pennsylvania, the production of bituminous coal fell by 50 percent in just three years, sparking bitter strikes and violence. Across the ocean, employment in British coal mines—racked by conflict between the miners and pit owners—slumped by nearly 30 percent in five years.

Nova Scotia—where coal output, which had peaked at 8 million tons in 1913, averaged just 5.2 million tons annually from 1930 to 1932—was also stricken. In the towns grown up around the collieries, it was as if a sacred trust had been broken; by 1931 the average miner worked just 140 days, compared to 230 five years earlier. Men still flocked to the industry; 11,000 on average toiled in the Nova Scotia pits that year, compared to 9,800 in 1926. The latest Royal Commission on coal mining, struck in 1932, estimated that some 2,000 young people living in those coal-mining communities had never worked—and, the way things were going, never would— as colliers.

Dorothy Duncan met her future husband—who had yet to ascend to CanLit godhood—in 1932, aboard a ship sailing from Europe to North America. Glace Bay–born Hugh MacLennan, it's clear from his writing, had mixed feelings about the mining folk of Cape Breton. It was a view that his American wife, who must have made her first visit to the island in the years after the Great Depression, seemed to share. Cape Breton's industrial centre, she wrote in *Here's to Canada*, was a "Scranton of Canada." Duncan deemed the view from Sydney harbour fine once the Atlantic winds dispersed the smoke, "but everywhere, for miles in the vicinity of the mines and the huge steel works, is the cast of coal dust and the smell of collieries and mills." The people, she sniffed, were Scotch émigrés who had abandoned the island's idyllic countryside for the mines—work which "took no more than one generation to lower the stature of those men who continued to earn their living this way." The men became "scrappy and combative because they are by nature courageous." After the Irish arrived, she wrote, things got even worse, as "Glace Bay became known as one of the toughest towns on the continent."

Yet somehow the Demont boys—Russell fourteen by 1937, Eric ten and Earl eight—survived. Clarie, their father, still had his production supervisor's job at the *Gazette*, and moonlighted looking after the hall at Knox United Church down on Commercial Street. The cruel winds of the Great Depression seldom seemed to enter the front door at 31 York Street, located right across the road from Central School, which all three boys attended before moving on to Glace Bay High. From their house it was possible to stand in the screened-in porch and see the transmitters that Guglielmo Marconi had used to send the world's first complete transatlantic radio signal, in 1902, and to hear the colliery whistle indicating that there would be work in No. 2 mine the next day.

Nostalgia ignores the banal and magnifies the notable. So my father seldom reminisced about walking out the front door and meeting the same church choir members, masons and store clerks who populated any Depression-era Canadian town. Instead, he recalled Glace Bay as a place with music, best considered, sometimes ruefully, often ironically, with eyes and ears wide open. The way he told it, when you stepped into the street, within a few blocks you'd meet an engineer on the Sydney and Louisbourg Railway, the local fire chief, a future member of Parliament, one of J.B. McLachlan's sons, the owner of the Russell movie theatre and a colliery man who walked out in the street at midnight every New Year's Eve and fired his rifle into the air. One minute you'd be waving to a young woman who would soon drown in the Mira River, the next you'd be nodding to a star athlete who one day, for no obvious reason, just went out into the woods and stayed there. You might meet a Great War veteran who would sidle up behind unsuspecting citizens and startle them with the news that they were "too tall for the trenches." Or a man lugging a sack of bootleg coal—a practice that thrived during the Depression years, when employment was scarce and heating the house took precedence over the nuances of resource ownership. You'd glimpse the halt and blind, victims of the moonshine from Reserve Mines, making their damaged way.

Maybe you'd see my grandfather, who would walk the six blocks from Senator's Corner without once looking up from the *Boston Globe*. His job at the newspaper made Clarie Demont something of a rarity in a town where most adult males still worked in the mines, or at some other job that depended upon the collieries. Consequently, my people may have been a shade better off than some of their neighbours; dinner was bologna, sausage or fish—usually cod from the fishmonger who went door to door. Since it was a teetotalling house, everything was washed down with milk delivered in glass quart bottles by a man in a horse-drawn carriage. There wasn't much in the way of ice cream or store-bought sweets, but Mabel was a prodigious baker. Date squares, dinner rolls and something known as Cape Breton sugar pie, a sort of fudge in pastry that was so sweet it would make your teeth ache, would come steaming from the kitchen.

The house teemed with life: the MacKeigans and Demonts, Clarie's buddies from the paper, Boss Wilson, the athletic director at the YMCA, who showed up every Saturday night for beans, the bank managers and ballplayers who boarded upstairs. You can see my father and uncles sitting there in the low buzz of kitchen-table talk, inhaling the smells of food, tobacco, liniment and coal dust. My father, until I pointedly asked him, never once mentioned the fact that he had grown up during the Great Depression. Nor did he make much of the fact that he and his brother Eric both caught tuberculosis and had to spend eighteen months in a sanatorium receiving pneumothorax treatment—essentially collapsing part or the entire damaged lung, then allowing it to sit unused and heal inside the chest cavity. (Although my father did once concede that it took a long time for his self-confidence to recover from this affliction with a disease that was usually associated with abject poverty.)

What he mostly talked about were the simple, goofy joys of small-town life in a happy home: getting a milkshake at Medical Hall, the pharmacy favoured by the Protestants; browsing through the comic books at Charlie MacLeod's bookstore as their father shot the breeze about politics and current events with the philosophical proprietor. After supper they huddled around the big Westinghouse radio with the trio of dials, listening to *Myrt & Marge* and *One Man's Family*. Saturday meant a movie matinee and a practised ritual that began at the kitchen table with the boys saying how much they wanted to see the latest Tom Mix or Hopalong Cassidy offering. Clarie or Mabel would say it wasn't really a good time, or maybe baldly state that they didn't have the money. The boys would beseech, the parents would equivocate. But invariably, when they went to clear away the dishes from the table, Russ, Eric and Earl would find a nickel—the price of admission in the 1930s—under each of their plates. During summer vacations they'd jump off a bridge on the Mira River with their buddy Dougie Holmes, who was blind, and float down the river with the current as blithely happy as dogs cooling off on a hot day. When my dad got older, sometimes they'd go to a dance at Spain's Pavilion, out on the Mira. Then a bunch of them would walk back at one or two a.m., laughing and yakking in the dark, Holmes lightly touching someone's elbow for directions.

Usually what they did when they weren't in school was play sports. They were, after all, Clarie Demont's boys. Though his playing days were over, Flash still kept time during road races and officiated at some of the local wrestling matches. (He also ran the local bingo game at a hall diagonally across from Knox Church, where he and Father Nash would split the profits—half to the YMCA and the other half to the parish up the hill.) In colliery towns, playing or watching sports was like going to the movies, the dance or the tavern—a way to while away the leisure hours, which seemed to grow immeasurably during the Depression thirties. Having your own hockey, baseball or rugby team provided a sense of separateness between those cookie-cutter towns. My father and uncles crowded into bone-snapping-cold rinks to watch their dad's old team, the Glace Bay Miners, take on their nearby rivals the Sydney Millionaires. They sat in the wooden bleachers as Sandy McMullin, dead a few years later from electrocution, and Alex MacDonald and "Coot" Maclean, who both died while serving in Italy during the Second World War, led the magnificent Caledonia Rugby Club to victory after victory.

The Demont boys were no slouches. As they got older they played basketball, hockey, and rugby, boxed, wrestled and ran track. If they saw a ball, they just had to kick, bounce or throw it. Some days my father would rush home from school, drop his books, then grab a worn leather baseball glove with no more padding than an oven mitt and go out on the front lawn to play catch with his idol, Roy Moore, star of the Glace Bay Miners, who boarded at 31 York Street. The Cape Breton colliery league wasn't just a bunch of pick-and-shovel men tossing around the horsehide. In 1935 the league allowed each team to sign three imports. A year later, as Colin Howell recounts in his book *Northern Sandlots: A Social History of Maritime Baseball,* the Cape Breton Colliery

League broke with the Nova Scotia Amateur Baseball Association and began signing on unlimited numbers of paid imports.

Sydney Mines added Bob Ayotte, slugging outfielder George Foster, Elliot and Charley Small from Maine; New Waterford had a young club led by shortstop Lennie Merullo, who later played seven years with the Chicago Cubs; the Dominion Hawks leaned heavily upon George Michaels (formerly of the Boston Royal Giants) and Gene Lumianski, who had pitched for Toronto in the International League; Sydney signed Rube Wilson, a big left-hander from South Carolina, and Guido Panciera, who had taken the field for the New York Yankees, the Boston Braves and the Boston Red Sox. The Glace Bay Miners had their own trio of stars: Billy Hunnefield, a switch-hitting infielder who had once finished second in the National League in stolen bases; first basemen Adolphial (Del) Bissonette, who one year hit .320 and dinged twenty-five home runs for the precursor to the Brooklyn Dodgers; Roy Moore, a left-handed pitcher who did a couple of seasons in the Big Show with Philadelphia and Detroit.

I've heard descriptions of their getting off the train that first time, arriving from dusty little American Midwest towns and broad-shouldered east coast cities, some of them has-beens looking for another paycheque, others younger, maybe college-educated, still hoping to get a shot at the big time. None of them, probably, knew quite what to expect when they learned about this new league up in Canada. But they would have understood that, though the slow recovery had begun, not a corner of this continent was untouched by the Great Depression. The down-at-the-heels dress of the people at the railway station must have seemed mighty familiar. Same with the lean faces—Englishmen, Scots, Irish, Lebanese, with a smattering of Italians, Slovaks and other Europeans thrown in—of men and women who never forgot the work camps and soup kitchens along with the hunger, cold and damp of that fretful time.

The ballplayers' very presence whipped the surrounding towns into a frenzied state. Games began with balls falling from airplanes, marching bands and speechifying politicians. Seasons ended like the one in 1938, when the members of the league-winning Glace Bay Miners were honoured by a parade that went through downtown Sydney and included a pipe band and over two hundred decorated cars. In between, hundreds of fans would slap down the forty cents to watch a game. Entire shifts at the colliery had to be cancelled because too many men had skipped work to attend a critical playoff contest—which might have been broadcast live over the radio.

Baseball, with its bracing combination of beauty, skill and joy, helped people rise above the hardscrabble reality of their everyday lives. As Jim Myers—who played on those same fields decades later—points out in his Saint Mary's University master's thesis on the colliery leagues, even those who didn't actually like the sport were touched by it. Townspeople held "theatre parties," dances, socials and bingo games to raise money for the community-owned teams. With the Depression still on, miners set aside money from each paycheque to help their team stay in operation. When one team faced financial trouble, the others in the league helped pay their costs.

The locals honoured their heroes. The players were introduced to the community at receptions at the start of the season, and feted with banquets and parades when it closed. Their willingness to sign every autograph and visit every sick child in the hospital cemented their celebrity status. So did a fastball between the shoulder blades, or arriving cleats-first trying to steal second base. A winning ball team helped shore up a community's self-esteem in troubled times. Which meant that there was more at stake than a *W* in the win column whenever two teams took the field.

Sometimes, players climbed into the stands to get at a fan who had been pelting them with rocks or throwing mud into their water buckets. Then all hell would break loose, as it did on July 30, 1939, at New Waterford's Dodger Field. By the seventh inning the Sydney manager was asking for protection from bleachers full of threatening, cussing fans. The umpire called two policemen to act as a buffer between the Sydney bench and the unruly crowd. When a pair of Sydney players lost it and took to the stands, the fans responded by ripping down the wire fence and storming the ball field. A full-scale riot ensued.

Umpires often took the brunt of the abuse. At one game in Sydney Mines, Umpire-in-Chief Stewart MacDonald was knocked down and kicked by fans. Somehow he made it to his car, where the beating continued and his driver was also attacked, until the police finally arrived. Another time, police protection had to be summoned in New Waterford after an umpire named Flemming was attacked during a game and a disgruntled fan threw a rock through his windshield. One day in the same town, a Glace Bay umpire named Gordon MacInnis made two successive bad calls against the home club. The president and manager of the New Waterford club tried right then and there to have him removed from the field. MacInnis refused. With the game tied in the ninth inning, the fans could restrain themselves no longer. It took the chief of police, a contingent of his constables, and ballplayers from both teams to escort MacInnis to a waiting truck as fans pelted him with sticks and stones. In the melee that followed, his father was beaten and five men were arrested.

On the other hand, the hapless Hugh Beshore did such a terrible job at a July 20, 1936, game that the managers for both the Reserve Mines and Glace Bay teams refused to play another out until he was replaced. Johnny Lafford, a pro boxer, was enlisted to finish the game behind the plate, while Beshore was relegated to the bases. "His calls on the bases were no better than his ability to call balls and strikes," recounts Myers, "upsetting the Reserve team who had to be restrained by the R.C.M.P."

In the mind an image starts to form: half-in-the-bag miners and steelworkers taking pulls on their barely hidden bottles of 'shine and store-bought hooch; fans openly gambling in the stands; as they baited umps and opposing players; local kids so pesky and cantankerous that they had to be penned in cordoned-off areas in some parks. And yet I bet the ballplayers, used to the nomadic life of the Depression-era athlete, hardly noticed. I'm not one of those who think that the baseball diamond offers a metaphor for life. But the essence of the game—blue sky, newly cut grass, a white ash bat colliding with a seamed horsehide orb—does seem to transcend time and place. I imagine that's why, whenever a sportswriter later caught up with some leather-faced colliery league vet—by then selling cars on commission or rocking away the hours in a retirement home—they always spoke kindly about their Cape Breton days.

If an interview with Roy Moore exists in some archive, I failed to turn it up. He was thirty-eight when he signed on with the Miners, a husky Texan at the tail end of a career that had peaked with three years with the Philadelphia Athletics, a two-year stint with the Detroit Tigers and an overall big-league record of thirteen wins and twenty-six losses. From then on it was the journeyman's life. Eventually he ended up playing for the minor-league Toledo Mud Hens. In 1935 he was barnstorming with the House of David, a Jewish touring team that had started signing players not of the faith.

I found a picture of the championship Glace Bay Miners squad of 1938. Moore was forty by then—living in a house where the only way he could guarantee a quiet afternoon nap was by bribing my father and uncles to stay quiet with a small purple bag of chocolates left dangling from the doorknob outside his room. With his raccoon eyes and old-guy slouch, he might have peered at himself in the mirror on a bad day and seen a middling athletic career that had just about run its course. Or he may have said, I'm a grown man who still gets to play a child's game for a living—even if it isn't a good living—and been happy with that. It's anybody's guess. I just like to picture him and my father lobbing the ball back and forth on the small front lawn: Moore moving with that fluid, exaggerated motion that natural athletes use when they're warming up; my dad, sixteen, nervous at first, then relaxing as time seemed to slow down.

Years later, when I was younger than he was in 1938, my father and I used to go out in our driveway in Halifax and play catch. One day he seemed to feel I was ready to learn how to throw a curveball. I didn't know much about Roy Moore then. I just understood that a long time ago he had shown my father how to grip the seams of the ball with index and middle finger and give it a clockwise spin. One minute the ball is going straight; then, with no warning, it twists and dips as if it's fallen off the edge of a table. I can't tell you how many hours I spent that summer trying to make a tennis ball break even a little as I chucked it against a school wall. It deviated not one inch from its prescribed path. I kept at it anyway, even after the street lights went on and the ball's echo dissolved like a thought in night air as thick and salty as ocean brine.

CHAPTER THIRTEEN

The Darkness of All Darknesses

The spirit does not soar driving through Springhill's downtown. Context alters perspective. And so—armed with a little backstory—a visitor begins to glimpse resolve in the rough little streets, allegory in the weathered cemetery headstones, resilience in the faded wooden houses. I'm here because of a phobia. I have more than my share. As long as I can remember, I've been unable to lie on my back and stare up at the sky without a terror-inducing vertigo. I worry way too much about taking out one of my eyes with a backcast from a fly rod. The sight of a plastic bag in the branches of a tree is enough to send me back to bed in an existential funk. Far as I know, the latter is a rare kind of dread. Stats, on the other hand, show that half of humanity is plunged into a heart-thumping, pupil-dilating panic at the thought of being buried alive.

While writing this book I started keeping a desktop file of coal-mine disasters around the world: blood-splattered items about droves of men who never made it out of mines in West Virginia, Alabama, Siberia, Serbia, China, Japan, Turkey and Czechoslovakia.

There's a forlorn pattern to the stories: the fire, explosion or roof collapse out of nowhere; the desperate rescue effort; the excruciating wait; the grief; the recriminations. Yet whenever I heard of a mine disaster, my first thoughts were always with the living, not the dead.

One day I headed for the best place I could think of to ask what being buried alive was really like. In the rolling hills outside of Springhill there's little sense of the sweep of the the area's story: its humble beginnings as a coal centre during the GMA monopoly, the late-1800s ascent when a new rail spur opened up markets for Springhill coal in Ontario and Quebec. By 1891, local historian Roger Brown recounts, the sleepy hamlet of nine hundred had swelled to a boom town five times that size.

From the start, there was blood on the coal in Springhill which has been forever beset by explosions and seismic jolts that cause roofs to cave in and tunnels to implode. From 1876 to 1969, 142 miners died in over 180 different incidents there. A disproportionate number of those deaths occurred in No. 2 mine, one of the deepest in the world by 1954, when Ken Melanson went inside at the age of seventeen. The son and grandson of miners, he didn't do it for the love of tradition; a new man in the mines got $9.74 a day compared to the $4 that a day in the woods, the other local employment option, offered. Melanson's first job was shoving empty one-ton boxes down to the coal face, waiting for them to be loaded, then coupling them together so they could be hauled to the surface. He worked a few months, was fired due to the inexorable slump that had begun in the coal industry, and then, a few months later, was rehired to reinforce the mine roof. On a whim he decided to try his fortune in Toronto. "When I got there I discovered the streets was not paved with gold," he told me one rainy afternoon in early 2008. "I spent four months washing dishes and I was never so happy to get back to Springhill in my life."

He's sitting at his kitchen table as he tells me this, a tall, high-strung guy with a character actor's basset-hound face. It's easy to picture him on Thursday November 1, 1956—just nineteen and still living with his parents—as he got ready for work on the afternoon shift at the No. 4 mine. At about 1:45 p.m. he picked up his lunch can and the towel he used to wipe away coal dust and walked out the door. Along the way, he stopped at the miners' hall and spent fifteen minutes yakking with a couple of his buddies. "It was a beautiful Indian summer day," he says, "and we sat there and thought it would have been a great day to take off and go hunting." Instead, they headed for the wash house, changed into their overalls, climbed into a trolley car and began the hour-long trip to the coal face.

Mining, in theory, was safer by then. The deeper the workings, the greater the pressure on the roof and sides of the mines, and the greater the cost of extracting the coal. Instead of the old grid-like pattern, mine interiors began to resemble ebony corridors. Long roadways supplied access to the coal "walls," hundreds of feet long and wide. Miners, at first using picks, worked along the face, extracting coal that was shovelled into cars and moved to the surface. In 1950 the Dominion Coal Company built an automatic cutting machine—the "Dosco Miner"—which could extract a tonne and a half of coal, load it into a container belt and ship it to the surface.

Everything seemed normal when Melanson started working along the east side of the mine. Then, at 5:07 p.m. he felt a powerful gust of wind blowing through the shaft. The subsequent investigation concluded that an empty train had derailed within the mine, cut an electrical line and ignited a fire in the roof of the supports. The explosion that followed shot a fireball through the shaft and out through the mouth of the mine. "The men working on the bank head—where the coal is piled on the surface," wrote the *New York Times* the following day, "got the full blast."

Down at the 5,400-foot level, all Melanson noticed was that the pans into which the men loaded the loose coal had stopped moving. He sat down and had a drink of water. About fifteen minutes later he heard someone down below say, "Knock off," the signal that the day's shift was over, for one of countless possible reasons. Taking different routes, the men began the walk back to the main slope to board the cars that would take them to the surface. Melanson didn't even get to the bottom of the slope before coming upon men from the other side of the mine. "They hollered, 'Don't go out there,'" he said. "I looked ahead of me and there was a man laying dead."

Melanson could smell smoke, but he knew the real threat was carbon monoxide, the colourless, odourless gas that stops men in their tracks and makes them keel over and die. For long minutes there was chaos in the pit. Melanson, who speaks patiently in an undulating voice, says he and some others found a trap door, went in and shut it behind them. Inside was a line carrying air from an above-surface compressor to run the mine's machinery. Someone found a big air hose. They cut holes in the sides and connected it to the compressor line and inhaled the clean air. Without the compressed air, he figures, they wouldn't have lasted three hours. "I can't describe that feeling you get, right down through you," he says. "It's a shock. It's like if someone came up to you and told you that you were going to be hanged in ten minutes. You shake, you quiver. You wonder, how did this happen to us?"

A natural leader emerged within the group of men: Com Embree, an overman or shift supervisor whose father had survived the

1891 blast and who had himself lived through two mine explosions. ("We knew anyone in trouble with Com Embree was going to come out of it," a miner named Harold Tabor later told the Halifax *Chronicle-Herald*.) With the help of another miner, Embree fashioned a makeshift barrier out of an old trap door to divert the gas. On the outside of the structure someone scribbled in chalk, "FOR GOD'S SAKE COME AS FAST AS YOU CAN—47 MEN ALIVE HERE."

More men found their way to the shelter. Some just said the hell with it, soaked their shirts with stagnant water, opened the door and headed for the slope. A while later Melanson and the others glimpsed a light in the distance, but in time it dimmed. Then the light, which one of the men making a run for it had dropped after inhaling gas and dying, finally went out, leaving Melanson and the rest to sit there in the "darkness of all darknesses" hoping someone would come. The only food was a few crumbs someone salvaged from a dead man's lunch tin. They starved, but with their throats coated with coal dust the thirst was worse. Some of the men prayed. They sang a little to pass the time. "You say all this stuff to yourself about how—if I could just get out and see the blue sky—how I would change my life," Melanson says. "But by Saturday I just gave up."

On Sunday evening, Embree said he planned to write no more in his diary. He offered the leftover pages to the men to write wills, and several of them took him up on the offer. According to Brown, a few of them sang a tune from the era: "Don't worry about tomorrow/ Just be real good today;/ The lord is right beside you/ He'll guide you on his way." Melanson didn't bother. "I remember a friend of mine in town, he died just before the explosion. I went to see him in the hospital, he was dying choking on his teeth and I couldn't understand why they didn't take them out. So that afternoon I just laid down and I took my teeth out and put them in my pocket. If I was going to die I wasn't going to choke to death."

Melanson wasn't expecting the noise they heard outside their door after more than sixty hours underground. They were scared that the toxic gas would get in if they looked out. But someone opened the door anyway and the draegermen from Springhill walked in. Melanson stops talking at this point. He lets out a sound that's partway between a shudder, a whinny and a sigh, then does it again and resumes his story: how the crowds had gathered at the pithead along with the announcers from CBC radio—broadcasting live—to wait for the survivors. "This went on all night. I got out of the mine, I don't know, two or three o'clock in the morning. And later in the morning the radio said, 'Ladies and gentlemen, that is the last survivor.'"

The death toll hit thirty-nine. Most of the bodies were still underground when it was decided to seal off the mine for fear of another explosion. In January the mine was reopened so that the bodies could be placed in steel coffins and brought to the surface. "There were no funeral homes back then," Melanson recalls. "And I remember all these funerals every day for a while, with all those crepes on the doors. It was sad—sad, sad, sad, sad."

All told, eighty-eight miners emerged alive from the depths, many encrusted with so much coal dust that they were unrecognizable. Some were never the same after that. Joe MacDonald had to sleep with the nightlight on for the rest of his life; "When I wake up in the night," he told his wife, "I want to see light." For two years after the cave-in, Hughie Guthro's fingers shook when he tried to button his shirt in the morning. Some men never went back underground. Many had no other choice.

Melanson headed for the mine in nearby River Hebert, where the seams were thirty inches wide and the conditions seemed like a hundred years ago. A considerable number opted for the No. 2 mine, the last one operating in Springhill. Which meant they were inside two years later when the mine's floor and rock ceiling clapped together. Within twenty-four hours eighty-one of the men had been rescued, although one of them later died in hospital. All told, seventy-four died in the mine and their bodies were eventually recovered. Another nineteen remained trapped underground—twelve in one group, six in another and one unfortunate soul alone.

Their predicament boggles my mind. The Washington-based National Academy of Sciences felt much the same way. Right after the bump, they dispatched a team of psychiatrists and sociologists to Springhill to see how the miners behaved while trapped underground.

In fragments, the story emerged. The air was hot, stagnant and full of carbon dioxide. The stench of death was everywhere; "Oh it was terrible the last two days," one miner recounted. "The smell, that is what I was scared of." Many of the men were badly injured, including a pinned and dying miner—whom the others were powerless to help—who slipped into delirium, pleading for someone, anyone, to amputate his arm. The lights died. By the third day the food—the group of twelve had a few sandwiches, a doughnut and some pieces of chewing gum—was gone. When the water disappeared, some of them tried drinking their own urine to stay alive. "They adapted themselves to it by stages," the researchers reported. "They first wet their lips, then rinsed out their mouths, and then drank." Some of them, unable to choke it down, added coal and bark to disguise the taste.

Both groups included men who had survived the 1956 explosion, and knew enough to keep their heads near the ground as a precaution against the gas. Few seemed overly worried about another bump. Instead, "the fear of not being rescued was uppermost in the minds of the trapped miners." Most of them focused on banal everyday things—unpaid debts, hunting trips—to keep their thoughts from their families and their situation. Before long, though, their spirits plummeted. The pleas of the trapped man and the smell of the rotting bodies drove some of the miners to the breaking point. Suspicion over the rationing of the water spiralled into paranoia. Ten of the eighteen men didn't have a bowel movement during the entire period. Most could only sleep for an hour or two. Many suffered from hyperventilation and heart palpitations.

Cut off from all light, they started to see weird things. "There were times that my eyes were shining like headlights in a car," one said. "I began to see a red—a yellow glow," added a second, while a third said, "When we lay down, we would see like little spots, like little fellows running away." Another said, "I'll tell you what they reminded me of—these kaleidoscopes, I think they call them, with all the little cut glass in." One miner, suffering from a fractured femur, seemed delusional: "I began to think of my leg as if it wasn't part of me, and I would keep on saying, 'My poor old leg! My poor old leg!' I began to feel sorry for it. But I didn't think it was part of me at the time. Maybe that was a good thing."

The sounds of the rescue operations were interpreted by some as the sealing off of the mine, sparking panic. "In some miners, fear changed to resignation during the last few days when the sounds of rescue occasionally stopped for an hour or two at a time as the rescuers in the long, narrow tunnels changed shifts," the researchers wrote. "These were the periods when most anxiety and pessimism were expressed."

Over in the group of twelve, the miner known to the researchers as Q12 declared, "The last day [before contacting the rescuers] we were all saying good-bye to one another as we thought we were dying, we would not see one another again." Another said, "I really gave up. I thought to myself—after what we had tried, the conditions I had seen, all the walls in—I can't get out and I am just as good an experienced man, how are they going to get in?" One of the group of six recalled:

> I sat there and thought, "Now I wonder how long?" Of course, I just said to myself, "Well, I'll likely not know much about it because I'll keep getting weaker all the time." The way I figured we would just keep getting weaker all the time, and I didn't think we was going to get out because I didn't think they were going to get to us. I figured we would just lay there when we got that weak. Well, in fact, the last day we couldn't hardly stand up.

And yet, against all reason—their food and water gone, in absolute night, the smell of death everywhere—some of them held on to a scrap of optimism. There were few if any times when there wasn't at least one miner expressing hope, even if just as a conscious counterweight to the deepening despair. ("I said, 'They will get us out.' I never thought they would. I was just telling him that.") Some of them, despondency simply could not crush. ("And then all at once, oh . . . F6 said . . . 'You still got hopes?' And I said, 'Yes I've got hopes . . . I got good hopes and I will until I draw my last breath.'") Others were pragmatists, displaying a composure that, to a person who has never been underground, seems incomprehensible. ("I couldn't understand us living though and living that long [unless rescue was to come]. We were in fairly good condition. Nobody went haywire. We were all talking sensible, ordinary conversations.")

The "miracle miners" who emerged alive were marked by it for the rest of their days. Some, according to Melissa Faye Greene, who wrote a book about the bump of 1958, felt survivor's guilt, men plummeted into depression, a few experienced an epiphany and tried to alter the course of their lives. Others were swept up by forces beyond their control. The media, desperate for a hero, seized on the story of Maurice Ruddick, a "mulatto" miner whose singing in the long days of darkness kept hope alive, and inflated his role in the drama. A poll in the Toronto *Telegram* chose him as "Canada's 1958 Citizen of the Year." Ruddick fantasized about some kind of ambassadorship, but the governor of Georgia showed him his place. The virulently racist Marvin Griffin invited eighteen of the Springhill survivors to be his personal guests at a new luxury resort in his state. Ruddick, his wife and four of their twelve children spent the week in three house trailers on the "negro beach," three miles from the motels where his white co-workers were staying. Afterwards Ruddick explained that he had been well treated but admitted that he "wasn't pleased with anything that keeps people apart—it is something out of the past."

Back at home, where his old co-workers resented his hero status, Ruddick's fame quickly died. The mines were closed. He couldn't find work. In time his unemployment insurance ran out. The family allowance and the Springhill Disaster Relief Fund— $88 per month plus $35 per week, to support a family of fifteen— weren't enough. Ruddick and his children formed a musical troupe, the Harmony Babes, and sang cowboy songs throughout the Maritimes. In the end, he was reduced to gathering loose coal chunks from along the railway tracks and around the pitheads of the abandoned Springhill mines, to keep his family from freezing.

Which is why I like to imagine him and the others when the rescuers arrived—when they realized that, despite everything, the Springhill miners would rise Lazarus-like from the deeps. From the blackness they emerged into the blinding flash of camera bulbs and the sheen of burnished legend. The world had watched transfixed as the tragedy and rescue unfolded: Prince Philip arrived to encourage the survivors. A disaster relief fund swelled to $2 million as contributions poured in from around the globe. The drama lived on in a tune penned by American folksinger Peggy Seeger—and decades later, covered by U2—and a poem written by Richard Brautigan.

Above ground big-finned Oldsmobiles, Chevys and Pontiacs, skippered by men with hair pomaded to a brilliantine flourish accompanied by women in poodle skirts and stiff saddle shoes, tooled across Nova Scotia's roads. The car radio crackled with news of a war in Korea, a Russian satellite winking as it circled the earth and the faraway voice of a hound dog named Elvis. Cold War angst—thoughts of bomb shelters, spies and mutant giant insects—hung in the air. But this was also the age of big ambitions. The St. Lawrence Seaway allowed ocean-going vessels to travel inland to the Great Lakes, the TransCanada pipeline brought Alberta's natural gas as far east as Quebec, the Trans-Canada Highway joined all ten provinces.

The Maritimes, like so much of booming postwar Canada, seemed to be in transition in the 1950s. Pre-industrial jobs—farming, fishing, forestry, mining—were disappearing. New enterprises were slowly emerging: a New Brunswick university dropout named Kenneth Colin Irving now owned 1,500 service stations through the Maritimes and Quebec, and was buying forests, newspapers, oil tankers and cargo vessels. Grocery stores owned by a butcher from Stellarton named Frank Sobey seemed to materialize overnight throughout the province. After supper, Nova Scotians sat down in front of their boxy RCAs, tuned in to one of their two TV stations and seemed equally happy watching shows about American gunslingers or fiddlers from Prince Edward Island.

Increasingly, even in the most rural area in the land, people began to long for the big city. During the 1950s, 82,000 Maritimers left the region altogether. Russell DeMont—who, after a brief stint as an electrician's helper, had decided that wasn't for him—joined the exodus. The time in the TB ward meant that he got a late start at tiny, perfect Acadia University in Wolfville, Nova Scotia, where he became the first DeMont to enter a post-secondary classroom. But he made up for the lost time at the little Baptist school where he covered tuition and living expenses by waiting on tables in the cafeteria and coaching basketball. Russey also played rugby, ran track and headed up the yearbook committee. He took particular pride in the boater-and-cane soft-shoe routine he developed with Bill "Shaky" Stewart, which became a fixture at campus social events. Among other things they were known for their humorous "odes," one being done in the manner of Clement Moore's "'Twas the night before Christmas" and including the verse: "Down the chimney came Santa nice and fat/ I hit him with my baseball bat."

After graduation—a BA in economics and history, class of 1948—Russ headed for Toronto, where he set up house in an attic in the Bloor West area of town with a couple of other Nova Scotia boys. He found a job filling mail orders for the Simpsons department store chain. Gordon MacNeill, one of his roomies, said he never quite took to Toronto. By 1951 Russ was back in Nova Scotia, living in Halifax a couple of blocks from where I write these words, selling stocks and bonds door to door. On weekends he headed back to Cape Breton. There, at a dance, he met a woman—pretty, lively, dark-haired, barely into her twenties. Russ ended up giving Jack

Briers's youngest daughter, Joan, a drive back to her parents' house. The next day they met again on the ferry back to the mainland. (The causeway connecting Cape Breton to the mainland didn't open until 1955.) In Halifax, Joan, who worked as a secretary at Dalhousie University, lived in a big old Victorian house a few blocks away from where Russ boarded. They started dating—going to dances and drive-in movies in his Ford sedan.

Russ might not have realized it, but every time he got behind the wheel he was part of something big. It was the rise of oil. Cars ran on it. Trucks, which had replaced trains as the dominant form of industrial transportation, did too. Railroads—which even back in 1950 took 15 percent of Nova Scotia coal—were also converting to oil. So, increasingly, were home and commercial heating furnaces, another market once dominated by coal.

The Second World War brought an end to the relentless poverty of the Great Depression; shipyards boomed, as did railcar works like the one in Trenton, Nova Scotia, and the Dosco steel plant at Sydney, which made wire fencing for the battlefields and produced more than one-third of Canada's output of regular ship plate used to make or fix warships. For a moment the war effort had breathed life into the coal industry. In 1940, the first full year that Canada was at war, the province's coal production had hit 7.84 million tons, the industry's second-biggest year on record.

But coal's comeback was oh, so short. Oil increasingly was replacing it. New processes were also displacing coal from the metal-smelting industry, and although coke was still required in iron-making, improved technology decreased the amount of it needed to produce a ton of iron.

Poisonous labour relations were another part of the problem. The miners were as patriotic as the next man. Dosco, on the other hand, made much of its pride in being "Canada's Largest Industry" and the "Only Producer of Steel and Steel Products in Canada Wholly Self-Sustained within the Empire" while selling products that were "more nearly 100% Canadian than any similar products available anywhere." Alas, that nationalistic pride failed to translate into a willingness to let its workforce share in the wage increases experienced by most wartime industries. That meant inevitable conflict with the coal miners, with their avowed goal of recovering the wage reductions imposed on them during the 1920s and early years of the Depression. (In January 1942 the average miner's basic adjusted pay rate was $3.90 daily, against $5.00 in 1920.) During 1939 and 1940, ninety-four "outlaw" strikes occurred in Nova Scotia, accounting for half the strike activity in Canada. Most of them occurred in the coalfields. So in many circles, patience was running thin when most of the coal miners in Cape Breton—in a moment of questionable judgment and timing—began a slowdown on May 11, 1941, in defiance of the provincial and federal governments and their own union leadership.

The Toronto papers accused them of a "crystal clear case of deliberate sabotage of the national war effort" and urged Ottawa to "send in the troops" to "end the grotesque and indefensible situation at the Cape Breton coal mines." Partially, it was an issue of manpower; in the first few years of the war nearly 2,000 skilled and able Maritimers left the lousy pay, tedium and danger of the pits for active duty in the armed forces. By the end of 1941, Ottawa declared the decline in coal production a national emergency. Britain, facing the same problem, simply conscripted 48,000 Bevin Boys—named after Ernest Bevin, wartime minister of Labour and former leader of the Transport and General Workers Union—directly into the mines. The Canadian approach was different; the military stopped accepting coal miners and the government made it illegal for coal miners to work in any other job. Getting miners back into the pit wasn't a smooth process. Historian Michael Stevenson writes that of the 2,200 miners who had been authorized for release from the army by the fall of 1943, only 970 went to mines across the country. Even after the government agreed to across-the-board wage increases, the men's hearts weren't in it. Absenteeism increased; productivity slumped further. During 1944 Nova Scotia's production sank to 5.7 million tons, 1.6 million less than production from the mines of Alberta, Canada's ascendant coal province.

Perhaps that made the benign neglect by the federal government in the years that followed understandable. C.D. Howe, Canada's "minister of everything," saw to it that some industries and companies got direct grants, others tax incentives, during the war years; almost none of them were in Atlantic Canada. Historian Ernest Forbes has written that Ottawa virtually abandoned Maritime economic interests during the war. Pleas for capital equipment grants and depreciation allowances to fund new manu-facturing capability fell on deaf ears in Ottawa. Transportation sub-sidies for Nova Scotia coal were discontinued, allowing American coal to flood the central Canadian market.

Dosco's experience, in particular, is worth considering. Howe gave $4 million in tax money to help two of Canada's "big three" steelmakers—the Steel Company of Canada in Hamilton and Algoma Steel in Sault Ste. Marie—modernize and increase capac-ity during the war years. Arthur Cross—the president of Dosco, the third company in the trio—wrote to Howe that his unwilling-ness to provide any government assistance to the Nova Scotia com-pany would make inevitable the conclusion that Ottawa was intending "to discriminate against the post-war future of this cor-poration and in favour of its Central Canadian competitors." Howe seemed untroubled by the perception; in 1944 he advised Ottawa's steel controllers to use Dosco "to the minimum extent possible even if we have to buy the steel from the United States." The upshot: an enterprise that should have emerged from the war as a powerhouse was left weakened as its central Canadian competitors continued their unprecedented growth.

The numbers spoke for themselves: in 1944 Canada consumed 36 million tons of coal, 12 million of which came from Canadian mines, with the other 24 million via imports. Fourteen years later, however, Canadian coal consumption had dropped to less than 20 million tons; U.S. coal would still have 60 percent of the market, leaving 7.7 million tons for domestic producers. Of that, Dominion Coal's portion—essentially all of Nova Scotia's production—was 4.5 million, half of which was sold in Quebec, with most of the rest destined for the Sydney steel plant.

Coal markets elsewhere were in a state of pandemonium after the war: slumping in the United States, where oil and gas were taking away the market in industrial and home use; soaring in Germany's Ruhr as rebuilding gathered steam. In Britain the shortage was so acute that the Labour government of Clement Attlee nationalized the mines in 1947, making 700,000 miners employees of the state.

Geography was what had doomed Cape Breton coal. The farther the coal seams lay under the ocean floor, the more lost travel time there was for the miners, the greater the complexity of the structural and ventilation problems, the higher the cost of production. The mines were old, neglected and inefficient—desperately in need of capital investment but unable to generate the income to pay for what so clearly needed to be done. In 1958, the average cost at the pithead of Nova Scotia coal was $10.72. American producers could ship their coal into Canada for one-third of that. The 1960 Royal Commission on Coal noted that moving it by rail from Glace Bay added another $6.31 to the cost. At the same time, the

new St. Lawrence Seaway provided "a cheaper means of transportation for American coal to move into the central Canadian
market, and for large foreign oil tankers to sail into the same area."
Ottawa did what it could to make Nova Scotia coal competitive
with imports. The complex system of "subventions" or freight sub-
sidies was by its own admission "a prolonged emergency measure
that held little promise of effecting an acceptable solution." And
no amount of government intervention could do anything to alter
the fact that Cape Breton coal was high in sulphur, which made it
burn less efficiently than Pennsylvania coal. In 1959 this reality was
driven home in a particularly lamentable way: Dosco's new management began shipping in American coal for use in the Sydney
steelmaking operation.

Friggin' Dosco, Cape Bretoners used to moan. Goddamn Dosco,
as if everything that happened was all the company's fault. By then
it did seem omnipotent—a behemoth that owned collieries, railroads and fleets of steamships; the largest undersea iron ore works,
on Bell Island, just west of St. John's, Newfoundland; blast furnaces, coke ovens and rolling mills in Sydney; a railcar plant in
Trenton; shipyards in Halifax; a steel wire and nail plant in Saint
John, New Brunswick; and even outfits in Ontario that made nail
and wire products, or designed, engineered, fashioned and erected
bridges, transmission towers, cranes and other structural steel
shapes. "It is a great and valuable asset on our national balance
sheet," Lionel Forsyth, Dosco's first and only Nova Scotia–born
president, told the Toronto chapter of the Empire Club of Canada
in 1953. Then, that was certainly true. But Forsyth had always
warned Stellarton tycoon Frank Sobey that once Nova Scotians
"lost their toehold on Dosco, it would be finished." The Dosco

president, whose 1957 death left a power vacuum at the top of the company, was rumoured to be a bit of a booze artist, but truer words were seldom spoken.

Sobey wasn't the only person aghast at what happened next. Roy Jodrey was a rural grade-school dropout who became the province's richest man with his Warren Buffet–like investment genius. He was equally outraged to learn that a tight little cabal of shareholders and directors in Toronto and Montreal had struck a deal to sell Dosco to A.V. Roe Canada Ltd.—a company that owed its very existence to C.D. Howe's postwar ambition of developing a high-tech, homegrown aeronautical industry. That aspiration was shared by Sir Roy Dobson, managing director of A.V. Roe—a subsidiary of Hawker Siddeley Aircraft of Britain—and one of the designers of the Lancaster, the finest British bomber of the Second World War. In 1945, Dobson and C.D. Howe had struck a sweetheart deal. A.V. Roe (AVRO) Canada—which would later be known as Avro Aircraft Ltd.—was set up in a plant outside of Toronto, "to give Canada," as Dobson told the press, "a basic industry which, in our opinion, she badly needs. Canada will become the aircraft production centre of the British Empire within ten years."

Sobey and Jodrey were unimpressed that A.V. Roe was then one of the most glamorous corporations in Canada. They cared not that the company, thanks to a steady diet of government contracts, employed 21,000 and had annual sales of $200 million by 1957. The pair, who were large Dosco shareholders, knew their way around a balance sheet; the takeover offer—a complicated mix of A.V. Roe common shares plus cash that worked out to about $38 per share when Dosco stock was trading at about $29—might have sounded sweet, but it effectively gave the conquerors control of a $300-million industrial empire for $60 million.

I don't know whether Jack Briers shared their view that absentee management by a company of aircraft manufacturers was no recipe for Dosco's success. He may even, in his heart of hearts, have worried about losing control to Englishmen—Roe's majority owner, the British-based Hawker Siddeley Group, started by Sir Thomas Sopwith of Sopwith Camel fame—with no affinity for the coal towns and workingmen of Nova Scotia. He certainly didn't have the means to do what the notoriously parsimonious Jodrey did next: launch an expensive, all-out propaganda war in the hope of scuttling the deal. When that failed, Jodrey tried to line up enough shareholders to force Dosco to call a special meeting, but fell short. On October 9, 1957, Roe announced that it owned 77 percent of Dosco's 3.1 million shares. Three weeks later, at a special meeting, A.V. Roe exercised its right as majority shareholder and bounced Jodrey from the Dosco board.

His replacement was Dobson, now chairman of A.V. Roe Canada. And, Lord, he had big dreams. What he dreamed of was a fighter plane that could fly higher and faster than any in the sky, a jet that would catapult Canada to the forefront of the aviation world. The prototype for the Avro Arrow could do all of this. The precise reason John Diefenbaker killed the Arrow—spiralling costs? Political chicanery? Cold war intrigue? All of the above?—has spawned countless books, movies and conspiracy theories. For our purposes the important thing is that A.V. Roe had mortgaged its future on the project. When the Arrow was cancelled, the company immediately laid off 14,000 employees.

For Dosco, it was a crippling blow. A.V. Roe had promised to use its immense clout—along with its Ontario mills and factories—to help Nova Scotia steel and coal further penetrate the market in Upper Canada. "The two companies together would have been a major force," explains Arnie Patterson, Dosco's public relations director in those days. "After the takeover battle, the Roe people, including the belted English lords from Hawker Siddeley, predicted that Roe participation would bring greater prosperity to the many Dosco communities. This never happened. All was lost with the crash of the Arrow."

Raw-boned and restless, Patterson would go on to make a million bucks in radio and television, run twice unsuccessfully for Parliament and do a stint as Pierre Trudeau's press secretary. When he joined Dosco he was on the short side of thirty, a strapping ex–city hall reporter for the Toronto *Telegram* hired to buff up the company's image. The job started ominously; within months of signing on he was in Springhill, Dosco's man on the spot during the Bump of '58, which essentially marked the end of coal mining in Cumberland County. "I spent the next six years feeling like the purser on the *Titanic*," he recalls. "There was always trouble on some front or other."

In fact, when the Arrow program was cancelled, Roe had to be supported by Dosco, itself ailing. Dosco lost $3 million in 1959 and $1.2 million the next year. Its steel arm was running near capacity and in the black and its shipyards were just about breaking even. Dominion Coal was the problem. From 1952 to 1955 its coal operation lost anywhere from $750,000 to $4 million. In a submission to the 1959 Royal Commission on Coal, Dosco laid out its view of the predicament:

> The greatest difficulty confronting the Companies from an operating viewpoint at the present time is largely one of high operating costs. These costs can be materially reduced if every mine which continues in operation is worked on a full time basis and at peak capacity. . . . The present capacity of the collieries should permit an output of 5,500,000 tons. An estimate of sales

for 1960 indicates that 4,300,000 tons of coal will be sold. This means that idle time of approximately 60 days will be experienced by most of the collieries this year. The cost of maintaining the mines over such an extended period of idleness will be very high and will result in severe financial losses. Actually if the industry is to be saved from bankruptcy, some action must be taken to bring production more closely in line with disposals.

"Action" meant closing mines: Florence, Dominion No. 4, Caledonia (by then the oldest operating colliery on the continent), No. 16 in New Waterford. I could try to describe the sorrow—the despairing meetings in the union halls, the inflamed rhetoric from the pulpit, the haunted gaze of the wives and children who understood that, as much as they had suffered, more and greater agony must now follow—but any words would be sorely inadequate. No mine lives forever, they more than anyone understood. The sheer size of the seams, along with the unceasing subsidies, had made them forget this hard truth.

These weren't nomads who packed their bags every few years when a deposit was mined out. Generations had made their careers in the same pit, creating what Ivan Rand, who headed the 1960 Royal Commission on Coal, called an "assumed state of permanence." It's hard to say at precisely what point the delusion was shattered, but No. 16 was the eleventh coal mine to shut in industrial Cape Breton since the end of the war. The colliery labour force barely topped a hundred in the Inverness area on the western side of the island. The Springhill mines were all but silent. The Pictou County coalfield, Canada's most extensively exploited field, was nearly tapped out.

Jack Briers got out, pension intact, before Florence closed, leaving three mines operating in Sydney Mines. The town's population was stagnant—or at least, so it seemed to Joan and Russ when they came to visit from Sydney and brought their three-year-old son, a boy of uncommon poise, beauty and intelligence. Somewhere there's a picture of me taken around that time. I'm being lifted in the air by Clarie Demont, who seems googly-eyed with delight at having a grandson. (Five more and a single granddaughter would follow.) The photo can't have been taken much before the day he emerged from the basement on York Street, after tending to the coal stoker, complaining of chest pains. A truly unexpected way for a man who once could outrun a stallion to go. But it was 1959. The old certainties were gone. Everything, everywhere, seemed to be shifting. Things just kept moving on.

CHAPTER FOURTEEN

Don't Worry, Be Happy

O ne afternoon, years before starting to write this book, I sat on the hood of a rental car parked over the northern end of the Sydney coalfield and let my thoughts wander. It's a holy place; the entire history of coal mining in Cape Breton lies buried underneath, in the tunnels and shafts where the GMA sunk the first shaft in the area in the early 1800s, in the men who died there, in the names of the companies that pushed farther out, beneath the massive weight of the sea floor, following the seams toward Newfoundland. It would be months before the last whistle blew in 2001 and the Prince mine, which extended eight kilometres from where I sat out under the ocean, closed. But this story was sputtering to its melancholy climax. And so, on an Indian summer day, in the parking lot outside the final coal mine operating in the province, I sipped rotgut coffee and waited for the last of Cape Breton's fabled colliers to emerge into the sunlight.

I knew the impending event was a big deal, though I didn't know much, beyond the basics, about coal mining at that point.

I had no idea, for instance, that Cape Breton was Cape Breton still—its economy stagnant, its population dwindling—after the failure of the Avro Arrow. Or that by 1962 Avro Canada had disappeared, its remaining assets taken over by Hawker Siddeley Canada. By then any optimism about Dosco's future had dimmed to a single ember barely burning. When Roe took over in 1957, the flagship Sydney steel plant employed more than 5,000 and was bound for a record-setting production year. By 1960 the owner had stopped pouring money into infrastructure and begun selling off departments that required new investment. Soon the plant's workforce had shrunk to 2,300. Two years later Dosco announced that it wanted to build a new rod and bar mill, which could use Sydney steel, in Contrecoeur, Quebec. Nova Scotia premier Robert Stanfield begged the company to build in Sydney, even offering to pony up $22 million, so Dosco would see the light. The mill went to Quebec anyway.

Dosco made no secret of its desire to unload its money-losing collieries. In 1960, twenty-seven coal mines were operating across the province. Five years later only three collieries—the McBean mine (374 men), the Drummond Coal Company (108 on the payroll) and the Greenwood colliery (104 employees)—were working in Pictou County. In Cape Breton, Dosco announced it was closing New Waterford's No. 18 mine and estimated that the other five operating on the island had fifteen more years of life left apiece. A pair of British experts hired by Dosco concluded that a $25-million infusion of capital to rehabilitate the existing mines and to open a new state-of-the-art colliery at nearby Lingan would be needed to make its coal arm viable. The catch: Hawker Siddeley didn't have the dough. Without $25 million in public money, 6,500 Nova Scotia miners would be jobless.

The threat had a familiar ring. Atlantic Canada spent most of the twentieth century listening to some industrialist threaten to pull out of the region unless the government gravy train kept running. Ottawa again found the money. Dosco pulled out anyway, leaving the federal government in a quandary: let the industry collapse, find a private buyer or nationalize the mines? The government opted to save colliery jobs in the short run but took its lead from the latest in an endless string of royal commissions examining the Cape Breton coal industry. "Future planning should be based on the assumption that the Sydney mines will not operate beyond 1981," wrote J.R. MacDonald, who suggested the creation of a federal Crown corporation empowered to handle the phase-out of the coal mines and to find ways to diversify the island's economy. Thus, armed with $50 million in new capital and a mandate to gradually close the mines only after it had created alternative employment to stop the colliery communities from fading into ghost towns, the Cape Breton Development Corporation (Devco) was born.

One day around four p.m. I drove aimlessly back and forth along the town of Dominion's waterfront until the right street magically appeared. In front of a new townhouse, a compact man sat in a lawn chair reading a newspaper. Wearing a tank top and shorts and the deep tan of a Florida pensioner, he looked to be perhaps in his early sixties. Since it was about ten degrees Celsius at the time—parts of Dominion harbour were still encrusted in ice—I stopped the car, rolled down the window and yelled, "You must be Bull Marsh." The man who may have been the toughest president ever to lead District 26 of the UMWA turned out to be eighty-six and bore long scars on both legs from knee replacements to prove it. William Marsh, who has a good-humoured face and eyes that dance like water, was as interested in picking my brain as I was his. Eventually we got around to the arrival of Devco and whether it was a welcome thing. "Private enterprise ruined the Cape Breton coal industry," he said. "Government couldn't do any worse."

The feds had a rough start. A few months later came "Black Friday," the day Hawker Siddeley announced it was shutting down the Sydney steel plant, the island's other economic pillar. Some 35,000 people marched through the city's streets in despair. Only the creation of another Crown corporation—the Sydney Steel Corporation (Sysco), operated by the Nova Scotia government— kept the plant operating. To run it the province chose Robert Burns Cameron, a "tough, shirtsleeved, blunt, profane" former war hero and Pictou County steel man who, according to the *New York Times,* liked "fat cigars, good whiskey, a cool office and vice-presidents who rip off quick answers to questions hurled at them like medicine balls." To call Cameron one of the great characters in Nova Scotia business history would be a profound understatement. R.B. wore paper clips as cufflinks, and once cut off a tedious after-dinner speaker at the Bank of Nova Scotia annual meeting—Cameron was one of the bank's largest shareholders, and a board member—by flicking off the banquet room lights mid-speech. He got results, though. Dosco said the steel mill was losing $1 million a month when it got out of the business. By 1968 Sysco was making $2.5 million a year.

No such miracle occurred at Devco. The third year in business, 1,340 of its employees snapped up early retirement packages. Its industrial development arm tried building wharves and airstrips, developing an industrial park and attracting light manufacturing, all with questionable success. Meantime, the coal business was in an uproar everywhere. In the United States, production was climbing back to postwar highs—thanks, in part, to increased foreign demand for metallurgical-quality coal for steelmaking—but some mines were cutting back and others closing altogether. The problem: a growing uproar over air pollution, which increased demand for low-sulphur coal and boded badly for collieries yielding high-sulphur output like the ones from Nova Scotia. Another shift was under way south of the border: a movement away from deep underground mines toward safer, more productive strip mines, particularly outside of the Appalachian coal belt. The end result was that as the 1970s dawned, about 135,000 people worked in the American coal industry, compared to the half a million miners who had toiled there thirty years earlier.

By then, 4,500 people were employed in Nova Scotia's mines—less than half the workforce during the height of the Second World War. That was still way too many. So Devco pushed ahead with its strategy: shutting the inefficient older mines while softening the economic blow by opening modern new ones that required far less manpower. I don't have to search far for first-hand witnesses to what ensued. Sitting in a chair on his deck, Aloysius "Wishie" Donovan was chewing a toothpick and holding a steaming mug of coffee the day I went to see him. Back in 1967, though, he was just twenty-three, a tough, capable guy with only a grade nine education but two tours of peacekeeping duty in Cyprus under his belt. The son and grandson of Glace Bay colliers, Donovan grew up thinking, I'm getting the Jesus out of here. Yet when he left the army he decided to head back to Glace Bay, where he found part-time work as a postman.

Nobody encouraged him to go underground. When a job in the mines opened up, the recruitment officer told Donovan that coal mining's long-term prospects "didn't look good" and that he was probably better off going back into the army; his father implored him to stay out of the pit. One of his brothers even begged Donovan to join him in Grande Cache, Alberta, a new town being built to develop the area's coal reserves. He stayed put and started working as a mucker—loading the coal left behind by the cutting machines—in No. 20. Donovan, who spent thirty-two years with steadily increasing responsibilities underground, had a future. No. 20—too old, unsafe and inefficient—did not. In 1971 the mine breathed its last. So did the No. 2 across town in Glace Bay, and the No. 12 in New Waterford.

"We understood the mines were going to be shut down," recalled Abbie Michalik, who worked in Glace Bay's No. 4 pit until it closed in 1961 and he headed for No. 2 just in time for it also to shut down. "But it was hard to take. It used to be that a strong back and weak mind was all you needed. But if you had no education where were you going to go? How were you going to put food on the table, clothes on your back and get your kids an education?"

We talked outside, on a point of land a short walk from the company house where he grew up in grinding coal-town poverty with his seven siblings, mother and Polish-born dad, who lost an arm while underground. If such an upbringing tends to leave scars, Michalik, a fit seventy-year-old in a tracksuit, wears them easily. As we talked, we picked our way amongst pieces of discarded mine equipment—huge diesel generators, stupendous conveyor belts, monstrous hydraulic roof supports that had to be broken down above ground, taken into the pit and reassembled—scattered in low grass like the remnants of dismembered prehistoric beasts.

By the time we reached the shoreline, he was telling me about the amazing thing that happened next: how in 1973 the sheiks called an embargo on oil shipments against any countries supporting Israel in the Yom Kippur War. Then, as oil prices surged higher, how coal emerged throughout the industrialized world as one way to reduce dependence on Middle East petroleum. In Canada, output from the collieries of Alberta and Saskatchewan climbed by nearly one-third during the three-year embargo. Across the country, Nova Scotia Power, the provincial electrical utility, began turning to coal-fired power plants. Devco management stopped thinking about winding up coal operations and starting searching for ways to expand.

Over in No. 26, Sheldon MacNeil sure felt as though a new day had broken. Another miner's son, he had been working in the X-ray department at St. Joseph's Hospital in Glace Bay when he got the call to go underground. His father had gone into the mine at age nine at a time when trapper boys earned 50¢ for each ten-hour shift. In 1970 Sheldon started out as an electrical apprentice with medical benefits, paid vacation and a real pension plan. The men were even on the clock during the ninety minutes it took to travel the five and a half miles out under the ocean to the mine face, a right his father, Daniel T., never once enjoyed. "All I can say," MacNeil tells me, in a Glace Bay Tim Hortons, "is thank God for Devco."

The bottom line still glowed red. The losses mounted. The unfunded pension liabilities soared. Anyone who looked at things soberly, in the light of day, could see that political will—that most ephemeral of things—was all that kept Devco's coal mines in business. But hope is a truly irrational thing. Suddenly, a person who really wanted to could discern a future in the Cape Breton mines. What I'm trying to say is that I had a cousin.

At Glace Bay High School, they called Kenneth Demont "Mama"— an odd nickname for a guy with a torso like the Minotaur's, who liked rattling the cerebellum of any hockey opponent stupid enough to come skating over the blue line with his head down. The nickname's origin is theatrical. One day a high school teacher decided to mount an in-class performance of *I Remember Mama*. When it came time to cast the title role, someone with an eye for the absurd blurted out, "Ken Demont," and it stuck. Irony, you see, has never been unknown in this part of the world, where old-country Gaelic still hovered in the air as the first pictures arrived from Mars. By 1975, when he was in grade ten, the wilderness was receding across Nova Scotia, the forested hills sliced by roadways, the nocturnal darkness pierced by pinpricks of light. Suburbs had arrived; disco was here. Grown men, wild on Harvey Wallbangers, exhorted their befuddled children to "sock it to me baby, let it all hang out." Housewives in miniskirts bearing vertigo-inducing geometrical designs pored over Carlos Castaneda by the light of a lava lamp. Middle-class boys stripped off their polyester shirts and streaked naked and screaming through the snowy east coast streets.

In Nova Scotia everything looked possible if you happened to be a certain age in the last quarter of the twentieth century. A university education seemed mandatory as my family continued its upward climb. Ken's parents—my Uncle Earl and Aunt Rea, whose father went into No. 11 in Glace Bay at an early age—were both teachers. His brother Bruce was bearing down with single-minded determination on med school. After high school, Ken Demont headed for the shining alma mater of his father and uncles, Acadia University. He started out studying business, then switched to sociology. In 1981, two credits shy of his degree, he got a call from a buddy back in Glace Bay; after years of downsizing, Devco was hiring again. "The money was good," Ken, a little broader and greyer, told me twenty-seven years later. "I wasn't really a traveller and didn't want to go all across the country for work." Instead, he became a gandy dancer, looking after the maintenance on a Glace Bay section of Devco railroad that ran between the No. 26 pit and the coal-wash plant.

The summer before he moved back to Glace Bay for good, I found work on the island myself. My father's cousin ate lunch every week with the editor of the *Cape Breton Post*, the Sydney daily. One phone call and I was working the evening seven-to-two shift as a junior sports reporter, which was a bit like going home again; the first time I stuck my head into the composing room, one of the linotype operators asked me if I was any relation to Clarie Demont, since they had worked together decades earlier at the Glace Bay *Gazette*. I used to hitchhike over to Sydney Mines to see my uncle Ted Singer and Aunt Mora (née Briers), or bum a ride with a co-worker to the other side of the island, where Ken's parents had a cottage overlooking the ocean not far from the old Inverness mines.

In the summer of 1980—despite being beset by insomnia and living in a converted beauty salon in downtown Sydney—I certainly didn't catch the whiff of terminal decline in the air. Afternoons, when the weather was good enough, I'd head down to the harbour and watch the coal boats heading to and from the shipping piers. At the tavern on nights off I'd see miners and steelworkers standing in the middle of the floor, daring you to bump into them. I walked around. Anybody could see it was a giddy time for them.

"More coal sold than at any other time in our history," declared the headline inside Devco's breathtakingly optimistic 1980–81 annual report. In it, the Crown corporation revelled in the three million tons it had loaded in the past year, and the investments in equipment, techniques and technology that had resulted in a per-shift productivity level double what it had been when the company took over. Omitted in the prose was one relevant point: during the most notable year in Devco's fourteen-year history, the costs of producing and selling the coal still exceeded revenues by

$10.5 million. Surprisingly, nobody seemed too concerned. "For the first time in the short history of the corporation, and perhaps in the long history of coal on Cape Breton, a long range strategic plan has been developed," the next year's annual report trumpeted.

> The revolution in coal demand has compelled us to concen-
> trate on the creation of a long range plan—twenty-five years—
> that will permit maximum benefits to accrue to the island
> economy. The plan of action, a strategic overview, demon-
> strates that the Sydney coalfield can produce more than ten
> million tonnes of coal annually by the end of the century, and
> that the vast investment required is recoverable.

By then, No. 26 was nearly tapped out and feasibility studies had already started to see if new mines into the Harbour and Phalen seams in the same area made sense. Ottawa had approved a series of proposed upgrades for the Prince mine. There was loads of grand talk about the potential for the Donkin-Morien project, which was forecast to result in the biggest underground coal mine in Canada. Reading this all these years later, you have to wonder if anyone really believed these words—or if they were shaded and reconfigured until they sounded like precisely what the political masters in Ottawa wanted to hear. Maybe the Devco executives were like those optimistic souls who think that if they say something loudly and hopefully enough, it will be so. Because everywhere else, the coal business was obviously ailing.

The coalfields of Pennsylvania and Virginia were coming off a decade of overexpansion fuelled by the growth in demand that was expected to accompany soaring oil prices. The surge never materialized, and a slump in the steel industry, the second-largest user of coal after power utilities, was causing prices to drop and layoffs to soar. In the United Kingdom, a historic clash between a prime minister unwilling to prop up what she saw as a failing industry, and the colliers clinging to their jobs and a way of life shook the country. Britain had never seen anything like the 1984 miners' strike, sparked by the threat to close twenty mines employing twenty thousand workers. It took a year to wear down the pit villages and mining communities. Even so, as the miners began to trickle back to work, no one could doubt that Margaret Thatcher had taken on the strongest union in the land and won.

In fairness, the Devco executives had no way of knowing that in the early 1980s the world would slip into recession, taking the coal market with it. Or that in 1984 Devco would be hit by a pair of fires and a decision by Sysco to close its second coke battery, another blow to domestic sales. As the losses climbed, a new government with a free-market ethos swept into power in Ottawa. Brian Mulroney—perhaps with an eye on his British counterpart—decreed a commercial mandate for Devco; the industrial development function was handed over to a new Crown corporation. Now solely a coal company, Devco was ordered to make across-the-board cuts.

My cousin was one of them. In 1987, after finishing his BA at the University College of Cape Breton, he got on with a local brewer. A year later he received a call from Devco; a job had opened up. But it was underground. Turn it down and you'll be struck off the company books forever, he was warned. Ken was destined for the Prince colliery out at Point Aconi. Then, just as the month-long training ended, he learned that he was bound instead for the gassier Lingan-Phalen colliery.

He was twenty-nine years old and had never been underground in a real working coal mine, so his eyes itched from lack of sleep when he walked into the wash house the first day. It spooked him to hear the walls shift and creak during the walk from the rake to the workface. There, they took one look at his size and told him to start erecting the wooden chocks used to support opened sections of roof until steel arches could be inserted. "I was right down there on the battlefield the first day on the job," he recalls. "They just threw me to the wolves."

For six months he hated everything about the work. One night he was working the back shift—eleven p.m. to seven a.m.—on top of the wall, the dirtiest spot on the pit. It was so dark that he couldn't see his hand in front of his face. The wood was slick with ice: "It was like fighting with a harbour seal." If ever there was a moment when he said, I'm out of here, it was then. And at that precise moment, something magical happened. To this day Ken's unsure whether his buddy in the control room pumped radio station CJCB throughout the entire mine, or just in the section where he was working. All he knows is that suddenly, inexplicably, Bobby McFerrin's soaring falsetto a cappella voice—which was everywhere on the CJCB airwaves in 1988—filled his ears. "I said, if you're here, well, the hell with it—you're here," Ken recalled. "Don't worry. Be happy."

The mine was still a dangerous place. A man died in Lingan the same year Ken went underground there; a friend lost a ring finger, other miners busted limbs and suffered concussions. One day in 1993 Ken blew out his anterior cruciate ligament, forcing him to leave the steep slopes of Lingan and move over to the Prince mine—one of only two still operating in the province, now that Westray had shut for good.

By then, my work was taking me back to Glace Bay again. Even I could see that, without a single operating mine, the place lacked its muscular purpose. Charlie MacLeod's bookstore had disappeared. So had the Union Marketeria, Zilbert Bros. grocery store and the old stone wall near Knox Hall where the teens used to hang out when I visited on summer vacations. Some of the landmarks around Senator's Corner—Ellie Marshall's Store, Markadonis's Shoe Repair, the Savoy Theatre where I noticed, on one visit in the mid-1990s, that the old R & B crooners the Platters were set to perform—lived on. Wandering the streets, searching for the kinds of characters that populated my dad's stories, I now found mostly pensioners, the spring gone from their step, their wild days barely a trace in the wind.

So few of them were my people. The Briers connection on this island had dwindled to an aunt, uncle, first cousin and some distant relatives. The DeMonts were hanging in, but Ken—who had a long-time partner, Anne, but no children—might be the last relative of mine bearing that name to live here. Dispersed as we were to the mainland of Nova Scotia, Ontario, Quebec and the United States, we were plainly part of the Cape Breton diaspora. In the last twenty-five years, while the population of Canada has grown by one-third, Cape Breton has lost 14 percent of its people. Rural areas everywhere in North America are emptying out. People here were even leaving the Cape Breton Regional Municipality, the newly formed amal-gam of the island's colliery towns. An unnerving percentage of those left behind were senior citizens or people lacking the skills to make it elsewhere.

Coal couldn't save them. Globally its market continued to plummet; at home Nova Scotia Power continued to depend upon high-quality coal from abroad to run its thermal plants. Nova Scotians had run out of patience with the strikes, the rampant absenteeism and the poor productivity in the mines. They had had it with the staggering amounts of money—by some sources as much as $3 billion from Devco's creation until 2000—that successive federal governments had spent to keep the company afloat. As the millennial end loomed, coal miners, increasingly, were seen as idle deadbeats forever draining the public purse. No one could remember the time when Cape Breton coal had fired the war effort and industrialized the country.

By 2000, if Ken didn't quite love the work, he at least enjoyed the sense of accomplishment, the camaraderie and the decent wages. Like most of the newcomers, he had signed on thinking he might have a job for life. Anyone could see that that promise wasn't going to be kept. Instead, he took a severance package and headed for the local college to enrol in a course to become a residential community worker. His timing was impeccable; within months, the last whistle sounded at the Phalen mine and Devco management announced they wanted to sell the Prince. With no buyer in hand, they said they had no option but to close Cape Breton's last subterranean coal mine even though Devco had failed to fulfill its mandate to diversify the Cape Breton economy. Which is why, one summer day in 2001, I hopped in a rental car in Halifax and started driving toward Point Aconi.

On the way, I took a detour. I wanted a last glimpse of the Sydney steel plant. After pumping an estimated $2.8 billion into it, the provincial government was giving up—shutting the mill, auctioning off the assets and putting hundreds more out of work on an island where the jobless rate already approached triple the national average. Steel left another legacy; the old tidal estuary leading to the harbour, now so thick with raw sewage and poisons that a grown man could stand on the surface, had become one of the worst toxic waste sites in North America. Upstream from the Sydney tar ponds stood the abandoned coke ovens plant, polluted to a depth of twenty-four metres with tar, ammonia, light oils, benzol, ammonium sulphate and other by-products. Farther to the west, crowned by a handful of rickety wooden houses, loomed the city's landfill—sixty hectares of waste, in places sixty metres deep—accumulated over a century of uncontrolled dumping.

A few months earlier, an affable ex-serviceman named Eric Brophy had taken me for a spin through Whitney Pier, around the mill and coke ovens. Within the space of two blocks, Brophy reeled off the names of dozens of former and current residents who had died from cancer or heart disease. They weren't strangers, these names on the roll call of woe. Brophy pointed out where his old pal Charlie had lived, the place where his buddy Wally had grown up and the homes where his childhood cronies Fraser and Alex had resided before cancer took them. He drove by the house where his first wife, Lorraine, who had died from the disease in 1995, had been born, and the small home where his current wife, Peggy—who had contracted cervical cancer and had later lost her first husband to cancer—had grown up. Brophy even showed me the house where he had lived as a child, and where his father, Frank, another cancer victim, probably contracted the disease.

It was the bleakest possible symbol of post-industrial Cape Breton. Yet there were so many ways for a visitor to understand that this place was on a new trajectory: the humming silence of the vacant houses and boarded-up storefronts in New Waterford; the news that the UMWA's fabled District 26 had been placed in receivership because of a precipitous loss in dues-paying members. I kept hearing that Glace Bay was still a great place to grow up. The young were leaving in droves. Once boasting a dozen coal mines, Glace Bay was Devco's town no longer, a fact reinforced when a call centre—one of the few growth industries on the island—took over the Crown corporation's old offices there.

At Point Aconi—the air soft with summer heat—I screwed up my brow and tried to picture the men underground on those subterranean roads that ran out under the Atlantic Ocean. Mid-afternoon, which meant that the day shift would be on the way back, inside metal cars, maybe sitting silent instead of playing tarbish, the island's distinctive card game, and talking to pass the forty-five minutes it takes to reach the surface. Once there, take off the helmet and overalls, hang the work clothes on the hooks and head for the shower to wash off the grime. Then, hair still slick—dressed for all the world as blandly as a flock of Etobicoke accountants bound for Home Depot on a Saturday morning—they would emerge into the parking lot.

There was a time when they might have picked up speed heading for their cars. Today, they seemed in no hurry to board their Dodge Dakotas, Ford Windstars and Honda Civics. I walked over to a couple of them, reporter's notebook in hand, and asked how they felt about things. To a man, I can see from my notes, they were polite and patient—weary stoics more than disappointed cynics. They talked about the uncertainty over what was next, and how it was hard to know who you were when the thing that most defined you disappeared. At that point, all they knew was what was about to vanish—not what the future, which has a tendency to take care of itself, would bring. I came from a world of five-year plans, high-fibre diets and the dream of a cushy retirement. Words fail me when I try to say how much I admired them standing there on the cusp of the new millennium, in a world bereft of all certainty.

One of them was a year older than me. His name was Steve Woods and his people had been going underground in Cape Breton for five generations. As we talked I discovered that his folk, like mine, came from England, where home was likewise Lancashire. Our ancestors, in both cases, would have arrived in a swirling haze of desire. The pioneer days were over. All they had was a setting and a sense of urgency. For a time their lives continued in parallel, until something caused them to diverge. And maybe all that separated us—a man with uncallused hands trying to make some sense of his past and another, who worked in a tunnel under the ocean, with a question mark for a future—was a choice here and a road not taken there. Writing these words years later, at a desk in Halifax, I'm still not sure. Yet I do remember that day: the light filling the afternoon, the rank taste of the coffee, and the stiff-legged walk of the miners before they climbed into their cars and vans and disappeared into legend.

EPILOGUE

Way Down in the Hole

Outside of Westville, just off a Pictou County back-country road in a place where pavement, field and forest convene, I found a spot where the land had been peeled back and chunked out. Three strip mines operated in Nova Scotia in the spring of 2007, the year a ton of coal topped the heretofore unheard-of price of $125 U.S. From an embankment hundreds of feet up and away, I watched earthmovers the size of scallop draggers scrape off layers of topography until the exposed terrain glowed black and blighted. They worked inland, in sections, a slab of wall a few football fields high marking their farthest advance. It was shot through with holes; clustered tightly together, some of them pierced the rock so unexpectedly that you could imagine the wonder when some future citizen encountered them, like cliffside caves from an ancient culture. I imagine their faces looking a lot like my own, as I stand here as shocked as Pizarro before the Incan Sun Temple. It had been six years since a Nova Scotian had gone into a coal-mine shaft. Weekly I perused the obituaries of the last generation of the province's coal miners.

Meanwhile, the final physical remnants of its coal-black past—the pitheads, shipping piers and old railway lines—were being eroded, buried and carried away. Before long, the only above-ground hints that something extraordinary had once occurred here would be some songs and books, and a scattering of museums, plaques and memorials sprinkled through the old towns.

Way down in the hole, though, tunnels lurked. From where I stood it was only possible to see a cross-section of the underground maze where all those personal stories connected. Inside the rock, I knew, were passageways where heroes had battled, tragedies had transpired and time had hung stubborn and heavy. At the Nova Scotia Department of Natural Resources library I found a map that showed every abandoned shaft, hillside tunnel, trench and other mine opening in the province. I spread it out on top of a couple of filing cabinets. Then I counted the black triangles marking coal-mine remnants, in parts so numerous they threatened to blot out the map below, until my eyes started to cross. But I still lacked a sense of how much of this province had been anthilled in the search for coal.

One day I called Ross McCurdy, the president of once-mighty Devco, who now spent his time selling off what remained of the dismantled steel mill, coke ovens and battery plant for scrap. He told me that 3,200 kilometres of mine workings streaked the Cape Breton landscape. The sheer magnitude of that number—equivalent to the distance from Halifax to Saskatoon—set my brain buzzing. I started to collect stories about island schools, backyards and seniors' clubs suddenly sinking into the ground, claimed by abandoned mine shafts underneath. Throughout my travels—like a war buff visiting places where lots of blood had been spilled—I made it a point to go and see places where I knew these pathways ran underfoot. They were surprisingly easy to find. In some places there were signs to show me the way. In others, I'd just get directions and drive through the towns that had grown up around them, passing some of the last company houses, still unmistakable despite the layers of paint, steering my car along streets named after old mines and all-but-forgotten managers, through ethnic enclaves, past beds where rail lines once lay and the final ruins of some wrecked foundry slumped.

Eventually, in the middle of these communities, I'd come upon the rolling terrain once home to No. 4 in Glace Bay, the Princess in Sydney Mines and No. 2 in Springhill, where birds now called and winds carried the smell of wet stone. Ghosts, if they walked anywhere, surely trod here, on which nothing loftier than scrub grass, low bush and heather seemed to grow. In the long run, Devco's plan was to "reclaim" eleven thousand of these acres. With time the old mine properties would be returned to forestland or transformed into ball fields, nature trails or other community green spaces.

Often when I moseyed around the old colliery lands it seemed as though the narrative was complete: my people, like so many others touched by coal, scattered to the winds; whole sections of Nova Scotia—their economies more redolent of the nineteenth century than the twenty-first, their industrial towns fading, their resources forever enriching folk elsewhere—locked in a slow, sad spiral. Sometimes I looked ahead and saw a Glace Bay, Westville or Springhill ravaged by drug abuse, crime and woeful health statistics.

Some days, though, I saw a different kind of future, one that would involve the kind of fundamental change necessary to alter the coal communities' predestined path. I'd see glimpses of what could be, in funny places: sitting in a car overlooking Sydney harbour as a local lawyer, as if under the influence of some powerful hallucinogen, described the bulk freighters, post-Panamax container ships and cruise lines he envisioned transforming the harbour into an economic driver for the region; slicing into a strip loin at a restaurant in a new Sydney-area trade and convention centre owned by the Membertou First Nation. One time I took a tour of the old tar ponds site. Though the mountains of leftover steel slag resembled a moonscape, clear land now stood where the coke ovens and steel plant had once loomed. Whole sections of the site—along the brook being rerouted to carry clean water into the tar ponds, on the old dump site turned grassy knoll, at the tidal lagoon where ducks and gulls floated—seemed leafy, alive, almost tranquil. Another day, driving on the outskirts of Glace Bay over a labyrinth of abandoned tunnels, I came upon a line of wind turbines, sleek, white and ten storeys high. I pulled up even with a car stopped on the shoulder of the road and asked how long they'd been there. "Since yesterday, I think," an older man in the driver's seat said. And then we both turned and watched the giant blades run the lights in the surrounding community.

On still another day, not far from there, my cousin Ken and I went for a spin. We stayed on the highway until we hit the community of Donkin, then took a sharp left over a little causeway by a stretch of craggy beach. From there we followed a neat gravel road until we reached the chain-link fence and "No Trespassing" sign. A quarter-century ago—during Devco's headiest days—the Crown corporation spent $100 million on a couple of exploratory tunnels into a seam thought to contain more coal than the combined tonnage of everything mined in the island's history. Then the price of coal tumbled. The tunnels were allowed to flood with water. The big corrugated metal storage shed and concrete pithead portals were left to the fog and salt air.

Until, that is, China's coal-powered economy started to sizzle. Across North America, fears intensified about the safety of supplies of natural gas, electricity's other main fuel source, pushing coal to the fore yet again. Let Al Gore yak about the costs of releasing all that carbon dioxide into the atmosphere—by 2008, as I was putting the finishing touches on this book, coal, for better or worse, was back, baby. Even in Nova Scotia, where the government had handed a consortium headed by a Swiss multinational the right to develop the Donkin seam, which would create three hundred underground mining jobs.

Nobody in his right mind expected coal to rule the future as it had dominated the past. Yet these towns were always essentially acts of faith, where dreaming of the impossible was all that ever made sense. So when my cousin Ken, car idling outside the gates into the Donkin pit-head, said he'd be willing to go back underground if a job came up there, he was simply proving that the dream still lived in this time and place. It wasn't a dream that appeared ripe with promise, that spoke of new beginnings or a glittering future. But I now knew that this had never been coal's lesson anyway. Geography is fate, my search had taught me, and only liars say the world is fair or that things will necessarily turn out all right. But these things too: watch your buddy's back; hold onto hope. Most of all: onward.

Acknowledgements

The most obvious debts of thanks for this book are to the coal miners of Nova Scotia and my family members who lived the story contained within these pages.

An immense thanks goes out to my parents, Joan and Russ DeMont, for countless reasons. But I'm also deeply indebted to my aunts, uncles and cousins on the Briers and DeMont sides of the family who, over the years, filled my mind with the stories you've just read. My uncles Earl Demont and Eric DeMont, my aunt Rea Demont and my cousins Kenneth Demont and Lynda Singer were particularly generous with their time, thoughts, experiences and hospitality. I also want to thank my brother Philip and cousins Frank DeMont and Wendy Clattenburg for their insights.

I'm forever indebted to the family genealogists Allen DeMont and Frank V. DeMont and Andrew Alston for their help in charting the family narrative. Andrew's generosity—he also supplied knowledge about Lancashire life—will forever stand as the standard by which such a thing is measured.

The open-heartedness of the great Nova Scotia labour historians Daniel Samson, David Frank and Donald MacGillivray—who
endured my rudimentary questioning, read long portions of the
book and supplied invaluable insights—will not easily be forgotten. Nor will the kindness of John Calder, who helped me understand the big picture and what Nova Scotia means to the geological
world—or of Jim Myers, who shared his knowledge of sporting life
in Cape Breton. My immense thanks, also, to the writers Peter
Moreira and Arnie Patterson, Elizabeth Beaton of Cape Breton
University and historian Howard MacKinnon, all of whom who
read parts of the manuscript and provided key corrections.

Dean Cooke, the wisest of agents, came up with the idea for
the book and made it happen. At Doubleday, Tim Rostron, and
freelance copyeditor, Gena Gorrell, took my unhewn lumber and
fashioned it into something. Susan Burns willed it into being.

A big shout out to my children, Belle and Sam, for their encouragement and keeping me grounded in the here-and-now. The
biggest thanks of all to Lisa Napier, just for everything.

Notes

PROLOGUE: A COLONY OF MINERS

The concept of coal being a book that speaks through fossils comes via geologist Anita Harris as quoted in John McPhee, *Annals of the Former World*, p. 156.

The quote about the nature of fossil energy comes from Bill McKibben, *Deep Economy: The Wealth of Communities and the Durable Future*, (New York: Times Books, 2007), p. 15.

The information about the first white settlers in Pictou comes from Reverend George Patterson, *History of the County of Pictou*, 1877.

The theory about the first white man to use coal comes from Cameron, *The Pictonian Colliers*, p. 16.

The Mi'kmaq relationship with coal comes from Richard, Report of the Westray Mine Public Inquiry, *The Westray Story: A Predictable Path to Disaster*, Vol. 1, p. 3.

The dimensions of the Pictou Coal field come from John Calder, *Coal in Nova Scotia*, a document prepared for the Nova Scotia Department of Natural Resources, Mineral Resources Branch, 1995.

The quote about the Stellarton seam comes from Richard, *The Westray Story*, Vol. 1, p. 6.

The early days of the General Mining Association in Pictou come from Cameron, *The Pictonian Colliers*, p. 8, and Richard, *The Westray Story*, Vol. 1, p. 8.

The "colony of miners" quote comes through Samson, "Industrial Colonization: The Colonial Context of the General Mining Association, Nova Scotia, 1825–1842," p. 19.

The information about how heavily mined the Pictou seams were relative to others comes from Cameron, *The Pictonian Colliers*, p. 3.

The total coal tonnage mined in Nova Scotia comes from an email exchange with John Calder, a geologist with the Nova Scotia Department of Natural Resources.

The figure on coal mining deaths and the descriptions of the causes comes from the Nova Scotia Mine fatalities 1838–1992 database, Nova Scotia Archives and Records Management.

The estimate on Nova Scotian deaths in the Great War comes from the Nova Scotia archives.

The description of the damps comes from Richard, *The Westray Story*, Vol. 1, p. 13.

The estimate on deaths in the Pictou Mines comes from Cameron, *The Pictonian Colliers*, p. 170.

The description of the Drummond disaster comes from the *Presbyterian Witness* of May 1873, by Richard MacNeil, as quoted on Pictou County GenWeb.

The notion of coal bringing the world out of the agrarian age comes from Freese, *Coal: A Human History*, p. 14.

For the entire interview with Frame see John DeMont, Carl Mollins and John Daly, "Clearing the Air," *Maclean's*, April 19, 1993.

For more on the political background to the Westray disaster and Eugene Johnson see John DeMont with Glen Allen, "Legacy of Despair: As the first anniversary of a tragedy approaches, controversy still swirls around the Westray case," *Maclean's*, April 19, 1993.

The description of what actually happened in the Westray mine on the day of the disaster comes from Richard, *The Westray Story*, Vol. 1, pp. 206–207.

CHAPTER ONE: NO VESTIGE OF A BEGINNING

The "big picture" line comes from McPhee, *Annals of the Former World*, p. 62. His elaboration of the concept comes from the same book, p. 63.

Biographical information about Gesner comes from Loris Russell's entry on Gesner in the *Dictionary of Canadian Biography*.

The quote from Gesner's *Remarks on the Geology and Mineralogy of Nova Scotia* is from the Gossip and Coade edition, 1836, p. 4.

The quote about Gesner's lack of business acumen comes from Loris Russell in his entry about Gesner in the *Dictionary of Canadian Biography*.

The theory that the world came to be after a collision between the sun and a comet comes via the incredible French nobleman Georges-Louis Leclerc de Buffon, a naturalist, mathematician, biologist, cosmologist and author who, a century before Darwin, published a forty-four-volume encyclopedia of natural history that, among other things, explored the similarities between man and apes.

The cooling gas cloud theory of creation was hatched by Pièrre-Simon Laplace, a brainy astronomer and mathematician who sat around thinking about such things in the late 18th and early 19th centuries.

Lyell's "the present is the key to the past" quote comes from a variety of sources.

Darwin's take on the formation of coal comes from John H. Calder, "'Coal Age Galapagos': Joggins and the Lions of Nineteenth Century Geology," *Atlantic Geology*, 2006, pp. 44–45.

The background on Logan comes from Charles H. Smith, "Sir William Logan, Father of Canadian Geology: His Passion was Precision," in *GSA Today*, May 2000, pp. 20–23.

The quote about Lyell's enthusiasm to see Joggins comes from Lyell, *Travels in North America* (1845), pp. 177–178 (quoted in Calder, *Coal Age Galapagos*, pp. 39–40).

The explanation of tectonic plate theory is based on McPhee, *Annals of the Former World*, pp. 115–126, and author's interviews with John Calder.

The information on the early natural history of Nova Scotia comes from *The Last Billion Years, A Geological History of the Maritime Provinces of Canada*, Atlantic Geoscience Society (Halifax: Nimbus Publishing, 2001).

Lyell's letter to his sister is quoted by Andrew Scott, "Roasted Alive in the Carboniferous," in *Geoscience*, March 2001.

The idea of coal as ancient sunlight comes from Freese, *Coal: A Human History*, pp. 3–7.

The information on how coal was formed comes from a variety of sources including *The Last Billion Years*, p. 109–116, Freese, pp. 17–21, and the author's interview with Calder.

The anecdote and quotes about Lyell and Dawson's meeting comes from Dawson, *Fifty Years of Work in Canada, Scientific and Educational*, pp. 50–51.

The general biographical material about Dawson comes from Peter R. Eakins and Jean Eakins, *Dictionary of Canadian Biography* online, from Howard Falcon-Lang and John Calder, "Sir William Dawson (1820–1899): A very modern paleobotanist," *Atlantic Geology*, 2005, pp. 103–114, and from Dawson, *Fifty Years of Work in Canada*.

The quotes about Dawson's introduction to geology comes from Dawson, *Fifty Years of Work in Canada*, pp. 34–36.

The story of the discovery of *Hylonomus lyelli*, comes from John H. Calder, "'Coal Age Galapagos': Joggins and the Lions of Nineteenth Century Geology," p. 46 and S.J. Davies, M.R. Gibling, M.C. Rygel, J.H. Calder and D.M. Skilliter, "The Pennsylvanian Joggins Formation of Nova Scotia: sedimentological log and stratigraphic framework of the historic fossil cliffs," *Atlantic Geology*, 2005, p. 116.

The analysis of the importance of the discovery—and its influence on Darwin—comes from Calder, "'Coal Age Galapagos': Joggins and the Lions of Nineteenth Century Geology," pp. 38 and 44, and Davies, Gibling, Rygel, Calder and Skilliter, "The Pennsylvanian Joggins Formation of Nova Scotia: Sedimentological log and stratigraphic framework of the historic fossil cliffs," p. 116.

The first Darwin quote comes from *The Origin of Species*, Plain Label Books (http://tinyurl.com/5uzyw5), accessed May 2007, p. 441. The second comes from Allan J. Tobin and Jennie Dusheck, *Asking About Life: Exploring the Earth* (Belmont, Calif.: Thomas, Brooks/Cole, 2004), p. 305.

Dawson's description of his rock-hounding days comes from Dawson, *Fifty Years of Work in Canada*, pp. 79–81.

Dawson's appraisal of the various coalfields of Nova Scotia comes from Dawson, *Acadian Geology, The Geological Structure, Organic Remains and Mineral Resources of Nova Scotia, New Brunswick and Prince Edward Island*, pp. 20, 408 and 410.

The dimensions of the Sydney coalfield come from a monograph, *Origins of Coal*, Nova Scotia Department of Natural Resources.

The description of the Stellarton formation comes from Calder, *Coal in Nova Scotia*, a monograph for the Nova Scotia Department of Natural Resources, Mineral Resources Branch, Series ME 8, 1995.

Dawson's appraisal of the coalfields of Nova Scotia come from Dawson, *Acadian Geology*, p. 4.

CHAPTER TWO: BENEATH THE GOLDEN SALMON

The early global history of coal comes from Bruce G. Miller, *Coal Energy Systems*, Academic Press, 2005; Freese, *Coal: A Human History*; John Hatcher, *The History of the British Coal Industry*, Vol. 1 (Oxford University Press, 1986). For more on the extent of the timber famine in

16th century England see Hatcher, *The History of the British Coal Industry*, Vol. 1, pp. 16–22.

The quote from Marco Polo comes from *The Travels of Marco Polo*.

The information about Henry VIII, the break with the church and its influence on coal comes from Freese, *Coal: A Human History*, pp. 28–29.

The descriptions of the Cape Breton voyages by Captain Strong, Captain Leigh, Samuel de Champlain and Nicholas Denys come from Richard Brown, *The Coal Fields and Coal Trade of the Island of Cape Breton*, pp. 32–34.

The information on Jean Talon comes from André Vachon's entry on him in the *Canadian Dictionary of Biography*.

The information on the early French usage of coal in Nova Scotia comes from a 2004 CBC online background report on Cape Breton coal miners (http://www.cbc.ca/news/background/capebreton/) Accessed November 2007.

The line about British and French stopping in Cape Breton in the 1700s and Admiral Walker's visit comes from Brown, *The Coal Fields and Coal Trade of the Island of Cape Breton*, p. 35.

The information about the very earliest extraction methods comes from Hugh Millward, "Mine Locations and the Sequence of Coal Exploitation on the Sydney Coalfield, 1720–1980," which appears in *Cape Breton at 200, Historical Essays in Honour of the Island's Bicentennial 1785–1985* (Sydney, N.S.: University College of Cape Breton Press, 1985), p. 190.

The section about founding and history of Louisbourg is gleaned from William Wood, *A Great Fortress: A Chronicle of Louisbourg, 1720–1760* (online edition); Jim and Pat Lotz, *Cape Breton Island* (Vancouver: Douglas David & Charles, 1974); Lesley Choyce, *Nova Scotia, Shaped by the Sea: A Living History* (Toronto: Viking Books, 1996), and the *History of the Fortress of Louisbourg* (Louisbourg, N.S.: Louisbourg Institute).

The quote from Louisbourg's Governor Pontchartrain comes from Choyce, *Nova Scotia, Shaped by the Sea: A Living History*, p. 62.

The information about the English efforts at Burnt Head comes from Brian
Tennyson and Roger Sarty, *Guardian of the Gulf: Cape Breton and the
Atlantic Wars* (Toronto: University of Toronto Press, 2002), pp. 15–17.

For the details of the lease changes over the years I depended upon historian
J.S. Martell, "Early Coal Mining in Nova Scotia," in *Cape Breton Historical
Essays* (Sydney, N.S.: College of Cape Breton Press, 1980) and Hugh
Millward, "Mine Operators and Mining Leases on Nova Scotia's Sydney
Coalfield, 1720 to the Present," in *Nova Scotia Historical Review*, Vol. 13,
number 2, 1993.

For the section on the creation of the steam engine I used Freese, *Coal: A
Human History*, pp. 43–69, and Bill McKibben, *Deep Economy, the Wealth
of Communities and the Durable Future*, pp. 5–8.

The figures for coal production in Nova Scotia in 1820 come from Brown, *The
Coal Fields and Coal Trade of the Island of Cape Breton*, p. 55.

The information about the coal industry in the early 1800s comes from
Stephen J. Hornsby, *Nineteenth-Century Cape Breton: A Historical
Geography* (Montreal: McGill-Queen's University Press, 1992), pp. 15–16.

The quote from Brown about the government's approach to leasing comes
from *The Coal Fields and Coal Trade of the Island of Cape Breton*, p. 67.

The information about Crown ownership of land in Nova Scotia comes from
Martell, "Early Coal Mining in Nova Scotia," p. 41.

The quote from Francis W. Gray comes from Gray, *The Coal-fields and Coal
Industry of Eastern Canada*, completed for the Department of Mines,
Ottawa, 1916.

The anecdote about John McKay comes from Cameron, *The Pictonian Colliers*,
pp. 17–18.

The figures about the state of the 1825 Nova Scotia coal industry come
from Brown, *The Coal Fields and Coal Trade of the Island of Cape Breton*,
pp. 148–149.

The description of Mount Rundell and the illustrious list of visitors comes
from Cameron, *The Pictonian Colliers*, pp. 24–25, and "Stellarton House

Considered One of the Most Historic in N.S.," *New Glasgow Evening News*, New Glasgow, N.S., April 8, 1973.

I learned of Fox's history of Rundell, Bridge and Rundell from Robert W. Lovett, "Rundell, Bridge and Rundell—An Early Company History," published in the *Bulletin of the Business Historical Society*, March, 1949. I also consulted J.S. Martell, "Early Coal Mining in Nova Scotia" and Edwin T. Bliss's paper "Albion Mines," read before the Nova Scotia Historical Society, March 7, 1975. I'm particularly indebted for the thoughts of historian Daniel Samson and also his essay "Industrial Colonization: The Colonial Context of the General Mining Association of Nova Scotia, 1825–1842."

The line about "the sign of the golden salmon" comes from Lovett, "Rundell, Bridge and Rundell—An Early Company History," p. 152.

The material about Rundell Bridge and Rundell's appointment as royal goldsmiths comes from Christopher Hartop, "Royal Goldsmiths: The Art of Rundell and Bridge and Its Successors," *The Magazine Antiques*, June 1, 2005.

The extent of Rundell Bridge and Rundell's operations in the 1820s comes from an entry on Rundell and Bridge Silver on the Georgian Index website (http://www.georgianindex.net).

The Duke of York's "By God I'll have everything the same at mine" quote comes via Martell, "Early Coal Mining in Nova Scotia," p. 48.

The quote about his spendthrift ways comes from Maev Kennedy, "Duke's Silver Service on Show," *The Guardian*, Nov. 27, 2002.

The information about the Duke's debts in 1825 comes from Martell, "Early Coal Mining in Nova Scotia," p. 48.

The story of the Duchess of York approaching Christie's to sell the Duke's silver collection is from Eva Czernis-Ryl, "The Duke of York Baskets," in *World of Antiques & Art*, online edition (http://www.worldaa.com).

Information about the state of the British investment world in the 1820s is from Samson, "Industrial Colonization: The Colonial Context of the General Mining Association of Nova Scotia, 1825–1842," p. 5.

The information on the formation of the Columbian Pearl Fishery Association comes from Lovett, "Rundell, Bridge and Rundell—An Early Company History." p. 160.

The Columbian Pearl Fishery Association's decision to abandon South America comes from Samson, "Industrial Colonization: The Colonial Context of the General Mining Association of Nova Scotia, 1825–1842," p. 6.

Martell, "Early Coal Mining in Nova Scotia," p. 48, is my source for information about the Nova Scotia minerals lease.

A copy of the Duke's lease for the mineral rights of Nova Scotia, signed 11 July 1826, London, by Liverpool, F.J. Robinson and G.C.H. Somerset, by His Majesty's Command is on file with Nova Scotia Archives.

The analysis of the Duke's lease swap with Rundell Bridge and Rundell comes from Samson, "Industrial Colonization: The Colonial Context of the General Mining Association of Nova Scotia, 1825–1842," p. 4.

The information about the assessment of Nova Scotia's mineral wealth conducted for the General Mining Association comes from Brown, *The Coal Fields and Coal Trade of the Island of Cape Breton*, p. 56.

CHAPTER THREE: A PONDEROUS PYRAMID OF RUINS

The description of the GMA's arrival in Stellarton comes from Cameron, *The Pictonian Colliers*, pp. 21–25.

The drawing of Smith is found in Cameron, *The Pictonian Colliers*, p. 138.

The biographical information about Smith comes from David Frank's entry on him in the *Dictionary of Canadian Biography*.

The derivation of Albion comes from Cameron, *The Pictonian Colliers*, p. 22.

The early history of Albion Mines comes from Richard, *The Westray Story*, p. 8.

The quote from *One Hundred Years of Solitude* comes from the Harper & Row edition, 1970, p. 233.

The description of Albion Mines circa 1830 is found in Joseph Howe, *Western and Eastern Rambles, Travel Sketches of Nova Scotia*, edited by M.G. Parks (Toronto: University of Toronto Press, 1973), pp. 159–167.

Brown's background in England comes from the Brown Family fonds, on file at the Nova Scotia Archives.

The description of Sydney Mines in 1836 emerges from Brown, *The Coal Fields and Coal Trade of the Island of Cape Breton and The History of Sydney Mines*, p. 168.

The picture I saw of Richard Brown was in volume 17 of the Nova Scotia Historical Society Collections, 1913, p. 99. The description of his career and the quote from the Canadian mining journal comes from *The History of Sydney Mines*, pp. 19–20.

Brown's discovery that most of the land in Nova Scotia was already leased comes from Brown, *The Coal Fields and Coal Trade of the Island of Cape Breton*, p. 57.

The quotes from Smith and Liddell come from Samson, "Industrial Colonization: The Colonial Context of the General Mining Association Nova Scotia, 1825–1842," p. 9.

The information about the GMA's sweetheart deal come from Marilyn Gerriets, "Impact of the General Mining Association on the Nova Scotia Coal Industry, 1826–1850," in *Acadiensis*, Autumn 1991, pp. 62–63.

I based much of the summary of the mass migration from Scotland to Cape Breton that follows on Stephen Hornsby's book, *Nineteenth-Century Cape Breton, A Historical Geography* (Montreal and Kingston, Ont.: McGill-Queen's University Press, 1992).

I based my musings on Alexander Beaton on correspondence between Beaton and British MP Charles Grant—stamped received June 15, 1830—which includes a list of emigrants on an unnamed ship from Skye who settled in Margaree. It's found on The Ship's List (http://www.theshipslist.com), an online compendium of ship's passenger lists to North America, Australia and South Africa. The description of the ship is extrapolated from Hornsby's book *Nineteenth Century Cape Breton*, where the quote by the Nova Scotia MLA appears on p. 47.

The information attributed to Gesner comes from Robert Morgan, *Early Cape Breton from Founding to Famine*, (Wreck Cove, N.S.: Breton Books, 2000), p. 138.

The description of the coal extraction methods of the day come from Hugh Millward, "Mine Locations and the Sequence of Coal Exploitation on the Sydney Coalfield, 1720–1980," in *Cape Breton at 200, Historical Essays in Honor of the Island's Bicentennial 1785–1985*, pp. 191 and 199.

The description of the Sydney Mines and the work conditions there come from Brown, *The Coal Fields and Coal Trade of the Island of Cape Breton*, pp. 50–54.

I'm indebted to Daniel Samson for an explanation of how the truck system worked.

CHAPTER FOUR: WHO COULD LIVE IN SUCH A HOLE?

The Briers biographical material comes from genealogical records, many of them hunted resolutely down by Andrew Alston, who also provided information about the topography of Lancashire.

The information about St. Helens comes from *A Brief History of St. Helens*, published by St. Helens Council and Tim Lambert, "A Brief History of St. Helens" (http://www.localhistories.org/sthelens.html)

For the section on the growth of the weaving industry of Lancashire, I'm indebted to Manchester City Council's website "Spinning the Web: The Story of the Cotton Industry" (http://www.spinningtheweb.org.uk).

The information about spinning mills in 1830 comes from John Simkin, "Cotton Industry," Spartacus Educational online encyclopedia (http://www.spartacus.schoolnet.co.uk/TEXcotton.htm).

I based much of the description of urban life during the Industrial Revolution upon Andrew Taylor's entry in "Cottontown," a web history compiled by the Blackburn with Darwen Borough Council (http://www.cottontown.org/page.cfm?pageid=257prepared).

De Tocqueville's description of Manchester is quoted in Murray Bookchin, *The Ecology of Freedom, The Emergence and Dissolution of Hierarchy.* (Oakland, Calif.: AK Press, 2005), p. 390.

The quote from Charles Dickens comes from *Hard Times.*

The quote from the nobleman visiting Manchester is found in the Mill Workers section of "Spinning the Web: The Story of the Cotton Industry 1760–1820."

The figures for women working in coal mines comes from Lynne Mayers's *Bal Maidens and Mining Women* website (http://www.balmaiden.co.uk/). The numbers for children come from Simkin, "Cotton Industry".

The information about compulsory schooling comes from "School Leaving Age May be Raised," BBC News, Nov. 10, 2006 (http://news.bbc.co.uk/1/hi/education/6135516.stm), along with *The Cambridge History of English and American Literature in 18 Volumes* (1907–21), Volume XIV, The Victorian Age, Part Two.

Peter Gaskell's description of the cotton mills comes from Gaskell, *The Manufacturing Population of England*, (London: Baldwin and Cradock, 1833), pp. 161–162.

John Wesley's view of child labour comes from Carolyn Tuttle, "Child Labor during the British Industrial Revolution," EH.Net Encyclopedia (http:/eh.net/encyclopedia/article/tuttle.labor.child.britain)

The information about the growth in the British coal industry during this period comes from Sidney Pollard, "A New Estimate of British Coal Production 1750–1850," in *The Economic History Review*, Vol. 33, No. 2 (May 1980), pp. 212–235.

The quadrupling of British coalmines during the 1842–1856 period comes from Freese, *Coal: A Human History*, p. 67.

The growth of the British coal-mining labour forces comes from John Benson, *British Coalminers in the Nineteenth Century: A Social History*, p. 7.

The figure about children in the coal mines comes from Tuttle, "Child Labor during the British Industrial Revolution."

The portrait of life for child miners is gleaned from *The Children's Employment Commission of 1842* and Benson, *British Coalminers in the Nineteenth Century: A Social History*. The quote about the initiation of child miners comes from Benson, the same source, p. 32.

The list of mining tragedies comes from a list compiled by English mining historian Philip Clifford on his website, www.heroes-of-mine.co.uk. The information about the death toll being higher for young miners comes from Benson, *British Coalminers in the Nineteenth Century: A Social History*, p. 38. The list of mining ailments comes from the same source, pp. 40–45.

The number of child miners in 1881 comes from Tuttle, "Child Labor during the British Industrial Revolution."

The description of mining techniques comes from ex–coal miner turned historian Bill Riley's website, www.pitwork.net.

The information on nineteenth-century boozing in colliery towns is culled from Benson, *British Coalminers in the Nineteenth Century*, pp. 142–171.

The figure about illiteracy in nineteenth-century English towns comes from Edwin G. West, "Literacy and the Industrial Revolution," in *Economic History Review*, No. 3, August 1978.

The information about the St. Hilda's colliery band comes from Alan Hindmarch's entry on the band on the Brass Band Reference website (http://www.harrogate.co.uk/HARROGATE-BAND/misc22.htm).

The description of the Parish Church of St. George, Chorley comes from the church's website (http://www.marcalcomputing.co.uk/stgeorge).

Andrew Alston provided information on courtship rituals in eighteenth-century Chorley as well as the descriptions of the pubs during that period.

The information on the Miners' Federation of Great Britain comes from the online history of the National Union of Mineworkers (http://www.num.org.uk).

The newspaper clippings about the state of the coal industry come from the *Chorley Guardian*, May 10, 1902, p. 7, and June 21, 1902, p. 6.

CHAPTER FIVE: GREED AND THE GILDED AGE

The biographical information and general summary of Whitney's career are culled from Donald MacGillivray, "Henry Melville Whitney Comes to Cape Breton: The Saga of a Gilded Age Entrepreneur," in *Acadiensis*, Volume IX, Autumn 1979; MacGillivray's entry on Whitney in the *Dictionary of Canadian Biography* and Thomas W. Lawson, *Frenzied Finance: The Crime of Amalgamated.*

The description of Whitney's business organization comes from Thomas W. Lawson, *Frenzied Finance: The Crime of Amalgamated*, p. 151.

My source for the GMA's deal is Samson, "Industrial Colonization: The Colonial Context of the General Mining Association Nova Scotia 1825–1842."

The 1838 figure on GMA coal production comes from David Frank's entry on Richard Smith in the *Dictionary of Canadian Biography*. The 1858 figures come from Gray, *The Coal Fields and Coal Industry of Eastern Canada*, Department of Mines and Energy.

I'm indebted to historian Daniel Samson for an advance read of sections of his book *The Spirit of Industry and Improvement: Liberal Government and Rural-Industrial Society, Nova Scotia, 1790–1862* (Montreal and Kingston, Ont.: McGill-Queen's University Press, 2008), which is my main source about the animus towards the General Mining Association. The information on the GMA's lease arrangements comes from Samson, "Industrial Colonization: The Colonial Context of the General Mining Association Nova Scotia 1825–1842," p. 18.

Information on how the GMA restricted competition comes from Marilyn Gerriets, "The Impact of the General Mining Association on the Nova Scotia Coal Industry 1826–1850," p. 74. The quote from John Archibald comes from the same source, p. 72.

The GMA's decision to hire ships to hunt down coal smugglers—as well as the quote from Matthew Roach—comes from Ian McKay, "The crisis of dependent development: class conflict in the Nova Scotia coalfields, 1872–1876" in *Class, Gender, and Region: Essays in Canadian Historical Sociology* (St. John's: Committee on Canadian Labour History, 1988).

The figure for the GMA's annual investment into Nova Scotia comes from Samson, "Industrial Colonization: The Colonial Context of the General Mining Association Nova Scotia 1825–1842," p. 22. The notion that the GMA's investments failed to materialize comes from p. 21 of the same source.

The quote from Cameron about Mount Rundell comes from *The Pictonian Colliers*, p. 24. The information about the renaming of a GMA steamship comes from the same source. p. 28.

David Frank's *Dictionary of Canadian Biography* entry on Richard Smith refers to the Nova Scotian paper's statement about his cantankerous nature.

Most of the description of the 1832 election battles comes from Brian Cuthbertson: *Johnny Bluenose at the Polls: Epic Nova Scotia Election Battles 1758–1848.* (Halifax: Formac Publishing, 1994), pp. 276–280.

The figure on coal imports to the United States comes from Brown, *The Coal Fields and Coal Trade of the Island of Cape Breton*, p. 76.

The account of the Pictou strike of 1842 comes mainly from Cameron, *The Pictonian Colliers*, pp. 141–42.

The information on Samuel Cunard's role in the GMA controversy comes from Phyllis Blakeley's entry on Samuel Cunard in the *Dictionary of Canadian Biography* and Cameron, *The Pictonian Colliers*, pp. 28–30.

Williston Northampton School has a new school song. I found the words for the old one, sung in Whitney's day, on the Wikipedia entry on the school (http://www/en.wikipedia.org/Williston_Northamption_School), which I truly hope to be true.

The information about Enos Collins's career comes from his entry as an inductee in the Nova Scotia Junior Achievement Hall of Fame.

For the information on the troubles in Cape Breton I depend upon Robert
Morgan, *Early Cape Breton from Founding to Famine.* (Sydney, N.S.:
Breton Books, 2000). The quote from the woman from Loch Lomond is
found on p. 141 of the same book, where the first quote from Norman
McLeod is also found.

The appraisal of Norman McLeod comes from Rev. George Patterson, *History
of the County of Pictou, 1877*, chapter 15. The other quote about McLeod
comes from Rev. G.W. Blair, in "The Rev. Norman McLeod, Founder of
the Waipu Charge," *The Outlook*, September 23, 1929.

The moral dictator quote comes from the Canadian Encyclopedia's entry on
McLeod (http://www.tinyurl.co /5voorc).

Information about the speculative period following the GMA's pullout
comes from Hugh Millward, "Mine Operators and Mining Leases on
Nova Scotia's Sydney Coalfield, 1720 to the Present," in *Nova Scotia
Historical Review*, Vol. 13, number 2, 1993, pp. 69–77; Brown, *The Coal
Fields of Cape Breton*, p. 138; and Hope Harrison, "The Life and Death of
the Cumberland Coal Mines," *Nova Scotia Historical Review*, Vol. 5,
number 1, 1985, pp. 73–83.

Brown's estimates of exploration licenses come from *The Coal Fields and Coal
Trade of the Island of Cape Breton*, p. 87.

CHAPTER SIX: LET THERE BE A TOWN

The railway information comes from John Cameron's article "A Legislative
History of Nova Scotia Railways," which can be found in the Railways of
Canada online archives (http://www.trainweb.org/canadianrailways/
articles/LegislativeHistoryOfNSRailways.html).

The figures for mine production, employment and locomotive employment
come from the Nova Scotia Department of Mines' Annual Report, 1871.

The anecdotes about coal mining's arrival in Springhill are from Pat Crowe,
"The Beginning of Coal Mining," *Springhill Record*, Jan. 11, 2006.

Springhill's population growth comes from Ian MacKay, "The Realm of Uncertainty: The experience of work in the Cumberland coal mines 1873–1927" in *Acadiensis*, Autumn, 1986, p. 10.

The information about exploitation of the Cape Breton seams comes from Millward, "Mine locations and the Sequence of Coal Exploitation on the Sydney Coalfield, 1720–1980," pp. 186–194.

The information about Hussey and the development of the Inverness mines comes from J.L. MacDougall's *History of Inverness County, Nova Scotia*, 1922, Chapter XI, The Town of Inverness, and Douglas F. Campbell: *Banking on Coal: Perspectives on a Cape Breton Community Within an International Context* (Sydney, N.S.: University College of Cape Breton Press, 1997).

Hussey's con game is recounted in Pamela Newton: *The Cape Breton Book of Days: A Daily Journal of the Life and Times of an Island* (Sydney, N.S.: University College of Cape Breton Press, 1984).

The fact that by 1870 North Sydney was the fourth-busiest port in Canada comes from Brian Tennyson and Roger Sarty, *Guardian of the Gulf: Sydney, Cape Breton, and the Atlantic Wars* (Toronto: University of Toronto Press, 2002), p. 98.

Information on Port Morien's growth comes from Kenneth J. MacDonald, *Port Morien: Pages From the Past* (Sydney, N.S.: University College of Cape Breton Press, 1995), along with John Udd, "Chronology of Mineral Development in Canada," found on the Natural Resources Canada website (http://www.nrcan.gc.ca/ms/pdf/chrono06_e.pdf).

The 1871 populations of Port Morien and Lingan come from the 1871 Census of Canada. The population of Glace Bay, twenty years later, is quoted in Frank, *The 1922 Strike and the Roots of Class Conflict in the Cape Breton Coal Industry*.

The list of occupations in the 1871 Census of Canada is quoted in appendix VI, Del Muise, "The Making of An Industrial Community: Cape Breton Coal Towns, 1867–1900," in *Cape Breton Historical Essays*, (Sydney, N.S.: University College of Cape Breton Press, 1980).

The mobility of the colliery work force comes from Richard K. Fleishman and David Oldroyd, "The Development of British and Canadian Coal-Mining Enterprise: A Comparative Study of Costing Methods, 1825–1900," a paper which they presented to the Interdisciplinary Perspectives Conference, Manchester, U.K., July 2000.

The quotes about worker shortages come from the Immigrant Report of 1864, Halifax Arrivals, from Journals of the Assembly of Nova Scotia, as quoted on The Ship's List website.

The impact of the end of the Civil War and the end of the Reciprocity Treaty with the United States comes from Mary Jane Lipkin, "Reluctant Recruitment: Nova Scotia Immigration Policy, 1867–1914," master's thesis, Carleton University, May 21, 1982, p. 10.

The exodus from Cape Breton is documented in Muise, "The Making of An Industrial Community: Cape Breton Coal Towns, 1867–1900," appendix II. The notion that the Highlands clearances were being repeated in Cape Breton comes from p. 82 of the same source.

The MacKeen family background comes from David MacKeen's great grand-son, the journalist and author Peter Moreira. For information on MacKeen's early career also see Donald MacGillivray's entry on MacKeen in the *Dictionary of Canadian Biography* as well as Morgan, *Early Cape Breton from Founding to Famine*, p. 147.

An explanation of the iffy nature of the market for Nova Scotia coal can be found by perusing Frank, "The Cape Breton Coal Industry and the Rise and Fall of the British Empire Steel Corp," in *Acadiensis*, Vol. VII, No. 1, 1977; Muise, "The Making of an industrial Community, Cape Breton Coal Towns 1867–1900," appendix 1; and Brown, *The Coal Fields and Coal Trade of the Island of Cape Breton*, p. 88.

The line about Cape Breton coal mines having a one-in-four chance of succeeding comes from MacGillivray, "Henry Melville Whitney Comes to Cape Breton: The Saga of a Gilded Age Entrepreneur," p. 52.

The stuff about coal duties comes from Frank, "The Cape Breton Coal Industry and the Rise and Fall of the British Empire Steel Corp," p. 113.

The information about Whitney's ascendance in Nova Scotia comes mainly from MacGillivray, "Henry Melville Whitney Comes to Cape Breton: The Saga of a Gilded Age Entrepreneur," which is also the source of Fielding's quote on p. 55 and the information about the stock offering on pages 55–56.

Whitney's acquisition of most of the mining leases in the Sydney areas comes from *The Canadian Mining Review*, August 1894.

The details of the Boston Syndicate's strategy came from Frank, "Coal Masters and Coal Miners: The 1922 Strike and the Roots of Class Conflict in the Cape Breton Coal Industry," p. 13; Brown, *The Coal Fields and Coal Trade of the Island of Cape Breton*, pp. 125–127; and MacGillivray, "Henry Melville Whitney Comes to Cape Breton: The Saga of a Gilded Age Entrepreneur," pp. 56–57.

The piece in the *Canadian Mining Review* appeared in August 1894, p. 132.

Information about Dominion Coal's recruitment plan—including the advertising campaign—comes from the Cape Breton Miner's Museum website (http://www.minersmuseum.com/history_of_mining.htm). Nova Scotia's immigration recruitment plan is detailed in Lipkin, "Reluctant Recruitment: Nova Scotia Immigration Policy, 1867–1914," pp. 16–22.

CHAPTER SEVEN: LAZYTOWN

The information from the passenger list for the *Siberian* is filed with Library and Archives Canada's collection of passenger lists, 1865–1922, viewable on the Library and Archives Canada website (http://www.collectionscanada.gc.ca/databases/passengers/index-e.html).

The description of the early days of the Princess mine comes from Frank, *J.B. McLachlan: A Biography: The Story of a Legendary Labour Leader and the Cape Breton Coal Miners*, p. 49.

The background on the town of Sydney Mines comes from *The History of Sydney Mines*. Sydney Mines: 1990. p. 11.

The story of the Briers family in Sydney Mines comes from my mother, Joan DeMont, and cousin, Lynda Singer.

Joseph Desbarres's encouragement of the United Empire Loyalists to come to Cape Breton comes from Robert Morgan's entry on DesBarres in the *Dictionary of Canadian Biography*.

The arrival of the Gaels in the Sydney area comes via Stephen Hornsby, *Nineteenth-Century Cape Breton: A Historical Geography*, p. 41.

For the story of the end of Whitney's Nova Scotian adventure I depend upon Donald MacGillivray, "Henry Melville Whitney Comes to Cape Breton: The Saga of a Gilded Age Entrepreneur," and Lawson, *Frenzied Finance: The Crime of Amalgamated*.

Information about the 1896 Smoke Nuisance Law is from James R. Alexander, *Jaybird: A.J. Moxham and the Manufacture of the Johnson Rail* (Johnstown, Pa.: Johnstown Area Heritage Association, 1991), supplement to the epilogue.

Most of the information about Whitney's ornate scheme comes from Lawson, *Frenzied Finance: The Crime of Amalgamated*, pp. 151–161.

The connection between the Whitney fiasco and its aftermath is made by Frank, *Coal Masters and Coal Miners: The 1922 Strike and the Roots of Class Conflict in the Cape Breton Coal Industry*, p. 11.

The Acheson quotes come from his article "The National Policy and the Industrialization of the Maritimes 1880–1910," *Acadiensis*, Spring 1972, p. 3.

The summary of the Canadian economy at the start of the twentieth century comes from William Thomas Easterbrook and Hugh G.J. Aitken, *Canadian Economic History*. (Toronto: University of Toronto Press, 1988), pp. 381–409.

The New Glasgow as "the Birmingham of the Country" line—along with the information about the Nova Scotia Steel Company—comes from Acheson, "The National Policy and the Industrialization of the Maritimes, 1890–1910," *Acadiensis*, pp. 20–21.

Laurier is quoted in Ron Crawley, "Off to Sydney: Newfoundlanders Emigrate to Industrial Cape Breton 1890–1914," *Acadiensis*, Volume XVII, no. 2, (Spring 1988), p. 147.

Whitney's arrangement for the steel plant, along with the subsequent stock issue, comes from MacGillivray, "Henry Melville Whitney Comes to Cape Breton: The Saga of a Gilded Age Entrepreneur," pp. 65–67.

The information on James Ross comes from *Montreal, Pictorial and Biographical.* (Winnipeg: S.J. Clarke, 1914).

The figure for Sydney coal production in 1902 comes from Frank, "Coal Masters and Coal Miners: The 1922 Strike and the Roots of Class Conflict in the Cape Breton Coal Industry," p. 15.

The Briers information in section 4 comes from the 1891, 1901 and 1911 censuses of Canada and genealogical information.

The 1901 population of Cape Breton County and Sydney comes from the Census of Canada, 1901. So does the occupational information.

The information about the exodus from Newfoundland comes from Ron Crawley, "Off to Sydney: Newfoundlanders Emigrate to Industrial Cape Breton 1890–1914," *Acadiensis*, pp. 27–51. The ditty from the St. John's *Daily News* is quoted on p. 28 of the same source.

The information about Sydney Mines circa 1902 comes via the Sydney Mines Online website and The History of Sydney Mines.

The stuff about Arthur Lismer's east coast excursion comes from Jeremy Adamson, *Lawren S. Harris: Urban Scenes and Wilderness Landscapes 1906–1930* (Toronto: Art Gallery of Ontario, 1978), pp. 110–114.

The Hugh MacLennan quote comes from *Each Man's Son* (Macmillan of Canada, 1951), p. 7.

The Ann-Marie MacDonald quote comes from *Fall On Your Knees* (Toronto: Seal Books, 2003), p. 1.

The information about the company houses in Pictou County is from Cameron, *The Pictou Colliers*, p. 104.

The names of the Sydney Mines houses come via "Looking Back," a pamphlet published by the Sydney Mines Historical Society.

The thousand company tenements in 1901—along with the quote from Ralph Ripley—comes from Ralph Ripley, "The Growth of a Mining Town," a pamphlet published in 1977.

I learned about the connection between miners and gardening from Robert McIntosh, *Boys in the Pits: Child Labour in Coal Mines* (Montreal and Kingston, Ont.: McGill-Queen's University Press, 2000), p. 114.

The anecdote about the Sydney Mines bathing practices—and about miners finally being able to fix up their homes—comes from "Looking Back," published by the Sydney Mines Historical Society.

My main source on the company store is John Mellor, *The Company Store: J.B. McLachlan and the Cape Breton Coal Miners 1900–1925* (Toronto: Doubleday Canada, 1983). The Bill McNeil quotes are from the same source, pp. x and xi.

Among other places the material about the pervasiveness of the company in colliery towns comes from Chyrssa McAlister and Peter Twohig, "The Check-off: A precursor of Medicare in Canada?" in the *Canadian Medical Association Journal*, December 6, 2005.

The Alexander MacGillivray quotes come from his testimony to the Royal Commission on the Relations of Labour and Capital, April, 1888—quoted in *Cape Breton's Magazine*, 46 (August 1987), pp. 54–57—as does Duncan MacIntyre's testimony.

The description of the company store is from Mellor, *The Company Store: J.B. McLachlan and the Cape Breton Coal Miners 1900–1925*, pp. 12–15.

The Gordon MacGregor quote about the company stores comes from "The Pluck Me . . . Life and Death of the Company Store," *Cape Breton's Magazine*, Number 3, p. 3.

The general information about Harris comes from Robert Tuck, *Gothic Dreams: The Life and Times of a Canadian Architect, William Critchlow Harris, 1854–1913* (Toronto: Dundurn Press Ltd. 1978), pp. 230–231. The section about Broughton mostly comes from pp. 165–174 in the same book.

The date of the mine closure comes from a Canadian Press story from July 2007 and the website of the Cape Breton Highlanders Association (http://faculty.uccb.ns.ca/highlanders/index.htm).

CHAPTER EIGHT: HE WAS THAT YOUNG

My main sources about child miners were Robert McIntosh, *Boys in the Pits: Child Labour in Coal Mines* (Montreal and Kingston, Ont.: McGill-Queen's University Press, 2000 and Ian MacKay, "The Realm of Uncertainty: The experience of work in the Cumberland coal mines 1873–1927."

The material about young miners crying on the way to the pits, etc., comes from a variety of sources including family members. This anecdote about young miners still believing in Santa Claus comes from Ian MacKay, "The Realm of Uncertainty: The experience of work in the Cumberland coal mines 1873–1927," p. 27.

The photo of the young miners appears in *Cape Breton's Magazine*, issue no. 3, p. 9, where the fact that Allie Mackenzie died in a World War I gas attack was also noted. The information about Tius Tutty comes from *Cape Breton's Magazine*, June 1974, pp. 5–11.

The quotes from Edgar Bonnar, George Dooley, Lybison MacKay, Ray MacNeil, Bob Hachey, Joe E. Tabor, Jimmy Johnson and Archie MacDonald come from Lawrence Christmas, *Coal Dust Grins: Portraits of Canadian Coal Miners* (Calgary: Cambria Publishing, 1998).

The quote about the changing status of boy miners comes from MacKay "The Realm of Uncertainty: The experience of work in the Cumberland coal mines 1873–1927," p. 26.

The constitution and by-laws of the Sydney Mines Friendly Society is on file with Nova Scotia Archives.

The quote from the federal Department of Mines report comes from Gray, *The Coal-Fields and Coal Industry of Eastern Canada, A General Survey and Description*, pp. 51–52.

The numbers of deaths inside the Nova Scotia colliers come from the Nova Scotia Mine Fatalities 1838–1992 database compiled by the Nova Scotia Archives.

The quotes from Gerald McGregor comes from *Cape Breton's Magazine*, no. 3, p. 3 and p. 9.

The newspaper account of the young miners morning ritual is quoted in MacKay, "The Realm of Uncertainty: The experience of work in the Cumberland coal mines 1873–1927," pp. 26–27.

The anecdote about Johnny Miles and the rats is found in Michael J. Bailey's obituary of Miles that appeared in the *Boston Globe* after Miles's death on June 14, 2003.

The Sid Timmons quotes come from *Another Night: Cape Breton Stories True & Short & Tall* (Wreck Cove, N.S.: Breton Books, 1995), pp. 185–94.

Dan J. McDonald told his story to Ed Payne in "Farewell to Coal: Into the mines as a Child" in *The Atlantic Advocate*, August 1967, pp. 21–23.

The description of coal mining in Nova Scotia in the early 1900s comes from MacKay, "The Realm of Uncertainty: The experience of work in the Cumberland coal mines 1873–1927," pp. 13–15.

The description of work and pay rates in the mines comes from Cameron, *The Pictonian Colliers*, pp. 107–111.

The information on Pictou Twist comes from Kevin Newman's article on the subject posted on the History of Pictou County website (http://www.rootsweb.ancestry.com/~nspictou/elect_text/pictou_twist.htm).

The words of Huey D. MacIsaac come from Lawrence Christmas, *Coal Dust Grins*, p. 238.

The line about roaming around in the dark comes from Dan J. McDonald as told to Ed Payne, "Farewell to Coal: Into the mines as a Child," p. 21.

The description of the Springhill disaster of 1891 comes from "A terrible mine disaster, probably one hundred lives at least are lost," *New York Times*, Feb. 22, 1891. The ages of the dead are noted in MacKay, "The Realm of Uncertainty: The experience of work in the Cumberland coal mines 1873–1927," p. 29.

The summaries of Cape Breton disasters are from Rennie MacKenzie, *Blast! Cape Breton Coal Mine Disasters* (Wreck Cove, N.S.: Breton Books, 2007). Con Hogan's narrative appears in *Cape Breton's Magazine*, No. 21, pp. 5–6.

The Inverness county mining history is gleaned from chapter 11 of J.L. MacDougall's 1922 *History of Inverness County, Nova Scotia*; Douglas Campbell, *Banking on Coal: Perspectives on a Cape Breton Community Within an International Context* (Sydney, N.S.: University College of Cape Breton Press, 1997); and Mary Anne Ducharme, "Coal Boom & Bust in Port Hood" on the Inverness County website (http://ww.invernessco.com/history_coalboom.html). She is also the source for the Port Hood information.

The information on the Port Hood explosion comes from Rennie MacKenzie, *Blast!* pp. 58–67. He's the source on the quote from the *Sydney Daily Post*.

The information on the flooding in 1911 comes from a 2003 community profile completed by the Nova Scotia government.

The information on the size and cost of pit ponies comes from Gray, *The Coal-Fields and Coal Industry of Eastern Canada, A General Survey and Description*, p. 41.

Much of the general information on the ponies' life in the pit comes from the Cape Breton Miners' Museum's website (http://www.minersmuseum.com). Patrick McNeil's quotes come from "Horses in the Coalmines," *Cape Breton's Magazine* 32 (August 1982), pp. 36–43.

CHAPTER NINE: I'M ONLY A BROKEN DOWN MUCKER

The information on John Briers's experience in World War I came from my grandfather's war records.

The figure for British coal production comes from Barry Supple, *The History of the British Coal Industry, Vol. 4, 1913–1946: The Political Economy of Decline* (Oxford: Clarendon Press, 1987), p. 4.

The "economic wonders of the world" line comes from Michael Dintenfass, *Managing Industrial Decline: the British Coal Industry Between the Wars* (Athens, Ohio: Ohio State University Press, 1992), p. 3.

The figure for Nova Scotia coal production is from S.A. Saunders, *The Economic History of the Maritime Provinces: A study prepared for the Royal Commission on Dominion-Provincial Relations, 1939*, p. 24. That is also the source for the information on the state of the coal industry post–World War I and why Nova Scotia's steel industry couldn't adapt to the changing environment.

Nova Scotia's 1913 coal production comes from "Canadian Production of Coal, 1867 to 1976," Historical Statistics of Canada, Statistics Canada, Table Q1–5, found at http://www.statcan.ca/english/freepub/11–516-XIE/sectionq/sectionq.htm.

Sydney steel plant and coalfield production figures come from David Frank, "The Cape Breton Coal Industry and the Rise and Fall of the British Empire Steel Corp.," pp. 122 and 123.

The minutiae of the Besco takeover comes from "Canada's Great Merger," *Saturday Night*, May 15, 1920, p. 18; an article in the *Monetary Times*, Nov. 14, 1919; David Frank, "The Cape Breton Coal Industry and the Rise and Fall of the British Empire Steel Corp.;" and David Schwartzman, "Mergers in the Nova Scotia Coalfields: A History of the Dominion Coal Company 1893–1940," doctoral thesis, University of California, submitted Aug. 1, 1953.

The information about the miners' growing political influence comes from M. Earle and H. Gamberg, "The United Mine Workers and the Coming of the CCF to Cape Breton," in *Acadiensis*, Fall 1989, pp. 3–26, and David Frank, "Company Town/Labour Town: Local Government in the Cape Breton Coal Towns, 1917–1926," in *Histoire Social—Social History*, May 1981.

The quote from Paul MacEwan comes from his book *Miners and Steelworkers, Labour in Cape Breton*, p. 59.

The information on strikes in Nova Scotia comes from Ian MacKay, "Strikes in the Maritimes, 1901–1914," in *Acadiensis* 13, 1982, pp. 3–56.

Information about the Italian experience in Cape Breton comes from Sam Migliore and A. Evo DiPierro (editors), *Italian Lives: Cape Breton Memories* (Sydney, N.S.: Cape Breton University Press, 1999).

I learned about the Jewish experience from the Glace Bay Synagogue website.

Epstein's story comes from *Pier Ties*, a historical newsletter published by Cape Breton University's Beaton Institute.

My primary sources for the section on Whitney Pier were *From the Pier, Dear!*, Whitney Pier Historical Society, 1993, and issues of *Pier Ties*. I also obtained information from Maude Barlow and Elizabeth May, *Frederick Street: Life and Death on Canada's Love Canal* (Toronto: Harper Collins, 2000); Elizabeth Beaton, "An African-American Community in Cape Breton, 1901–1904," in *Acadiensis*, Spring 1995, pp. 83–84; and Craig Heron, "The Great War and Nova Scotia Steelworkers," in *Acadiensis*, Spring 1987, pp. 3–34.

The source for the material about the Whitney Pier bar proprietors packing pistols on their hips is Elizabeth Beaton, "An African-American Community in Cape Breton," p. 95.

Mayann Francis's stories come from her Lt. Governor's Community Sprit Awards website (http://www.communityspiritaward.ca/).

The figure for British colliery bands in 1900 comes from the St. Austell (U.K.) Band's website (http://members.lycos.co.uk/staustellband/).

General information on the history of brass bands in Cape Breton is from William A. O'Shea, *The Louisbourg Brass Bands* (Louisbourg, N.S.: Louisbourg Heritage Society, 1991).

The Nina Cohen quote comes from John C. O'Donnell, *And Now The Fields Are Green: A Collection of Coal Mining Songs in Canada* (Sydney, N.S: Cape Breton University Press, 1992), p. xi. The list of coal-mining song titles comes from the same source, as do the following excerpts from songs found there:

"I work in the pit, it's a terrible hole . . ." ("I Work in the Pit," collected by Ron MacEachern from the singing of Stan Deveaux)

"I gave my best to Besco/ They gave me their worst." ("The Soreness of My Soul," words and music by Leon Dubinsky)

"Deep down in the earth where we take out the coal/ The chill of the mine will soon enter your soul . . ." ("Down Deep in the Mine," Marie MacMillan)

George Alfred Beckett from "Old Perl'can" is the title character in "George Alfred Becket," collected by Ron MacEachern, which is also found in O'Donnell's collection.

Archie MacInnis appears in "Coal Mining Days," collected by John C. O'Donnell, in his book *And Now The Fields Are Green*.

The Dawn Fraser poem reproduced is "He Starved, He Starved I Tell You," found in Fraser, *Echoes From Labor's War: Industrial Cape Breton in the 1920s* (Wreck Cove, N.S.: Breton Books, 1992), pp. 29–30. The autobiographical information about Fraser comes the same source, pp. 9–23.

My main source on the strike of 1922 was the *Sydney Record*, August-September 1922, and Donald MacGillivray, "Military Aid to the Civil Power: The Cape Breton Experience in the 1920s," in *Cape Breton Historical Essays* (Sydney, N.S: College of Cape Breton Press, 1980).

Dawn Fraser's poem "Merry Christmas to You Jim" is found in *Echoes From Labor's War: Industrial Cape Breton in the 1920s*, p. 43.

CHAPTER TEN: JIMMY AND THE WOLF

All of the DeMont family material comes from the genealogical experts of the clan: Frank V. DeMont of Vermont and Allen DeMont of New Glasgow. The spelling of the various related names come from section on the 1751 Gale in The Palatine Project's genealogical website (http://www.progenealogists.com/palproject/ns/1751gale.htm).

The account of the Great Windsor Fire of 1897 comes from the Windsor Fire Department (http://www.fierygifts.com/wfd/fire1897.html).

The stories about Clarie DeMont come from my father and uncles. A summary of his athletic accomplishments is found on the Nova Scotia Sport Hall of Fame website (http://www.novascotiasporthalloffame.com/inductee_view.cfm?InducteeID=73).

The infant mortality figures come from Donald MacGillivray, "Cape Breton in the 1920s: a Community Besieged" in B.D. Tennyson (ed.), *Essays in Cape Breton History* (Windsor, N.S: Lancelot Press, 1973), pp. 49–67.

The sources for the New Waterford disaster of 1917 were Rennie MacKenzie, *Blast! Cape Breton Coal Mine Disasters*, pp. 79–81, and Men in the Mines: Disasters in the Mines, a Nova Scotia Archives and Records Management website (http://www.gov.ns.ca/nsarm/virtual/meninmines/disasters.asp?Language =English).

The information about Humphrey Mellish comes from Philip Girard, Jim Phillips and Barry Cahill, *The Supreme Court of Nova Scotia, 1754–2004: From Imperial Bastion to Provincial Oracle* (Toronto: University of Toronto Press, 2004), pp. 164–166.

The information on strikes in Nova Scotia comes from Ian McKay, "Strikes in the Maritimes," pp. 10–19.

The account of the Matewan and Blair Mountain coal mine wars come from "West Virginia's Mine Wars" on the West Virginia Archives and History website (http://www.wvculture.org/hiStory/minewars.html).

The figure for coal mine strikes in Nova Scotia during the 1920–25 period comes from Christina M. Lamey, "Davis Day Through the Years: A Cape Breton Coalmining Tradition," in *Nova Scotia Historical Review*, Vol. 16, No. 2 (1996), pp. 23–33. Reprinted by permission of the author and the Royal Nova Scotia Historical Society (publisher of the *Collections*, successor journal to the *Review*).

The McLachlan biographical details that follow come mainly from *Frank J.B. McLachlan: A Biography: The Story of a Legendary Labour Leader and the Cape Breton Coal Miners*, the author's interviews with Frank and with McLachlan's daughter-in-law Nellie McLachlan.

The "greatest living question" quote comes from Frank via an email exchange with the author. McLachlan's quote about wisdom is an inscription on the J.B. McLachlan memorial in Glace Bay.

The information about the start of the Provincial Workmen's Association and the biographical material about Drummond comes from Ian MacKay, "'By Wisdom, Wile or War': The Provincial Workmen's Association and the Struggle for Working-Class Independence in Nova Scotia, 1979–97," in *Journal of Canadian Labour Studies*, Fall 1986, and MacKay's entry on Drummond in the *Dictionary of Canadian Biography*.

The comment about soaring profits comes from a perusal of the *Morning Chronicle* (Halifax) in 1909.

The pattern of harassment of the UMWA membership comes from Paul MacEwan, *Miners and Steelworkers: Labour in Cape Breton*, pp. 23–38, and Philip S. Foner, *History of the Labour Movement in the United States: The T.U.E.L to the End of the Gompers Era* (New York: International Publishers Co., 1991), pp. 230–235.

The Lewis quote is from *The Morning Chronicle* (Halifax), June 11, 1909. Wanklyn's quote is found in the same paper, July 6, 1909. The arrival of the troops is also noted in the *Morning Chronicle* (Halifax), July 8, 1909.

The march anecdote and general information about the strike comes from Paul MacEwan, *Miners and Steelworkers: Labour in Cape Breton*, pp. 23–38.

The Wolvin quote occurred on June 22, 1923, and is noted in "The 1923 Strike in Steel and the Miners' Sympathy Strike," in *Cape Breton's Magazine*, no. 22, June 1979.

The accounts of the first few nights of the strike come from coverage of the events in the *Sydney Post*.

The anecdote about the face-off between the strikers and the machine gun comes from Donald MacGillivray, *Military Aid to the Civil Power: The Cape Breton Experience in the 1920s*, p. 102.

The account of the riot in the Whitney Pier area comes from the *Halifax Herald*, July 2, 1923.

Bernie Galloway and Doane Curtis's story and quotes come from "The 1923 Strike in Steel and the Miners' Sympathy Strike," in *Cape Breton's Magazine*, no. 22, June 1979.

CHAPTER ELEVEN: SILENCE PROFOUND AND SINISTER

McLachlan's letter was reprinted in its entirely in "MacLachlan Incites Strike by Circulating Lies Regarding the Conduct of Provincial Police," in the *Sydney Record*, July 6, 1923.

The details of McLachlan's arrest come from various stories in the *Sydney Record*, July 7, 1923.

The anecdote about the meeting with Byng comes from Frank, *J.B. McLachlan: A Biography*, pp. 307–08.

Lewis's comments about the "red element" are found in the *Sydney Record*, July 11, 1923.

The excommunication of McLachlan and Livingston is noted in the *Sydney Record*, July 18, 1923.

The source for the change of charges is Frank, *J.B. McLachlan: A Biography*, p. 326.

For coverage of the trial I read the (Halifax) *Morning Chronicle*, Oct. 16–18, 1923.

Cahill's "miscarriage of justice" quote is found in Philip Girard, Jim Phillips, Barry Cahill, *The Supreme Court of Nova Scotia, 1754–2004: From Imperial Bastion to Provincial Oracle*, p. 165. Mellish's legal background is found in the same source, pp. 164–166.

The information about the length of the trail comes from the (Halifax) *Morning Chronicle*, Oct. 18, 1923.

The detail on McLachlan's jail term and his triumphant return comes from Frank, *J.B. McLachlan: A Biography*, p. 338.

The quotes from his New Waterford speech comes from the *Sydney Post*, March 17, 1924.

The 1925 coal production figures come from Report of the Royal Commission
Respecting the Coal Mines of the Province of Nova Scotia 1925,
Appendix B, and the Cronyn quotes from pp. 63–64.

McLurg's quote—as well as the average wage for a miner—comes from the
Glace Bay Miners' Museum website (http://www.minersmuseum.com/
history_of_mining.htm).

The detailed deductions from the miner's pay envelope can be found in Report
of the Royal Commission Respecting the Coal Mines of the Province of
Nova Scotia 1925, Appendix E.

The line about the 2,000 idle families comes from Donald MacGillivray,
"Cape Breton in the 1920s: A community besieged," pp. 55–56.

The detail about the destitution during the 100 percent strike comes from a
number of sources: the *Sydney Post*, the Halifax *Morning Chronicle*, Frank
J.B. McLachlan, A Biography, Donald MacGillivray, "Cape Breton in the
1920s: A community besieged."

Randolph Paiton's story actually appeared in the *Sydney Post*, April 15, 1925.

Cronyn's view is found in the Report Royal Commission on Coal Mines,
1932, pp. 41–46.

The source for Sara Gold's account is "A Social Worker Visits Cape Breton,
1925," in *Cape Breton's Magazine*, no. 38 (no date given), pp. 22–50. *The
Halifax Herald*'s editorial was reprinted in the same source on p. 47.

The *Ottawa Citizen* editorial was reprinted in March 18, 1925, *Sydney Post*.

Most of Prime Minister King's labour background is detailed in H. Blair
Neatby's entry on William Lyon MacKenzie King in the *Dictionary of
Canadian Biography*.

For my account of the events of June 11, 1925, I used Frank, *J.B. McLachlan,
A Biography*, pp. 382–383, and coverage in the *Sydney Post* beginning on
June 12, 1925.

CHAPTER TWELVE: MOORE THE MAGNIFICENT

Some of the Cape Breton nicknames come from my own ever-evolving list and some from William Davey and Richard MacKinnon, "Nicknaming Patterns and Traditions among Cape Breton Coal Miners," in *Acadiensis* (Spring 2002), pp. 71–83.

My apologies for repeating the Biscut Foot anecdote which I've already included in one book and a magazine column, but I like it so much that I'm likely to keep telling it until the day I die.

The *Time* magazine quote about Besco comes from "Empire's Steel," *Time*, June 2, 1930.

The biographical information on Holt—including the Newman quote— comes from an entry on Holt on the McCord Museum's website (http://www.mccordmuseum.qc.ca).

My main source on Depression-era Atlantic Canada is Ernest Forbes, *Challenging the Regional Stereotype, Essays on the 20th Century Maritimes* (Fredericton, N.B.: Acadiensis Press, 1989).

The figure about the decline in coal production in Pennsylvania comes from the ExplorePAHistory.com website.

The decline in colliery employment in Britain is noted by the United Kingdom Department of Business Enterprise and Regulatory Reform.

Coal production figures in this chapter come from "Canadian Production of Coal, 1867 to 1976," Historical Statistics of Canada, Statistics Canada, Table Q1–5, found at http://www.statcan.ca/english/freepub/11–516–XIE/sectionq/sectionq.htm; the Report, Royal Commission on Coal Mines, 1932 (Appendix C and p. 24); and from the Nova Scotia Department of Natural Resources.

The fact that Dorothy Duncan and Hugh Maclennan met aboard a ship is noted in *The Small Details of Life: Twenty Diaries by Women in Canada, 1830–1996* (Toronto: University of Toronto Press, 2002), p. 394.

The Duncan quotes come from Dorothy Duncan, *Here's To Canada* (New York: Harper & Brothers, 1941), pp. 40–41.

The list of 1936 imports to the Cape Breton colliery league come from Colin
Howell, *Northern Sandlots: A Social History of Maritime Baseball* (Toronto:
University of Toronto Press, 1995), pp. 168–69.

For the day-to-day history of the colliery league and its impact on Cape Breton
I'm indebted to James D. Myers, "Hard Times—Hard Ball, The Cape
Breton Colliery League 1936–39," master's thesis, 1997.

Roy Moore's career statistics come from the online Baseball Almanac
(http://www.baseball-almanac.com/players/player.php?p=moore01).

CHAPTER THIRTEEN: THE DARKNESS OF ALL DARKNESSES

The background about Springhill's mining history comes from Roger Brown,
Blood on the Coal, The Story of the Springhill Mining Disaster (Hantsport,
N.S.: Lancelot Press, 1976).

The *New York Times* article on the 1891 calamity was titled "A terrible mine disaster, probably one hundred lives at least are lost," Feb. 22, 1891.

The figure on coal mine deaths comes from the database Nova Scotia Mine
Fatalities, 1720–1992, compiled by Nova Scotia Archives and Records
Management.

The description of the Dosco miner machine comes from a 1953 speech that
Dosco president Lionel Forsyth made to the Empire Club of Canada in
Toronto.

The New York Times story about the 1956 accident was "118 Men Trapped in
a Nova Scotia Coal Mine as Gas Explosion Smashes Pithead to Bits,"
Nov. 2, 1956.

The Tabor quote comes from Roger Brown, *Blood on the Coal, The Story of the
Springhill Mining Disaster*, p. 31.

The psychological impacts of the explosion of 1956 are noted by Melissa Fay
Greene in *Last Man Out: the Story of the Springhill Mine Disaster* (Orlando,
Fla.: Harcourt, 2003), pp. 20–21.

The findings of the National Academy of Sciences researchers are contained in H.D. Beach and R.A. Lucas, *Individual and Group Behavior in a Coal Mine Disaster* (Washington: National Academy of Sciences—National Research Council, 1960).

Melissa Fay Greene extensively documents the deification of Ruddick in *Last Man Out.*

The miners' experience in Georgia is detailed in "Rescued Miners Frolic in Georgia: 13 from Nova Scotia Savor the State's Hospitality—Lone Negro is Segregated," *The New York Times*, Nov. 21, 1958, and "Nova Scotia Miners Back From Georgia," *The New York Times*, Nov. 27, 1958.

The information on life after the bump for the Ruddick family comes from an unpublished manuscript about the disaster quoted by John Leeder in text accompanying "No More Pickin' Coal" by Valerie Hope MacDonald, Maurice Ruddick's daughter, published in *Canadian Folk Music Bulletin*, vol. 23.4, December 1989.

The description of K.C. Irving comes from John DeMont, *Citizens Irving: K.C. Irving and His Legacy, The Story of Canada's Wealthiest Family* (Toronto: Doubleday Canada, 1991), pp. 63–64.

The maritime exodus during the 50s is noted by E.R. Forbes and D.A. Muise in *The Atlantic Provinces in Confederation* (Toronto: University of Toronto Press, 1993), p. 384.

The information on the changing coal market comes from, among other sources, the submission by District 26 of the United Mine Workers of America to the Royal Commission on Coal (1959) pp. 2–3.

Dosco's role in the war years comes from Forbes and Muise, *The Atlantic Provinces in Confederation*, pp. 313–314.

Nova Scotia's coal production figure for 1940 come from "Canadian Production of Coal, 1867 to 1976," Historical Statistics of Canada, Statistics Canada, Table Q1–5, found at http://www.statcan.ca/english/freepub/11–516-XIE/sectionq/sectionq.htm.

The working mines figure can be found in the Nova Scotia Department of Mines, 1940 Report on Mines, tables 7 and 8.

Dosco's wartime boasts are noted in Michael Earle, "'Down with Hitler and Silby Barrett': The Cape Breton Miner's Slowdown Strike of 1941," in *Acadiensis*, Spring 1988, pp. 56–90.

The section on wartime labour squabbles in the collieries comes from Michael D. Stevenson, "Conscripting Coal: The Regulation of the Coal Labour Force in Nova Scotia during the Second World War," in *Acadiensis*, Spring 2000, p. 62, and Christina Lamey, "Davis Day Through the Years: A Cape Breton Coalmining Tradition," in *Nova Scotia Historical Review*, Vol. 16, No. 2 (1996), pp. 23–33.

The newspaper editorials criticizing the coal labour force in Nova Scotia come from Michael Earle, "'Down with Hitler and Silby Barrett': The Cape Breton Miner's Slowdown Strike of 1941," p. 56.

Michael D. Stevenson notes the difficulty in getting colliers back in the mines in "Conscripting Coal: The Regulation of the Coal Labour Force in Nova Scotia During the Second World War," p. 76.

The 1944 coal production figure comes from "Canadian Production of Coal, 1867 to 1976," Historical Statistics of Canada, Statistics Canada, Table Q1–5, found at http://www.statcan.ca/english/freepub/11-516-XIE/sectionq/sectionq.htm.

Forbes and Muise note the disparity of the government support in *The Atlantic Provinces in Confederation*, pp. 306–345.

Ottawa's abandonment of Dosco is detailed in David Kilgour, *Inside Outside Canada*, Chapter 2: (Edmonton: Lone Pine Publishing, 1990.)

The international coal situation is detailed in A.H. Raskin, "Survey Shows Coal Losing to Gas, Oil," *The New York Times*, March 8, 1950; Jack Raymond, "Ruhr Coal Output Faces New Hitch," *The New York Times*, Dec. 12, 1947; and "British Coal Pits are Nationalized," *The New York Times*, Jan. 1, 1947.

The Cape Breton mine quandary is noted by Allan Tupper, "Public Enterprise as Social Welfare: The Case of the Cape Breton Development Corporation," in *Canadian Public Policy*, Autumn 1978, p. 533; on p. 16 of the report on the

1960 Royal Commission on Coal; and p. 4 of the submission by District 26 United Mine Workers of America to the same royal commission.

The quote about subventions comes from Tupper, "Public Enterprise as Social Welfare: The Case of the Cape Breton Development Corporation," p. 531.

Dosco's decision to import coal for the steel plant is noted by Paul MacEwan, *Miners and Steelworkers, Labour in Cape Breton*, p. 336.

The extent of Dosco's reach is detailed in Dosco president Lionel Forsyth's 1953 speech to the Empire Club of Canada. The quote about Dosco's future comes from the same source.

Former Dosco public relations director Arnie Patterson pointed out the significance of Forsyth's death in an interview with the author.

For much of the information about the nasty squabble to fill the power vacuum left by Forsyth's death, I'm indebted to Harry Bruce, *Frank Sobey: The Man and the Empire* (Halifax: Nimbus Publishing Ltd., 1985).

The Dobson quote comes from David Orchard, *The Fight for Canada: Four Centuries of Resistance to American Expansionism* and can be viewed on the Avroland website (http://www.avroland.ca/ccaft-105.html).

Roe's acquisition of 77 percent of Dosco's shares is noted in *The New York Times*, "Roe wins Control of Dominion Steel," Oct. 10, 1957.

The source for Dosco's losses in the 1952–55 period is Paul MacEwan, *Miners and Steelworkers*, p. 294.

Dosco's self-appraisal is contained in the submission to the Royal Commission on Coal (1959) by Dominion Coal Company, Ltd., pp. 21–22.

The decline of the Nova Scotia industry is noted in the Submission of the Government of the Province of Nova Scotia to the Royal Commission on Coal (1959), pp. 16–50.

CHAPTER FOURTEEN: DON'T WORRY, BE HAPPY

My main sources for Roe's involvement in Dosco are interviews with Arnie Patterson; Tupper, *Public Enterprise as Social Welfare: The Case of the Cape*

Breton Development Corporation; and MacEwan, *Miners and Steelworkers: Labour in Cape Breton.*

The summary of coal production in Nova Scotia at this time comes from various annual reports of the Nova Scotia Department of Mines.

The quote about the future of coal mining in Cape Breton comes from J.R. MacDonald, *The Cape Breton Coal Problem* (Ottawa: National Energy Board, 1966), pp. 32–35.

The description of R.B. Cameron comes from Edward Cowan, "Volatile Nova Scotia Executive Pulls Steel Mill Out of the Red," *The New York Times*, Dec. 16, 1968, and from interviews with those who knew him.

Most of the information on Devco's state during this period comes from Cape Breton Development Corp., annual reports. As good a description as any of Devco's strategy during this period comes via its former president, Tom Kent, in his paper, "Cape Breton provides pointers for the adjustment programs required by the decline of the old economy," School of Policy Studies, Working Paper 14, February, 2001.

The appraisal of the U.S. coal industry comes from Michael C. Jensen, "King Coal's Comeback Bid," *The New York Times*, Oct. 15, 1972.

The British situation during the oil shock period is considered in Roy Reed, "Despite Falling Output, British Coal's Future Looks Bright," *The New York Times*, Aug. 2, 1977.

My source for the increase in U.S. production during the 1970s is Richard Bonskowski, William D. Watson and Fred Freme, "Coal Production in the United States—An Historical Overview," a document prepared for the Energy Information Administration, 2006, p. 1. The document is viewable online at: http://www.eia.doe.gov/cneaf/coal/page/coal_production_review.pdf.

Figures on Canadian coal production during this period come from "Canadian Production of Coal, 1867–1976," Historical Statistics of Canada, Statistics Canada, Table Q1–5, found at http://www.statcan.ca/english/freepub/11–516-XIE/sectionq/sectionq.htm.

The figures on population growth come from the Census of Canada from the years 1956 through 1981. Cape Breton statistics come from "Good Governance, a necessary but not sufficient condition for facilitating economic viability in a peripheral region: Cape Breton as a case study," prepared for the Cape Breton Regional Municipality by Wade Locke and Stephen Tomblin, Oct. 2003. It is viewable online at http://www.cbrm.ns.ca/portal/documents/GovernanceStudyReport.pdf.

Cape Breton's unemployment rate is found in the Nova Scotia Department of Finance's Labour Market Review 2004 for Cape Breton.

The figure for Devco subsidization comes from "Ottawa Dismantling Devco," CBC News, November, 10, 2000 (http://www.cbc.ca/canada/story/1999/01/28/devcoll990128.html). The comparable figure for Sysco comes from James Douglas Frost, *Merchant Princes: Halifax's First Family of Finance, Ships and Steel* (Toronto: James Lorimer & Company, 2003), p. 328.

I wrote about Brophy in "Letter from Sydney: A deadly legacy: The city's infamous tarponds still await cleanup," *Maclean's*, April 16, 2001, p. 32.

Bibliography

Benson, John. *British Coalminers in the Nineteenth Century: A Social History.* New York: Holmes & Meier, 1980.

Brown, Richard. *The Coal Fields and Coal Trade of the Island of Cape Breton.* London: S. Low, Marston, Low and Searle, originally published 1871. Reprinted Stellarton, Nova Scotia: Maritime Mining Record Office, 1899.

Calder, John. "Coal Age Galapagos: Joggins and the Lions of Nineteenth Century Geology," in *Atlantic Geology,* 2006.

Cameron, James. *The Pictonian Colliers.* Halifax: The Nova Scotia Museum, 1974.

Christmas, Lawrence. *Coaldust Grins: Portraits of Canadian Coal Miners.* Calgary: Cambria Publishing, 1998.

Dawson, John William. *Acadian Geology, The Geological Structure, Organic Remains and Mineral Resources of Nova Scotia, New Brunswick and Prince Edward Island.* London: Macmillan and Co., 1868.

———. *Fifty Years of Work in Canada, Scientific and Educational.* Edinburgh: Ballantyne, Hanson & Co., 1901.

Forbes, E.R., and D.A. Muise (eds.). *The Atlantic Provinces in Confederation.* Toronto: University of Toronto Press, 1993.

Frank, David. *J.B. McLachlan: A Biography: The Story of a Legendary Labour Leader and the Cape Breton Coal Miners.* Toronto: James Lorimer & Company, 1999.

———. "The Cape Breton Coal Industry and the Rise and Fall of the British Empire Steel Corp." *Acadiensis*, Vol. VII, No. 1, 1977.

———. "Coal Masters and Coal Miners: The 1922 Strike and the Roots of Class Conflict in the Cape Breton Coal Industry." master's thesis at Dalhousie University, Halifax, 1974.

Fraser, Dawn. *Echoes from Labor's War.* Wreck Cove, N.S.: Breton Books, 1992.

Freese, Barbara. *Coal: A Human History.* Cambridge, Mass.: Perseus Publishing, 2003.

Gray, Francis. *The Coal Fields and Coal Industry of Eastern Canada.* Ottawa: Department of Mines and Energy, 1916.

Historical Statistics of Canada, Statistics Canada. Table Q1–5, Canadian Production of Coal, 1867 to 1976. Found at http://www.statcan.ca/english/freepub/11-516-XIE/sectionq/sectionq.htm.

The History of Sydney Mines, Sydney Mines, N.S.: Princess Printing, 1990.

Hornsby, Stephen J. *Nineteenth-Century Cape Breton: A Historical Geography.* Montreal: McGill-Queen's University Press, 1992.

Lawson, Thomas W., *Frenzied Finance: The Crime of Amalgamated.* New York: Greenwood Press Publishers, 1968 (originally published in 1905 by The Ridgway-Thayer Company).

Lovett, Robert W. "Rundell, Bridge and Rundell—An Early Company History" in *Bulletin of the Business Historical Society*, March, 1949.

MacEwan, Paul. *Miners and Steelworkers: Labour in Cape Breton.* Toronto: Hokkert, 1976.

MacGillivray, Donald. "Cape Breton in the 1920s: A community besieged," from *Essays in Cape Breton History*, ed. by B.D. Tennyson. Windsor, N.S.: Lancelot Press, 1973.

———. "Henry Melville Whitney Comes to Cape Breton: The Saga of a Gilded Age Entrepreneur" in *Acadiensis*, Vol. IX, Autumn 1979.

MacKay, Ian. "'By Wisdom, Wile or War': The Provincial Workmen's Association and the Struggle for Working-Class Independence in Nova Scotia, 1879–97." *Labour/Le Travail*, Fall 1986.

———. "Strikes in the Maritimes, 1901–1914." *Acadiensis*, Vol. 13, 1982.

———. "The crisis of dependent development: class conflict in the Nova Scotia coalfields, 1872–1876" in *Class, Gender, and Region: Essays in Canadian Historical Sociology*, reprinted in a special issue of the *Canadian Journal of Sociology*, 1988.

———. "The Realm of Uncertainty: The experience of work in the Cumberland coal mines 1873–1927." *Acadiensis*, Autumn 1986.

MacKenzie, Rennie. *Blast! Cape Breton Coal Mine Disasters*. Wreck Cove, N.S.: Breton Books, 2007.

McPhee, John. *Annals of the Former World*. New York: Farrar, Straus and Giroux, 1998.

McIntosh, Robert. *Boys in the Pits, Child Labour in Coal Mines*. Montreal and Kingston, Ont.: McGill-Queen's University Press, 2000.

Mellor, John. *The Company Store: J.B. McLachlan and the Cape Breton Coal Miners 1900–1925*. Toronto: Doubleday Canada, 1983.

Millward, Hugh. "Mine Locations and the Sequence of Coal Exploitation on the Sydney Coalfield, 1720–1980" in *Cape Breton at 200, Historical essays in honor of the island's bicentennial 1785–1985*. Sydney: University College of Cape Breton Press, 1985.

———. "Mine Operators and Mining Leases on Nova Scotia's Sydney Coalfield, 1720 to the Present" in *Nova Scotia Historical Review*, Vol. 13, number 2, 1993.

Morgan, Robert. *Early Cape Breton from Founding to Famine*. Sydney, N.S.: Breton Books, 2000.

Muise, Del. "The Making of an Industrial Community: Cape Breton Coal Towns, 1867–1900" in *Cape Breton Historical Essays* (Donald MacGillivray and Brian Tennyson eds.). Sydney, N.S.: University College of Cape Breton Press, 1980.

Nova Scotia Mine Fatalities 1838–1992, Nova Scotia Archives and Records Management database. www.gov.ns.ca/nsarm/virtual/meninmines/fatalities.asp?Language=English.

O'Donnell, John C. *And Now the Fields Are Green: A Collection of Coal Mining Songs in Canada.* Sydney, N.S.: Cape Breton University Press, 1992.

Patterson, Rev. George. *History of the County of Pictou.* Pictou, N.S.: Dawson Brothers, 1877.

Report of the Royal Commission Respecting the Coal Mines of the Province of Nova Scotia 1925. Halifax: Minister of Public Works and Mines, 1926.

Report of the Royal Commission Respecting the Coal Mines of Nova Scotia 1932. Halifax: Minister of Public Works and Mines, 1932.

Richard, Justice Peter. *The Westray Story: A Predictable Path to Disaster*, Report of the Westray Mine Public Inquiry. Vol. 1, November, 1997.

Samson, Daniel. "Industrial Colonization: The Colonial Context of the General Mining Association, Nova Scotia, 1825–1842." *Acadiensis*, Autumn 1999.

———. *The Spirit of Industry and Improvement: Liberal Government and Rural-Industrial Society, Nova Scotia, 1790–1862.* Montreal: McGill-Queen's University Press, 2008.

Tuttle, Carolyn. "Child Labor during the British Industrial Revolution" in EH.Net Encyclopedia.

Permission Credits

Grateful acknowledgement is made to the following for permission to reprint previously published material:

Library and Archives Canada:

Excerpt from *The Coal Fields and Coal Trade of the Island of Cape Breton* by Richard Brown (S. Low, Marston, Low and Searle, 1871). Reprinted with permission from Library and Archives Canada.

Quote from *Hard Times* by Charles Dickens (Harper's, 1854). Reprinted with permission from Library and Archives Canada.

Excerpt from *The Manufacturing Population of England* by Peter Gaskell (Baldwin and Cradock, 1833). Reprinted with permission from Library and Archives Canada.

Quote from *Remarks on the Geology and Mineralogy of Nova Scotia* by Abraham Gesner (Gossip and Coade, 1836). Reprinted with permission from Library and Archives Canada.

Excerpt from *The Coal-Fields and Coal Industry of Eastern Canada, a General Survey and Description*, by Francis W. Gray (Government Printing Bureau, 1916). Reprinted with permission from Library and Archives Canada.

Beaton Institute, Cape Breton University

Excerpt from "Katy Mary," unpublished manuscript by Florence R. MacLeod papers, in *Cape Breton from Foundling to Famine* by Robert Morgan (Breton Books, 2000). Reprinted with permission from the Beaton Institute at Cape Breton University.

Quote from *Cape Breton's Magazine* by Gordon McGregor. Reprinted with permission from Ronald Caplan.

Quote from *Cape Breton's Magazine* by Patrick McNeil. Reprinted with permission from Ronald Caplan.

Excerpt from *He Starved, He Starved, I Tell You*, by Dawn Fraser (New Hogtown Press, 1978). Reprinted with permission from Breton Books.

Excerpts from "I Work in the Pit," "The Soreness of My Soul" and "Deep Down in the Mine," reprinted with permission from John C. O'Donnell.

Grateful acknowledgement is made to the following institutions for allowing the reproduction of images from their archives and collections:

Nova Scotia Archives and Records Management

"Glace Bay, CB." Postcard sent by Mr. Brown to his daughter in 1906.

"Miner's home life" (Florence, Cape Breton, 1941). From the Helen Creighton Collection.

"The Springhill Colliery Explosion." Published in *The Dominion Illustrated*, 7 March 1891, F80 D71.

Nurse tending to a miner injured in the Springhill Mine Disaster, taken by Maurice Crosby, 1 November 1956. From the Maurice Crosby Collection NSARM 1997-254/005 no.33.13b.

Portrait of James B. McLachlan, circa 1930. From the Jefferson Collection NSARM 1992–304 n.124.

Museum of Industry, Stellarton, Nova Scotia

Photo of Mount Rundell, the home of the Manager of the General Mining
Association, circa 1880. From the Stellarton Mining Museum Collection,
no. I91.32.604.

Portrait of Richard Smith, from the Stellarton Mining Museum Collection,
no. I91.32.608.

Beaton Institute, Cape Breton University

"Pit pony and boy, Glace Bay," 1905. Photograph donated by David Frank. 80–
18–4198.

"Boy miners at Caledonia," circa 1900. Photograph donated by David Frank.
80–5-4185.

"Soldiers of Dominion No. 3, Glace Bay," 1909. Photograph donated by Hilda
Day. MG 12.16 (E): 78–735–2485.

National Coal Mining Museum of England

Drawing of child trapper working in the mine from the Children's Employment
Commission Report, 1842.

Drawing of woman carrying coal from the Children's Employment Commission
Report, 1842.

Index

A Note About the Author

JOHN DEMONT is the best-selling and award-winning author of *Citizens Irving: K.C. Irving and His Legacy* and *The Last Best Place: Lost in the Heart of Nova Scotia*. He has written for many publications, including the *Financial Times, Canadian Geographic, The Walrus* and *Maclean's* where he was Atlantic bureau chief for ten years.

A NOTE ABOUT THE TYPE

Coal Black Heart has been set in a digitized form of Caslon, a typeface based on the original 1734 designs of William Caslon. Caslon is generally regarded as the first British typefounder of consequence, and it is believed that these original fonts were used in the first edition of Adam Smith's *The Wealth of Nations*, a pioneering work in the field of systems thinking. Caslon is widely considered to be among the world's most "user-friendly" text faces.

BOOK DESIGN BY ANDREW ROBERTS